CW01510761

Tales of
CYPRUS

A TRIBUTE TO A BYGONE ERA

Constantinos Emmanuelle

Tales of Cyprus: A tribute to a bygone era.

Printed in China

First Printing, 2018

ISBN 978-0-64699240-2

A catalogue record for this
book is available from the
National Library of Australia

Written by Constantinos Emmanuelle
Book design by Constantinos Emmanuelle
Colour photography by Constantinos Emmanuelle

www.talesofcyprus.com

Tales of CYPRUS

A TRIBUTE TO A BYGONE ERA

Constantinos Emmanuelle

"We all lived together in harmony.
Muslims and Christians together like brothers
and sisters. Yes, we were poor, but we had the
love and support of our family and friends.
We were grateful for what we had. "

MILTIADES NEOFYTOU

DEDICATION

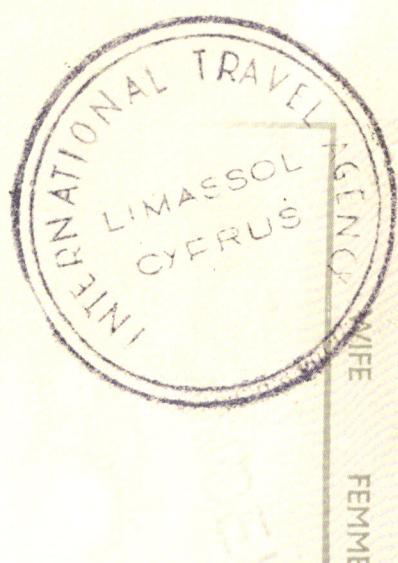

WIFE FEMME

PHOTOGRAPH OF BEARER

SIGNATURE OF BEARER.   SIGNATURE DU TITULAIRE.

INTERNATIONAL TRAVEL AGENCY
LIMASSOL
CYPRUS

To my father
Miltiades Neofytou
who always shared
his stories about the
past with me and
helped me to value my
cultural heritage.

You will always be
in my heart.

Contents

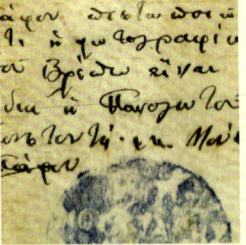

74

Agathi Constantinou
Stroumbi, Paphos

83

**Andreas and
Panayiota Nikolaou**
Kallepia, Paphos

87

Napoleon Pantazis
Ktima, Paphos

92

Ellou Nicholaidou
Trozena, Limassol

97

**Andreas and Panayiota
Aristovoulou**
Agios Athanasios,
Limassol

102

**Chloe and George
Gabriel**
Anogyra, Limassol

109

Theodoros Kyriacou
Monagroulli, Limassol

112

**Christos and Antigone
Apeitos**
Agros, Limassol

120

Gülten Erdoğan
Amiantos, Limassol

127

Jimmy Tsindos
Vasa, Limassol

134

Maria Frangou
Skarinou, Larnaca

141

Takis Ioannou
Kalavasos, Larnaca

146

Andreas Prastites
Aradippou, Larnaca

153

Nina and Michalakis Christou
Pano Lefkara, Larnaca

156

Andreas Pavlides
Kornos, Larnaca

164

Chrysanthi and Sotiris Charalambous
Famagusta

169

Stella Komodromou
Rizokarparso, Famagusta

174

Harry Shiamaris
Lefkoniko, Famagusta

181

Erol Eralp
Sygkrasi, Famagusta

186

Eleni Theodotou
Livadia, Nicosia

192

Stellios Panagiotou
Lagoudera, Nicosia

198

Taki Leptos
Morphou, Nicosia

207

Hakki Abdurazak
Yeni Jami, Nicosia

212

George Papouis
Nisou, Nicosia

Disclaimer
The names of people mentioned in this book are
spelt in accordance with the wishes of the storytellers.
Location names are spelt as they appear on maps pre-1950.
In addition, all the photographs have been scanned
in their original state and have not been digitally
altered or enhanced in any way.

ACKNOWLEDGEMENTS

Firstly, I would like to thank all the beautiful Cypriots who feature in this book and who welcomed me into their homes. I am humbled and privileged that you allowed me to record and transcribe your stories and memories for *Tales of Cyprus*. Your hospitality and humility are beyond compare. I will be forever grateful for the kindness you extended towards me.

Special thanks to my wonderful wife Christina Pavlides for all of her love and support with *Tales of Cyprus* over these last few years. I honestly could not have done this without you. Thank you for sharing this important journey with me and for allowing me to bounce my ideas and thoughts with you (even in the middle of the night). Your input has been invaluable. Thank you also for caring for our children while daddy goes off to conduct yet another interview or to stay up all night to work on his book. You are my rock.

I would also like to thank my youngest children Andrew and Katerina for being so patient with me during this quest. I owe you many outdoor adventures and a long overdue holiday.

Thanks to Camilla Eustance for her thoughtful proofreading and editing.

Lastly, I would like to thank all my friends and family, including my loyal online community. Your words of encouragement and praise have fuelled my desire to document and preserve the stories of this incredible bygone era.

I hope this book is reward enough.

"No matter how much poverty existed at the time, I believe that people back then were somewhat more grateful, more respectful and more pleasant. That's what I believe. That's what I know to be true."

SOTIRIS CHARALAMBOUS

Introduction

Our world has changed dramatically over the past century. All over the globe, we have undergone the transformation from a mostly rural self-sufficient society to a modern urban sprawl. This continuing process shows no signs of stopping anytime soon. Although it has brought many positive aspects with it, the endless march of progress quietly threatens to erase not only our environment but also our cultural identities and the already loosening ties to our individual ancestries.

This realisation of a changing world is what prompted me to create *Tales of Cyprus* around six years ago. It began as a personal quest, an investigation into what life was really like in my parents' homeland, Cyprus, before 1950.

As a modern society, we may be richer in terms of material wealth, but in many ways we are poorer than past generations. Take, for instance, the dispersed family unit and the fragmented communities that exist in many modern towns and cities today. Compare that to the connectedness of the people who once coexisted in self-contained village communities 'living with the land' and you will see that we have lost much in the exchange. In my opinion, family unity has been the first casualty. We simply do not receive the same level of support, comfort and care that was once commonplace in a village-based community.

As a teacher living in a vast metropolis like Melbourne, I see the repercussions of modern living every day. Besides the loneliness and isolation felt by many

of my students, they have grave fears about their future. They have legitimate unease about a vast range of concerns spanning from education and careers to relationships, starting a family and owning a house.

Tales of Cyprus is therefore a reminder that less is more. It is reminder that living a humble life can ultimately be more rewarding. It is a reminder that a close connection to family, community and culture can help shape and improve one's sense of identity, self worth and self esteem.

From the beginning, I had a single-minded ambition to document and preserve the oral histories and living memories of my parents' generation. When you speak to older Cypriots who remember Cyprus before 1950 you get the sense that they had a simpler, yet wonderful life. Yes, they were poor, perhaps even ignorant, and their life was hard but they seemed content with what they had. Once I realised that Cyprus in the past was a completely different world, I had to go and investigate.

I deliberately chose to focus on the period pre-1950 as I did not want to get into the political issues that arose on the island thereafter. Besides, the political ideology and propaganda that eventually divided Cyprus in 1974 is still furiously contested and I find the ongoing debate very counterproductive. I would much rather discuss the period pre-1950, that I often refer to as the golden era.

It may be rather cliché to admit, but once I became a parent I quickly developed a renewed respect for my own parents. I had been dismissive of their life before then and I never really appreciated that the intricate nature of their mindset was hardwired by their cultural beliefs.

It took a certain maturity for me to realise that both my parents belonged to a special generation and a unique period in time.

The quest to discover my ethnic roots and ancestral home began with a lengthy interview with my father. What a world I discovered. A world far removed from my own, with experiences I knew very little about. Although my father had always shared snippets of his past life with me, it wasn't until I asked him specific questions that he truly opened up.

My father arrived in Australia in early 1950, after the war, seeking a better life.

Three years later, he saw a photo of my mother and decided to bring her over to Australia with the hope of marriage. It was an arranged marriage, which was very common at the time. I have to say they really made it work. There was a respect and tolerance that you seldom see in couples nowadays. No matter how tough their life and their marriage was, my parents never threw in the towel. They never gave up. What fascinated me about my parents' life and the decisions they had to make was just how accepting they were with everything that happened to them. Compared to my generation, they were from a different planet altogether.

I have been intoxicated by my Cypriot culture from the time I first stepped foot on the island as a young boy. It's been quite a discovery and adventure ever since. Wandering through the mountains and along the cobblestone paths of a traditional Cypriot village. Sitting outdoors in the village square amongst a hundred relatives basking in the glory of a traditional home cooked feast. Accompanying my *vraka*-wearing grandfather to his vineyard to collect grapes as I rode on his donkey. Eating freshly baked bread cooked in a wood fire oven served with olives and home-made haloumi cheese.

In this book I have unearthed the recollections of those who remembered what the island was once like. This very creative generation made the most of what they had. It is not that I am romanticising the past - far from it. Things were undoubtedly tough;

poverty, unemployment, malaria, high infant mortality and disease all abounded. However, there existed a powerful connection between people and their community and I believe it is this attribute, that gave Cypriots the strength to survive such hardships. That is the essence of what I am trying to communicate through *Tales of Cyprus*.

At its core, *Tales of Cyprus* is also a story of migration, a story of how the Cypriot diaspora has managed to keep the customs and traditions of the past alive. In some cases, I have discovered that the Cypriot diaspora has maintained a more traditional moral code than many who chose to remain on the island. With regards to migration, it is amazing to contemplate how many Cypriots left their island to escape economic hardships or some form of persecution.

Throughout many of the interviews I conducted, there was an underlying sense of loss. I saw many tears and sad smiles. I believe that this grief was for the loss of the life people once knew. For many of my interviewees, this was the first time they had really spoken about their past. Opening up about their homeland was an emotional experience for them. They still missed their villages and loved ones, and they spoke about their past life with such fondness. There was a real sense of nostalgia and even regret for an era that no longer existed.

During the initial stages of my ethnographic research, I realised the importance of preserving the images of the past; namely, old family photographs. Each family that I visited had perhaps two or three vintage photographs that had travelled with them from their home. These precious keepsakes are the link between the past and the present. The presence of these photographs in *Tales of Cyprus* ensures that these images will not be forgotten.

For me, this project has been bittersweet. To be welcomed into peoples' homes to hear first-hand the accounts of their past lives was a real privilege, always a sweet moment. However, many of the people I met and interviewed were living lonely lives. They didn't have many visitors to their homes anymore, as many had lost their closest relatives and friends. Their children and grandchildren have their own lives, and are often too busy (or live too far away) to visit. I do try to go back and visit these people whenever I can. As I see it, they are now part of my community.

Tales of Cyprus has evolved into something quite different from its beginnings in 2014. Back then, my intention was to conduct interviews and scan old family photos to help inspire a series of drawings about the past. Along with the drawings, I also created a set of vintage-style travel posters, which formed the basis of my first-ever *Tales of Cyprus* exhibition in Melbourne. Over 1,500 people came to see my exhibition in December 2014. The majority were from the diaspora – both Greek Cypriot and Turkish Cypriot. It was a wonderful celebration of our combined heritage and intertwined past.

This book was written partly as a response to the public demand that resonated from my weekly posts online and partly from the realisation that there were very few publications of this kind. Any books that did examine Cyprus of old were written in either Greek or Turkish so there was also a need for an English book accessible to younger generations and people of other cultures.

Regardless of whether you have a connection to Cyprus through ancestry or otherwise, this book will appeal to anyone who appreciates how looking towards the past helps make sense of our present – and hopefully improves our future.

I hope the stories that I have documented within this volume provide a nostalgic appreciation of Cyprus of old. I hope they will help to validate the importance of a very special generation of people. Our lives have more meaning and purpose simply because of the sacrifices they have made.

Through these stories and the reproduction of old family photographs, I wish to pay tribute to a bygone era; an homage to a way of life that my parents and their generation knew and had been a part of. I have often said that my parents' generation will be the last to have lived and witnessed that way of life. That is why I also say that we shall, sadly, never see their kind again.

Tales of Cyprus is also a European story. Many countries in southern Europe have experienced the same breakneck transformation from the past to the present. This catapult into the 21st century can sometimes strip away the authentic cultural landscape of a traditional lifestyle.

The Cyprus that my parents knew is now a distant memory. This book recalls that beautiful time in the past through the images and voices of those who experienced it.

I hope you enjoy it.

About the INTERVIEWS

It is fair to say that interviewing elderly Cypriots has been quite an education for me. I have discovered many things about Cyprus-past that I simply didn't know before. As a Greek Cypriot-Australian born to migrant parents, I have had a long-distance and somewhat limited appreciation of my cultural heritage and ethnic roots. *Tales of Cyprus* has changed all of that. I now feel reconnected to my heritage. Even my Greek language skills have improved!

The people I chose to interview for *Tales of Cyprus* were mostly aged between eighty and ninety-five, born between 1920 and 1940. Many of them left Cyprus in the 1950s to start a new life in faraway places such as the United Kingdom, America, Canada, South Africa and Australia.

Many common topics and themes emerged during the course of my interviews. For instance, the severe poverty that existed at that time; the dependency on child labour; the lack of education; the value of eating what you grew; the unconditional respect for parents and village elders; the prevalence of arranged marriages; traditional gender roles - and of course, migration.

Nearly all the people I interviewed stated that although they were poor and suffered many hardships - they were ultimately content. By appreciating the little that they had, they reinforced the popular old adage that 'less is more'.

Through these interviews I was also able to confirm that Muslims and Christians on the island were friends and coexisted in peace. In fact, all the people that feature in this book spoke of endearing and loving friendships with all Cypriots regardless of their religious beliefs. They stated that apart from language and religion there were no cultural differences. "We even looked the same," was how one person put it.

Conducting these interviews has had its fair share of challenges. Firstly, I had to establish trust and credibility with my target group. To this end, I had prepared legitimate and clear answers to the question most often asked, which was: "Why are you doing this?"

I had to ensure that the people I interviewed knew that my desire to record their stories was honourable and that my primary objective was to record the truth about their past.

This was difficult, because recording objective truths is not a familiar pursuit and not widely understood by many subsequent generations, even in Cyprus.

Understandably, some people were sceptical about this project and indeed my intentions. Others appeared apathetic. Having a website and a Facebook page has been an effective way to communicate my message and lower some of the barriers. I also went to the trouble of designing information flyers and brochures in Greek, English and Turkish to reach more people.

Once I explained that my primary objective was to document the sacrifices made by past generations, most people

were more than happy to talk to me.

I had to be patient, and this was very difficult, knowing that my target group was getting older and frailer. Sadly, many elderly Cypriots died while I was waiting for the final approval to interview them. Remarkably I was able to conduct nearly all my interviews face to face. I did this for two simple reasons. Firstly, I believe that people feel more relaxed in their home setting, allowing their stories to flow more freely. Secondly, using the Internet or even the telephone would have made the interview static and impersonal thus creating a feeling of detachment. Most of my interviews were conducted in Melbourne, London and Cyprus.

Once I had established trust within the community, I had to ensure I could gather enough information to write an accurate and informative life story. My questions were deliberately phrased to avoid 'yes' or 'no' answers. I had to

become skilled in the art or prompting and probing for more information. My teaching background had prepared me wonderfully for this kind of challenge.

The idea of recording one's history seemed strange and pointless to some people. "Why do you want to know about my past?" was a common response. "Who cares about my story; who would want to read about my life?" Perhaps you could argue that a lack of education meant that older Cypriots did not appreciate or value the documented memoir.

On the contrary, I would suggest that many older Cypriots perhaps felt a sense of shame or even remorse about their past lives. Given that most had suffered great hardships and witnessed abject poverty, perhaps the memory of walking barefoot and hungry in a village full of basic mudbrick homes was not worth mentioning, let alone recording in print.

I quickly realised as I conducted each

interview that I was dealing with an oral, word-of-mouth society. With perhaps one or two exceptions, most people did not have any written accounts of their life story. There were no personal diaries, no letters, no transcripts from school, or work references, or travel documents. There were no certificates regarding property and marriage. Even the few photographs they had kept had no clues written on the back. For this reason, recalling the names of the people in the photographs and the dates and locations was quite an ordeal.

One of the most tragic confessions I often heard from older Cypriots was how all their personal documents and photographs were either lost, destroyed or deliberately thrown away by other family members. Others lamented that many of their treasured possessions were left behind and abandoned when they were forced to flee their homes during the troubles that engulfed the island in the 1960s and 1970s.

Given the advanced age of my target group, it was no surprise that many older Cypriots had difficulties remembering specific details and facts about their past such as the names of friends and relatives, the name of their school or the name of the migrant ship they travelled on. In some cases, the onset of dementia had started to diminish the clarity of their recollections. I have always known that this project would be a race against time and at a certain point, it seemed that patience was a virtue I could no

longer afford. I had to act fast and I had to extend myself in ways that made it possible for me to capture someone's story before it was too late.

While I cannot claim that the stories in this book state the complete historical truth, they are the reminiscences of my subjects. Sometimes it would be obvious during an interview that a person had made an error. For instance, it is very unlikely that someone might have earned five pounds a week in 1941 working as a waiter in Kyrenia, as they may claim. From my extensive research, it is much more likely they were paid around two shillings a week. I am also sure that some stories have been exaggerated.

But do these minor details matter? All I hoped to achieve in this book was a faithful translation of each interview that would then serve as an eyewitness account of the past. In other words, a

recollection of a bygone era as told by those who were there.

Tales of Cyprus is, at its heart, a collection of oral histories based on the living memories of a very special generation. Who am I to question or even doubt their stories. I am extremely grateful to have had the privilege of

recording their memories in this book. They speak of a time of strength and resilience in the face of extreme adversity. A time when the debt collectors loomed large in people's lives; a time when the vagaries of weather could ruin crops and destroy one's livelihood.

I was also very fortunate to have had the help of many people in the cross-referencing and checking of certain facts, and none more so than the living descendants of the people I interviewed. Sometimes key dates were disputed, or certain names and places, and it was the descendants of my subjects who would help sort through these details. Despite this help, I would often go back to a person's house two or three times to tidy up details and close any gaps in a story. In more than one case, the same story would be retold differently the second time, offering strange new facts

and information. The fallibility of memory is something I am, more than ever, fully aware of when interviewing an ageing population.

Sometimes during the course of an interview a family secret was revealed which surprised the descendants and family of my subjects. This is a most remarkable outcome for *Tales of Cyprus*. For instance, it was only after I interviewed my mother's sister that I discovered that my mother was in fact engaged to another man before she met my father. Similarly, when I interviewed my father's brother, I discovered that before my father had left Cyprus for Australia, where he married my mother, he had been in love with a Catholic girl. My parents never mentioned these relationships to me.

Then there are those memories that are just too painful to share. I was often taken into the confidence of my subjects and told personal stories that they did not want repeated or written down. In these cases an interview suddenly turns into a confession. I have heard some incredible things over the years, but I have been made to promise not to share them with anyone, not even with the person's immediate family. There have been stories told that are so fantastic and so unbelievable that it makes me wonder, what else do people keep to themselves and eventually take to their grave.

Even in my own family, I was told about a murder that was committed in my maternal grandmother's village of Arsos over a hundred years ago. Would you believe that even after all these years I still have trouble getting straight answers from some of my relatives?

Some people refused to be interviewed in case they said something that may offend a living relative. "What if someone reads what I have said about their grandfather?" I was once told. Some of the best stories I have heard cannot be published in accordance with the wishes of the storyteller.

And on the other hand, there are also those people who will tell you everything about their life and pour their hearts out during an interview. "Go ahead!" they tell me. "Write it all down. People need to know what happened to me. People need to know the truth." I once interviewed a ninety year old man who confessed openly that he visited brothels frequently in his youth. His family agreed to have this information published – purely to show how the strict moral code at the time forced many men to visit brothels rather than approaching or dishonouring the reputation of a girl from their village.

With all my interviews I deliberately focused on investigating life on the island as it existed between 1920 and 1950. I was not interested in peoples' individual opinions about the political turmoil that has engulfed Cyprus since the 1950s. I know that I upset people when I refer to the first half of the twentieth century as the golden era for Cyprus. "How can you say that, Costas?" they respond firmly. "Are you forgetting the poverty, the debt and the lack of jobs?" I tell them that according to all the people I have interviewed for *Tales of Cyprus*, they all tell me that life at this time was pretty good, despite all the challenges they faced. Furthermore, they remember their youth with great fondness, joy and longing.

After so many interviews I have come to appreciate that my parents' generation lived a humble life without any airs or graces. They had fears and concerns just like the rest of us, except that their fears and concerns were based on simple truths and practical matters such as making sure they had enough food to eat and staying alive long enough to get married and start a family. They weren't distracted by the consumption of goods, material gains and selfishness – in the way that so many of us are today. For me, there have been great losses in the transformation from a self-contained, self-sufficient rural society to a largely fragmented urban existence. We have lost our sense of community which was the heart of life in Cyprus at this time.

Tales of Cyprus has been a fantastic education for me, serving up many invaluable lessons on how I should live my life. I hope you too are as enthralled and enchanted by the life stories in this book and perhaps learn a thing or two about the way Cyprus used to be.

The
INTERVIEWS

> " *People were never idle in those days.*
> *Everybody worked – from six years old to eighty.*
> *My parents would take me out into the fields to help*
> *them water or tend to our crops. I would also*
> *collect small rocks to build low walls.* "

CHRISTOS APEITOS

Miltiades
NEOFYTOU

My father Miltiades Neofytou was a gentle man who led an honest and simple life. He was born in the village of Tsada in Paphos on the 6th of December 1921. He lived in a simple mud and straw brick house with his parents Neofytos and Pelayia Emmanouil and his older sister Eleni and younger brother Andreas.

My father never really spoke about his life unless I quizzed him. He did tell me often how desperately poor his family were. I guess that explains why he became so upset if I didn't eat all my food at the kitchen table.

I have lived a charmed life compared to my father. He only attended two years of school and from the age of nine was required to look after a small herd of goats. I am ashamed to admit that I used to tease him about this when I was young and naive.

At the age of fifteen, my father left home (and Tsada) to look for work. He told me he could not bear to see his parents suffering and struggling to make a living. "We were very poor. I walked around barefoot because my parents could not afford to buy me any shoes. I thought that if I left the village, my parents would have one less mouth to feed and one less child to worry about."

My father initially found work as a kitchen boy at a restaurant in Ktima and later, worked as a labourer building

roads and runways for the new airport at Geroskipou. In 1939, aged eighteen, he travelled to Nicosia where he worked as a kitchen hand in a food canteen for the Navy, Army and Air Force Institutes (also known as NAAFI).

During the Second World War my father was transferred to the mountainous region of Troodos and later to Varosi in Famagusta where he continued to serve the English soldiers their daily meals. "With one tin of bully beef and a dozen potatoes I could make one hundred *keftedes* (meatballs)," he boasts. "Everyone loved my *keftedes*."

Sometime in the early 1940s, my father spent time in a military prison for insulting the English King. Apparently, he was paid a shilling for a week's work in the NAAFI kitchen. Upset by his meagre wage, he threw the coin onto the floor in front of an English officer. He was immediately frogmarched into a prison cell after being charged with the offense of throwing the King onto the floor - the coin had the embossed head of King George on it. "What are you talking about? I told them. The King lives in London. Anyway, I spent two days in a British prison cell."

Following his work in the NAAFI canteen, my father moved to Nicosia where he worked as a waiter at a number of different restaurants and taverns.

In late 1949, he left Cyprus to go to Australia seeking the promise of

Miltiades Neofytou. Cyprus, 1947

employment and a better salary. He was twenty-eight years old.

Although my father spoke openly about his family and village life in general, he rarely discussed his days as a single bachelor man. I was told recently that before he left Cyprus in 1949 he was in love with a woman he had met at the NAAFI. The woman was English and Catholic and my grandfather Neofytos

Miltiades Neofytou with his grandson Andrew P. Emmanuelle. May 2010

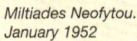

Miltiades Neofytou.
January 1952

time settling in with the local Cypriot community. He soon found steady work as a labourer in various factories around the city (including Everhot in South Yarra). He rarely spoke about his adventures as a young single man living in Melbourne. All I knew was that he shared a house (or was it a room) with a few other Cypriot bachelors. He did tell me that the inner city suburbs where he lived were gritty and dirty and he had to pay extra to have a hot bath.

Those who knew my father in his bachelor days have told me that he was a quiet and decent man. He was content to sit in the background at the Acropoli café in the city and just listen to the other migrants boasting or telling tall tales about their life. My father never bragged nor boasted about his life. He was probably the humblest man I have ever known. By all accounts he had a good circle of friends in the early 1950s and it

seemed that he thoroughly enjoyed their company.

In 1953, a Cypriot migrant named Christakis Miltiadous showed my father a photo of his wife's younger sister and suggested that he should marry her.

The woman in question was Panayiota Konnaris (my mother) who was still living with her parents in a tiny village called

did not approve of their union. This may have prompted my father to leave Cyprus. According to my uncle Andreas (my father's brother), my father had asked this Catholic girl to meet him at the port of Limassol on the day he was due to leave Cyprus but she didn't show up and he boarded the ship without her. It's strange how in the thousands of conversations I have had with my father, he did not (not once) mention this Catholic girl.

My father arrived in Melbourne in early March 1950 and wasted no

Mousere back in Cyprus.

My father agreed to marry the woman in the photo. He then instructed his parents to go to my mother's village to arrange their marriage. Once both sets of parents had agreed on the bridal dowry, my mother Panayiota was placed on a ship in December 1953 and sent to Melbourne to marry my father. Six weeks later they were married and exactly nine months later my

Miltiades Neofytou (back row, second from right) with his Cypriot migrant friends in Melbourne. c.1951

sister Eleni (Helen) was born. In 1958, my twin sisters Androula (Ann) and Neofytoula (Toula) were born. I was born in 1960.

My parents often joked about how they really didn't like each other when they first met. My mother stated that she was greeted by a skinny man on Station Pier in Port Melbourne wearing

Miltiades and Panayiota Neofytou on their wedding day in Melbourne. January 1954

Neofytos and Pelayia Emmanouil. Tsada, Paphos. c.1948

oversized pants, looking nothing like the photo he had previously sent her. My father also stated that my mother did not resemble her photo either and that he had no idea how religious she was. In fact, my mother's obsession with the church would annoy him for most of his life.

I often try to imagine what it must have been like to enter an arranged marriage, especially so far away from your family and country of origin. At least my father had travelled and worked for many years before getting married. What about my poor mother? She was taken straight

out of her village and shipped to a strange land on the other side of the world to marry a complete stranger.

Despite some initial hardships, my parents made the most of their situation and I can testify that their marriage was indeed a success. I am blessed to have witnessed how they were able to tolerate their differences and get on with the challenge of raising a family together.

My mother was a typical, dutiful Greek housewife who spent all her waking hours looking after her children and making sure our house was spotless. She was the product of cultural conditioning that epitomised her generation and her deep-

rooted traditional upbringing. From as far back as I can remember, my mother worked 18 hours a day, cooking and cleaning and making sure we had the best start in life with the little comforts my father could afford to give her.

It has to be said, however, that my father worked damn hard himself. I remember he would rise before the sun, catching trains in the darkness to go and work in dingy factories miles away from our family home. Despite the weather, he never took a day off.

I have fond memories of my father coming home on a Thursday night (his pay day) with a bag of Violet Crumble chocolate treats. Even then, my sisters and I knew that this simple gesture was a testament of his great love for us.

I only saw my father cry once in my life. He did well to shield his family from his worries and problems. On this particular day however, when I was around eleven or twelve years old, I overheard my father complaining to my mother about not having enough money to buy food for the family and to pay the mortgage on our house. I must have walked in at the wrong time or perhaps I said something inappropriate. In a fit of anger, he lunged at me and he started to beat me. Thankfully, my mother intervened and pushed him away. Moments later I saw him outside leaning against a brick wall, hands on his head sobbing uncontrollably. At that moment - all the anger I felt towards him evaporated. I was left only with a deep remorse for the man. As I grew older I started to put things into perspective and I grew to admire and respect my father even more.

In early 1974 my father decided to return to Cyprus with his family. For my parents, it was a long-overdue trip back to their birthplace. For us children, it was our first glimpse of this mysterious island we had heard so much about. Our trip to Cyprus was also based on my mother's secret desire that perhaps, just maybe, we could resettle in Cyprus and move there permanently. Unfortunately, things did not go as planned. It was evident from the time we landed that the political situation in Cyprus was unstable. In fact, there were weekly reports of killings amongst delusional Cypriots from both sides of the political debate, threatening to spark a civil war on the island.

As a teenager, I largely ignored the local news or the dinner table conversations about President Makarios and his arch rival General Grivas. I just wanted to have fun and explore the island. It wasn't until my parents rented a small flat in Limassol that tensions on the island really started to flare up. During the month of June, gunfire could be heard most nights on the streets of Limassol. Even our landlord would climb onto the roof of his house with a machine gun and start firing live rounds at the nearby police station. On the 20th of July my father's plan to evacuate our family to the airport in Nicosia was halted by the Turkish invasion that very morning. We had no choice but to escape to the mountains where we hid for a few weeks fearing for our lives. Eventually, some nice United Nations peacekeepers helped us to evacuate to England from the Akrotiri military base in Limassol and from there we flew back to Melbourne.

It's fair to say that my Cypriot adventure in 1974 (despite the troubles) has had a lasting impression on me.

I would forever swear my allegiance to Cyprus and use my creative skills to pay homage to this remarkable place. Looking back now, I can appreciate my parents' efforts to show us as much of Cyprus as they could afford. For the most part, our tour was largely governed by my mother's demands to visit every monastery and religious landmark all over the island.

My family on the 25th March 1965. We had just attended church in East Melbourne for Greek Independence day.

Miltiades Neofytou with his daughter Helen. c.1957

My parents plan to repatriate our family to Cyprus had failed. It turned out to be a very expensive lesson for my father. Back in Melbourne he was now disillusioned and unemployed. He felt both betrayed and embarrassed by the sorry state of affairs that took place on the island in 1974. I wished I had the foresight at the time to sit and talk to him: to try and comfort his tortured mind and alleviate his guilt. I can only imagine how he must have felt. It seemed like a lifetime before he found work again in a furniture-making factory near our home.

Slowly, my father was able to put the tragic events of 1974 behind him and he moved on with his primary objective of looking after his family. At times, I would often hear him saying to relatives, "Forget Cyprus. Cyprus is lost."

Around 1978, my father found a job as a storeman packer at the large Kodak factory in Coburg. Within a few months he was trained as a forklift driver. It was the first time I had even seen my father actually proud of his job. Being a forklift driver at Kodak was a big deal to him; especially since he never managed to learn how to drive a car.

As I finished high school, my father tried (in vain) to convince me to join him at Kodak. I wasn't interested. I wanted to become an artist or perhaps a graphic designer. "Forget this art rubbish," he would say to me sternly. "Learn to drive a forklift like me. It's a good job and you will make plenty of money."

I must admit, my father was forever trying to give me his good advice. Most of the time, he was simply imposing parental values he himself had inherited from his own parents. "You should think about getting dentures," he once told me after I announced I had yet another toothache. When I broke up with my girlfriend in 1985, he sat me down and calmly said; "Marry that good Greek girl down the road. Trust me, you will learn to love her." Much to his disappointment, I am sure, I did not take my father's advice.

Many years later, my father suddenly announced how proud he was of me. I was surprised. "But Dad," I said. "I didn't take any of your advice. I became a graphic designer; I still have my own teeth and I married a girl that I love. I didn't listen to a word you said." My father nodded slowly and smiled. He then looked at me with wet eyes and said. "It's true son. You have taught me that there is another way." In that moment, in that beautiful profound moment between a father and a son, we had bridged the generational and cultural divide and understood one another.

I had come to realise that all the advice my father had ever given me was just his way of trying to look out for me; that his advice was based on love. And he too had come to realise that I could be trusted to make my own decisions about my future; that sometimes doing something different can be good; or even better, than first thought.

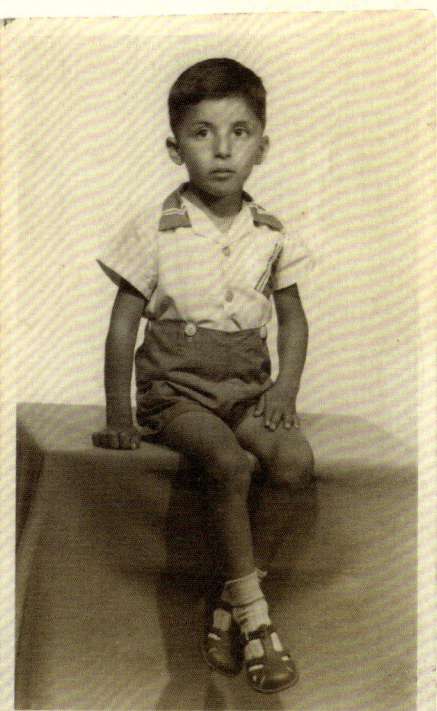

The author aged four. Melbourne, 1964

I am blown away by the contrast between my father's life and mine. He spent his childhood looking after his father's goats and later as a teenager washing dishes for a living. He left home at fifteen never to return and instead, travelled to the other side of the world to seek a better life. He married a woman he met through a photograph. He struggled for years working in factories as a labourer in what must have been truly horrid conditions and he earned a pittance for all his effort. When he finally earned enough money to take his family to Cyprus in 1974, some narrow-minded fanatics ruined his plans of resettlement for good.

Towards the last years of his life I am glad to say that I became even closer with my father. I would visit him at least twice a week and whilst sipping our Turkish coffee in his kitchen we would sit and talk for hours trying to solve the problems of the world. More often than not, we would spend our time comparing the past with the present. I would tell him about my world and he would tell me about his. I didn't realise it at the time but my father was helping me to hatch the idea for *Tales of Cyprus.*

My father passed away on the 10th of December, 2011. He had just turned ninety. I was glad to have made the effort to get to know him and to learn more about his life before he was gone. It was only after he died and I started to write down his life story, when I realised that I still knew very little about him and his past - and I still had a hundred more questions I wish I could have asked him.

The truly remarkable thing about my father was his ability to accept things as they were and carry on regardless. To not worry about the things you cannot fix. His catch-cry was always that 'things could be worse', which, surprisingly, was something I always remembered if I ever started to feel sorry for myself. Things could certainly be worse.

And so, Dad, I dedicate this book to you. You have showed me all the wonderful things about being Cypriot, and in doing so, I hope to live a better life.

Thank you, Sir.

Panayiota
NEOFYTOU

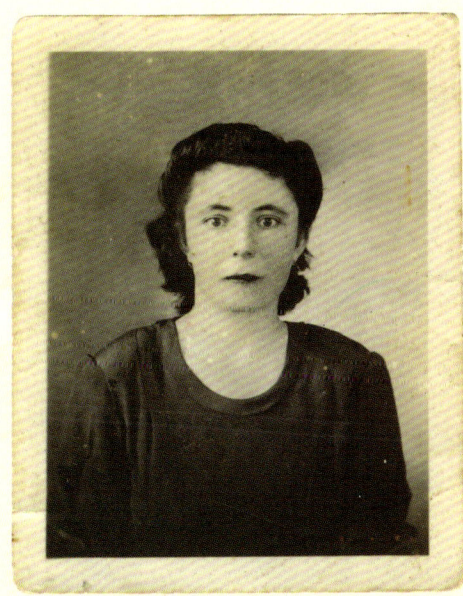

Panayiota Konnaris. c.1952

My mother Panayiota Neofytou (nee Konnaris) was born in the small village of Mousere, in the district of Paphos on the 29th May 1925. She is the second daughter of Konstantinos and Eleni Konnaris and sister to Despina and Augusta. Like so many women of her generation, my mother lived a life of servitude and obedience, supporting her parents in their rural environment as they tried to scratch a living from cultivating crops and grazing livestock in their pastures.

From an early age, my mother was drawn to the church and to the teaching of the Orthodox faith. She was a devout Christian. Throughout my life, I had witnessed many acts that have demonstrated my mother's incredible devotion to God. This includes praying before and after every meal, reading her bible every single night (often for a few hours), blessing the house three times a day with her *kapnistiri* (incense burner) and fasting for up to fifty days at a time during the holiest periods of the year. Though I admire this devotion, I have sometimes thought that she was perhaps a little too preoccupied by her religion.

My mother also managed to memorise every saint's day on the calendar. I remember how each morning she would remind me which particular saint was celebrated on that day and then provide a quick synopsis about the saint's life and

their proven miracles. I sometimes joked with my father that his wife should have been a nun. He would often nod his head in agreement.

In December 1953, my mother, aged twenty-eight, was sent by ship to Australia to marry a complete stranger (my father, Miltiades Neofytou). Though my mother did not quite settle into her new life all that well, she made the most of the situation and dutifully assumed the role that others had preordained for her.

Like most Cypriot newlyweds, my parents were keen to start a family. It was rare for Cypriot couples to prolong their engagement. Besides, sex before marriage was considered a moral and religious taboo. Three weeks after my mother arrived, she married my father on the 26th of January 1954. My sister Helen (Eleni) was born exactly nine months later. My twin sisters Ann (Androula) and Toula (Neofytoula) arrived next, in 1958. I was born in 1960.

Before I was born, my father sold his small and drab cottage in the inner-city suburb of Collingwood and bought himself a larger brick veneer house in the outer fringe suburb of Reservoir. The main reason my parents moved to Reservoir was because the new house had a big backyard. My mother hated the house in Collingwood because it was dark, narrow and damp. There were also many large rats. Whenever she suffered muscular

Panyiota's family in Mousere. She is standing second from the right. Her parents Konstantinos and Eleni Konnaris are on the far left. Mousere village. c.1952

ailments or arthritic pain, my mother would blame the 'rising damp' from that dreaded house in Collingwood. According to my mother, her mud and straw house in Mousere was much better insulated than the modern homes in Australia. I grew up listening to many of these blunt comparisons between modern Australia and old Cyprus.

By the time I turned four, our big backyard in Reservoir was transformed from a barren and desolate patch of land into a lush Mediterranean oasis. My parents had spent every weekend planting fruit trees, vines and an impressive array of vegetables. In the corner of the block, my father constructed a wonderful multi-level chicken coop out of sheets of tin and lumps of wood he had sourced from around the neighbourhood.

I have since come to appreciate that many migrants from Southern Europe have converted their 'Aussie' homes into a little piece of their homeland. The

local Australians must have experienced a collective shock at seeing each backyard transformed into a foreign-looking wonderland of exotic trees and vegetables. I am certain that our neighbours must have thought my mother to be some kind of witch doctor. If she wasn't chopping the head off a chicken, or blessing the fruit trees with her incense burner, she was seen collecting snails from under the *kolokasi* (taro) plant and placing them into a cooking pot.

I can now admit that my mother was indeed a 'superwoman'. She was always up at daybreak (even before our rooster) and willing to work all day long, often until midnight, cooking and cleaning and making sure our house was pristine and spotless. All our meals were homemade. She washed all our clothes by hand and even made most of our clothes by hand. She performed a thousand other tasks without complaint (well almost). As a Greek boy, I was groomed from

a young age to accept the so-called 'natural order of things'. Women did all the housework and child rearing and the menfolk drank coffee, talked politics and fixed stuff outdoors. I guess my parents were the same as the other migrants in my neighbourhood. Whatever their nationality, they all seemed to march to the same beat. When visitors arrived, I had the privilege as a male child to be allowed to join my father and the other men in the good room of our house, while my mother and sisters would wait on us and provide us with an obscene amount of food and drink.

To say that my mother was the homely type is an understatement. She didn't go anywhere other than her beloved church. I do remember, however, that during the first ten years of my life, she seemed to be more social and would take us shopping, to parties and weddings and even the occasional picnic. However, as I grew older she started to withdraw away from the outside world and seemed more content to simply stay at home.

My father was the exact opposite. He enjoyed going out and would plan to go somewhere new each day, which seemed to annoy my mother to no end. "Where's your father now?" she would complain. *'Kyrie Eleison!'* (Lord have mercy). That man never stays home. Always out. Does he think about me? No! Does he ever stay home to help me? No!" This was her constant lament throughout my life. In truth, my father did his best to help out around the house. The problem was, (according to my mother) 'his best' was never good enough.

I can honestly say, however, that I have never met anyone who worked as hard as my mother. Barely five foot tall, she was able to wash and hang large heavy blankets or curtains by hand. I tried to help her lift a wet blanket out of the washing trough once and I nearly broke my back. This tiny Cypriot woman

put us all to shame. How on God's good earth did she manage to keep our house spotless, wash and iron all our clothes and cook a multitude of complicated dishes and still find time in the evenings to bake *kourabiethes* (Greek shortbreads) or knit a six-foot scarf? How did she do it? For as long as I can remember, my mother spent an extraordinary amount of time at the kitchen sink. "Your mother doesn't just wash the dishes," my father used to joke. "She gives them a bath."

My mother was also full of contradictions. On one hand, she was kind to people from all races, often giving strangers bags of home-grown produce or fresh eggs or a basket of freshly baked *flaounes* (Easter cheese pies). On the other hand, she would forbid me from visiting our Australian neighbours. I think she was afraid that I might end up marrying an Australian girl. She often insisted that I should only marry a Greek Orthodox girl – unless of course I wanted to send her to an early grave. My mother also complained about being 'cooped up' inside her house all day but whenever we offered to take her out, anywhere – she would always refuse to go.

I know that my mother missed Cyprus terribly. Sometimes I think her self-inflicted isolation was largely a result of her homesickness. I remember her melancholy as she read and sometimes re-read a letter that was sent to her from a relative back home.

In early 1974, my family went on a fateful trip to Cyprus. I say

Konstantinos Konnaris. Passport photo. c.1956

fateful, because unbeknownst to us, the political situation in Cyprus was about to implode. My mother's dream to repatriate back to Cyprus was interrupted by a civil war instigated by ultra-nationalists and members of the Greek Junta which, tragically, prompted a Turkish invasion of the island. As the fighter jets flew overhead against a blood red sky, we fled from our rented house in Limassol to the relative safety of the mountainous village of Agios Theodoros. A few weeks later, thanks to our Australian passports, we were rescued by the United Nations Peacekeeping Force and transported to the Akrotiri Air Force base. From there we boarded a Hercules plane to England where we stayed with relatives before flying back to Melbourne. My mother never went back to Cyprus again. In fact, her seclusion and isolation in our family home increased after the troubles of '74. Having said that, she did seem content to stay at home.

Looking back now, I believe that my mother viewed our house as a sanctuary from a foreign world. Perhaps it was a safe haven that reminded her of her homeland. Furthermore, because she was a superstitious woman, I think she felt protected surrounded by her many religious icons.

Despite some interaction with other people (mostly migrants), my mother did not learn to speak English. She had

My maternal grandparents Konstantinos and Eleni Konnaris in Mousere. c.1952

to therefore rely on her children to act as interpreters when required. In the mid-to late 1970s, she was forced to look for work to help my father pay the bills and reduce our family debt. She found employment in a dim sim factory and then later in a confectionery factory. One of my most endearing memories is the day I accompanied my mother to her work (as part of a school project) and watched as she proudly fussed over me and introduced me to all the women on the factory floor. She looked radiant that day, and it pleased me greatly to see her interacting and laughing with the people on the factory floor.

Like millions of other Greek boys and men with their mothers, sisters and wives – I guess I took my mother for granted. She was always there for us. Family came first. In many ways, I believe my mother was simply conforming to ancient traditions that had compelled, bewitched and propelled her to assume the role of housekeeper, caretaker, cook, nanny, cleaner, nurse and more.

Panayiota Neofytou with baby Helen. Melbourne, 1955

So, on behalf of all the Cypriot men: the fathers and the sons - who have stuffed their mouths at the kitchen table without as much as a kind word or small gesture of gratitude, I would like to say "THANK YOU" to all the Cypriot women for their years of support and self-sacrifice.

My mother turned ninety-three years old in May 2018. She now resides in a Cypriot Nursing Home in the northern suburbs of Melbourne. Although she has dementia, she seems calm and comfortable in her world. You see, in her world, my father is still alive, and so too are her parents and all of her relatives. She often believes she is young again and living in her little village back in Cyprus. I try to visit her at least twice a week, despite juggling the demands of full time work and raising a family. I have learnt to deal with the dementia in my own way. When she asks me if I have fed the donkey or returned the goats to their pen, I tell her all the animals are fed and happy. If she asks me if I have seen my father, I tell her that he has just popped down to the market to buy a pumpkin.

Panayiota Neofytou will always be a superwoman in my eyes.

Panayiota's first cousin Lefkou Haralambos with her husband Nikos and their children. c.1946

Panayiota and Miltiades on their wedding day in Melbourne. January 1954

Despina
MILTIADOUS

Despina Miltiadous (nee Konnaris) was born in the village of Mousere on the 17th of October 1922. Despina was the eldest of three daughters and her parents Eleni and Konstantinos Konnaris expected her to help raise her siblings. She was also expected to perform a multitude of chores on the family farm. This included: cultivating the land, attending to the vines, threshing and milling wheat, collecting the fruits from the carob and olive trees, pressing the oil, feeding the animals and baking bread. Life was hard in those days and the constant toil to force a livelihood from the land certainly aged a person before their time. Her mother Eleni suffered with bouts of pneumonia and was often bedridden, placing the extra burden of running the household on young Despina's shoulders.

There were also tasks that extended beyond the family home. Twice a week Despina would visit her paternal grandfather Panayis Konnaris who was living on his own after his wife had died. Old Panayis was fiercely independent and refused to live with any of his eight children. Young Despina would cook for him, sweep his floor and generally clean his house. Like most Cypriots, she was taught from a very young age to revere and respect her elders. Panayis died peacefully aged ninety-nine years old, knowing that he was always cared for by his family.

When Despina turned fifteen she was sent to live with an aunt in Limassol.

The aunt's neighbour was a talented seamstress and was paid to teach young Despina how to sew. After an apprenticeship that lasted eighteen months, she had become an accomplished dressmaker. It was only during the holiest days of the year, such as Easter and Christmas, that Despina was able to return to her village to see her family.

Despina remembers her father Konstantinos Konnaris as an astute and industrious man. Like most farmers he was constantly at work tending to his crops, fields, orchards and vineyards. As the appointed *agrophylakas* (rural guard), it was his job to ensure that the village farm animals did not wander or trespass onto a neighbour's property - especially the goats. At night when most of the village was resting, Konstantinos could be heard tinkering in his courtyard on some personal project.

"My father worked day and night," recalls Despina. "I remember that my mother was tired of walking to the stream to wash our clothes, so she asked my father to build her a washbasin underneath the olive tree in the courtyard of our house. Instantly, my father collected some large stones and worked all night to build the washbasin. What else could he do," laments Despina. "He didn't have any sons to help him."

In fact, Despina's father did have a son. His name was Panayiotis. "The poor child died a few years before I was born," says Despina. "He was only nine months old. It was my father's greatest regret."

Despina Miltiadous with her daughters Sotiroula and Elenitsa. Limassol. c.1950

"How so?" I enquired.

"The child was sickly, and my father refused to take him to see a doctor." She speaks softly now. "Back then it could take days to go and find a doctor. Perhaps my father was concerned about how much time would be lost on the farm. In any case, the child died and my father would forever regret his decision to not take Panayiotis to the doctor."

When I asked Despina to describe the

people of Mousere, I was surprised to learn that unlike most of the other villages in Cyprus, not everyone got along so well. She recalls that some people were consumed by jealousy and often spewed out lies about the other inhabitants. It would seem that bad behaviour was usually caused by greed or envy and sometimes by sheer lunacy. Gossiping was also a popular pastime.

and stones, and sometimes even set fire to the fields of any farmer they had a dispute with. "Those men from Dora were bad news," she exclaims. "What do you expect from uneducated people? People often took matters into their own hands."

It seemed there were many family squabbles over land and animals. When twenty pounds was reported missing from the funds of a relative named

in her eye. "The day after he poisoned my father's animals, fourteen of his goats were found dead in their *mandra* (pen) without any sign of human intervention." She gazes skywards towards the heavens and does the sign of the cross.

Apparently, Solomi and his sons had intentions to kill Konstantinos but his older brother Christodoulos (Toulis), intervened and prevented the murder.

Despina's daughters Sotiroula and Elenitsa with their cousin in Mousere. c.1952

Despina remembers one particular goat herder, a rather cantankerous man, who would forbid other goat herders from using the same mountain track as the one used by his goats. "He would fly into a rage if he spotted anyone else on the same path."

She also remembers the night raids by bandits from the nearby village of Dora, who would come to steal wood

Solomi, Despina's father Konstantinos was quickly accused of stealing the money. As retribution, Solomi and his sons decided to poison a mule and two donkeys that belonged to her father. Despina, a devout Orthodox Christian, strongly believes that 'divine intervention' played a part in punishing Solomi. "You wouldn't believe what happened to Solomi," she whispers to me with a glint

Despina was home when the men came to her house brandishing knifes and hollering threats. "I remember my uncle shouting at them. 'You touch one hair on my brother's head and you'll see what will happen. It's not enough that you poisoned three of his animals and now you plan to make his three daughters orphans as well.' The men fled without causing any harm.

Despina (far left) with her sisters Augusta (middle) and Panayiota (far right). Mousere. c.1952

Mousere in the 1930s was a small village with around two hundred inhabitants. The nearest police station was in the neighbouring village of Archimandrita. As with many disputes at that time, village justice reigned supreme and the peasant folk nearly always settled matters their own way - ignoring the law of the land or the rule of the Church.

Despina recalls that her maternal step grandmother Panayiota was a mean-spirited woman who did not care for her stepchildren. She would often treat Despina's mother and her aunts with constant bouts of verbal and physical abuse. Apparently, the stepmother's jealousy became so great that she decided to poison two of her stepdaughters, Persephone and Efterpi, by feeding them soup that had rat poison in it. The older stepdaughter Eleni (Despina's mother) was spared because she was married and living away from home.

Panayiota got away with her terrible crimes, despite the suspicions of several villagers, who accused her of being the murderer and even threatened to kill

her. Eleni's father Nisiforos was a broken man thereafter. It is unclear if he too suspected that his wife had killed his two daughters. Life went on as it always did in the village. People died – but life went on.

In the 1940s, Despina's father Konstantinos was elected as the village *mukhtari* (headman). Despite his limited schooling, he was able to read and write and managed to intervene and settle most disputes with blinding confidence and efficiency. "As the village *mukhtari* my father would spend more time at his brother's *kafenion*," recalls Despina. "He loved to meet people and was a very social person. In fact, he had a habit of inviting every stranger he would meet at the *kafenion* to come to our house for dinner or even to stay the night, especially if they had travelled from afar and needed to rest. Our house was always full of guests. Even English soldiers were

invited to have dinner at our house. When that occurred, our cousin Panayi would be summoned to act as interpreter."

One fateful day in 1944, Despina went to meet a friend who was waiting for her at the village schoolhouse. Upon her arrival, Despina was surprised to

Back of passport photo stamped by the village mukhtari
Konstantinos Konnaris (Despina's father). c.1948

discover that her friend had brought along a male relative; a twenty-one year old man named Christakis Miltiadous who was from the nearby village of Vasa Koilaniou. Apparently, Christakis had come to Mousere looking for a wife.

Despina laughs as she recalls the memory of their first meeting. "My uncle Herakli knew Christakis and had already told him that there were far better girls to choose from in Mousere. My uncle was obviously referring to his own daughters. Men were sly and crafty back then. Thankfully, my other uncle intervened and told Christaki that the best girls in the village were in fact the daughters of Konstantinos Konnaris."

Despina's daughters Sotiroula and Elenitsa. c.1952

Despina's younger sister Augusta. c.1956

Despina and Christakis were engaged in 1945 and married a year later in 1946.

In 1948, they had a daughter Sotiroulla (Roula), followed by Elenitsa (Nitsa) in 1950. The children were only two years old and nine months old when their father decided to leave Cyprus and travel to Australia. Like so many other Cypriot men, he left by ship in 1952 to try and set up a new life for his family in Melbourne.

Christakis Miltiadous was quick to find work at an inner city automotive company in Melbourne working as a spray painter. He earned around sixteen pounds a week, which was three times the salary he would have earned in Cyprus. It would be three long years before his wife Despina and two daughters would see him again. Not surprisingly, her daughters did not

recognise their father when they were reunited with him in 1955.

In Melbourne, Despina and Christakis rented a small house in the inner city suburb of Northcote. Eight months later, they were able to place a deposit on their first home in the neighbouring suburb of Fairfield. Around this time, their third child was born; a son named Andrew. Soon after, Despina's parents and younger sister Augusta also emigrated from Cyprus and moved in with them. The Fairfield house was suddenly quite crowded. Unfortunately, after a few financial blunders, Christakis was unable to pay the hefty mortgage and the bank repossessed the house. In 1958, with the help of steady work and a loan from Despina's parents, they were able to purchase another house in the more affordable suburb of Regent. Their fourth child Maria was born in 1960.

During the 1950s, Christakis worked as an automotive panel beater and spray painter. By the mid-to-late 1960s, however, he found work as an untrained ward assistant working for a number of Mental Asylums (as they were called then) such as the Kew Lunatic Asylum, Pleasant View Asylum and the Larundel Asylum.

In 1963, Despina's father Konstantinos died after contracting Hepatitis. He was sixty-nine years old. By comparison, his twin brother Nikoli, who had remained in

Christakis Miltiadous' passport photo. c.1948

Despina Miltiadous with her daughters Sotiroula and Elenitsa. Limassol, 1954

The Miltiadous family. Melbourne, 1961

Cyprus and continued to enjoy the rural benefits of village life, would outlive him by thirty years.

There is a lot to be said about life in a mountainous village; breathing fresh air, eating a frugal home cooked meal every day, constantly moving and walking around the village and being surrounded by family and friends who shared the same culture. Konstantinos had immigrated to Australia to be close to his three daughters but unlike his twin brother he lived in a polluted city away from nature and with few friends to keep him company. By all accounts he was probably bored and lonely and perhaps even depressed.

Once her children had grown up, Despina joined her husband at Larundel where she worked as a cleaner before they both went to work at Janefield Colony (a centre for children with intellectual disabilities). Despina and Christakis worked together for many years throughout the 1970s until they retired in the late 1980s.

As I concluded my interview with Despina I asked her to share her opinion about the future of Cyprus. Her response was spiked with a fierce conviction. "Let me tell you something Costa *mou*. If Cypriot men listened to what their women said, Cyprus would be a hundred times better off. Things would have turned out far better for everyone. But men's attitude has always been 'why should I listen to a woman?' They go and do what they want. If only they listened to what women had to say, Cyprus would be much better off."

Despina Miltiadous passed away in November 2014.

ACKNOWLEDGEMENTS
Thank you Aunt Despina for all the kindness and goodwill you have shown me throughout my life. May you rest in peace. Special thanks to Rheya Linden and Andrew Miltiadous for their kind assistance in helping to check some of the facts in their mother's life story.

Andreas
NEOPHYTOU

Andreas Neophytou as a young soldier in 1944

Andreas Neophytou was born in the village of Tsada in Paphos on the 10th of December 1926. He was the youngest of three children born to Neofytos and Pelayia Emmanouil. His older sister Eleni married and stayed in Tsada all of her life whilst his older brother Miltiades immigrated to Australia in 1950.

From the age of eight, Andreas attended primary school and remembers being frequently beaten by the teachers with belts and sticks. "I must have been very cheeky to upset the teachers so much," he recalls. When Andreas was in grade five he had an argument with his teacher. Apparently, the teacher was offended when he mistakenly said 'Can I have a kiss' instead of 'Can I have the keys.' In order to avoid the punishment for his rude behaviour he hid all night in the village cemetery. After that episode he decided to quit school.

Andreas remembers that every Easter Sunday and Christmas Day his family would wear their best clothes (or at least their cleanest outfits) and spend the holy day visiting all their relatives in the village. Like most villages in Cyprus many of Tsada's inhabitants were all somehow related. Quite often, the relatives would gather at a designated house where they would all sit at long tables in the courtyard and celebrate and feast together all day and night. Christmas day was extra special as the menfolk would slaughter a pig that had been fattened throughout the year. Andreas remembers playing games with sticks called *lingri* and a game with sheep droppings called *scadouya*.

In the 1930s, during the Great Depression, many families in Cyprus (and indeed in Tsada) experienced great poverty and struggled to survive. From the age of eleven, Andreas decided to leave his village with his older brother Miltiades to find work in Ktima. "We both left our home because our parents were very poor and we couldn't bear to see them struggling day after day. It was common in those days for children to seek work elsewhere to help their parents – especially if their father had debts to pay off." Andreas found temporary work in a cake shop in Ktima, earning around five shillings a month. His brother Miltiades found work as a kitchen boy in a nearby restaurant.

Paphos was the poorest district in Cyprus at that time and trying to find steady work was next to impossible. The two brothers decided to leave Ktima and try their luck in Limassol, where they were fortunate enough to find work at neighbouring coffee houses. After a few months, the brothers were on the move again - this time to Nicosia. "In Nicosia, we worked at different restaurants as waiters and kitchen hands," recalls Andreas. "We were never far away from each other but

Andreas Neophytou in Egypt. c.1948

for some reason we always worked in different places. It would have been great for us to work together but that never happened."

Andreas often spoke about his relationship with Turkish Cypriots. "There was no difference between them and us," he says. "We were the same. In mixed communities, Christians and Muslims even attended each other's weddings. I remember that we ate, drank and danced together all night."

In 1940, with the outbreak of World War II, many men joined the Cypriot Volunteer Regiment (CVR) with the British Forces. "There were no jobs in Cyprus," exclaims Andreas. "It was difficult to earn a living so I joined the CVR earning myself about two shillings a day." Andreas was stationed in Egypt where he would witness the horrors of war up close. His main task was to transfer army supplies to the various army posts in North Africa.

the mouth. The military doctor examined him and checked his temperature and declared him unfit for duty. His superiors had little choice but to send him back home to Cyprus.

After the war ended, Andreas decided to become a builder. He worked at various places around the island and would return home to see his parents and sister once or twice a year. It was during one of these visits to Tsada when he announced his desire to marry a local girl named Kallistheni Xatzievagora.

Much to his surprise, her parents disagreed and would not give him their consent to marry her. Frustrated and deeply upset, Andreas went and stood beside a deep well and announced to Kallistheni's parents that unless they let him marry their daughter, he would climb into the well and never come out. Her parents immediately relented and gave their consent.

Andreas' uncle Konstantinos Stylianou. c.1918

Water wheel with donkey. Tsada, Paphos. Unknown person and year.

When Andreas became ill he was sent to a military hospital to recover where he saw many soldiers injured or dying. He was desperate to find an excuse to be discharged so he found some toothpaste and chewed on it until he was frothing at

In November 1952, Andreas and Kallistheni tried to get married but an altercation at the church interrupted the ceremony. An arrangement had been made with the village priest for an agreed sum of money to be paid in order for him

to conduct the church service. Halfway through the service, however, the priest stopped the proceedings and demanded more money. Andreas was furious. He called the priest a liar, grabbed his fiancé by the hand and stormed out of the church.

Undeterred by their church wedding ordeal, Andreas and Kallistheni lived happily together and had three children; Eleni born in 1955, Keti born in 1957 and Nicos born in 1959.

Andreas eventually left the building trade and began driving a taxi around Paphos. That was when he met one of the owners of the *Laiko Kafekopteio* (a large coffee grinding company) who gave him a job as a delivery man and travelling salesman. After that Andreas was given the nickname *Laikos*. The *Laiko* coffee business was located in Nicosia and was started by three professional coffee makers in 1948. The coffee makers were seeking a better alternative to the limited

ABOVE: Andreas and Kallistheni Neophytou. c.1961
BELOW: Andreas Neophytou. c.1951

Andreas Neophytou with his father Neofytos Emmanouil. Tsada, Paphos. c.1942

coffee bean supply offered by the British at that time.

Andreas was now happily driving all over Cyprus selling and delivering orders of *Laiko* coffee and sweets to various *kafenion* and café owners. He became very well known and made many friends, especially in the districts of Paphos and Limassol. He worked for *Laiko Kafekopteio* for three decades until he left the company in 1986. At the age of sixty he purchased his own car and continued to sell refreshments, *loukoumi* (Turkish

Delight) and other sweets for another two decades. He finally retired when he was seventy-five in 2001.

When asked if he regretted anything about his past, Andreas sighs and says, "I don't regret anything other than being separated from my brother Miltiades. We grew up together in Cyprus and we were always very close. When he left me in 1949 to travel abroad, I was twenty-three years old. I only saw my brother two more times after that. A family that is separated is the worst thing."

ACKNOWLEDEGMENTS
I would like to thank my uncle Andreas for allowing me to tell his life story. From my first visit to Tsada in 1974 Uncle Andreas and Aunt Kallou always made me feel welcome. I was glad to have visited Uncle Andreas one more time before he passed away in 2017.

I would also like to thank Sabine Neophytou and Eleni Neofytou for their assistance. Special thanks to Andri Christodoulou for conducting the first video interview with her grandfather back in 2012.

Froso
NEOFYTOU

MOUSERE-PAPHOS

F roso Neofytou (nee Solomou) was born on the 24th of January 1934. She grew up with her two sisters Panayiota and Anthoula, and her brother Charalambous (Humbi) in the tiny village of Mousere in the district of Paphos.

Froso's father Solomos Charalambous was born in Mousere in 1908. He was the eldest of seven children born to Xanthou and Haralambos *tou* Pethgari (also known as Humbi). Solomos was a farmer and *agrophylakas* (rural guard).

Although he was illiterate, Solomos used his natural charm and confidence to converse with all types of people. He loved to listen to traditional folk songs on the radio and was known to sing and dance without excuse. "I remember my father bought home a battery-operated radio and he would dance with (or without) my mother all the time. He was such a happy man."

Solomos married Eleni Petrou from the nearby village of Kato Archimandrita in 1929. She was eighteen and already an accomplished housekeeper and cook. Many Cypriot girls were taught by their mothers to cook an impressive repertoire of dishes and to manage a plethora of household tasks from a very early age, all in preparation for married life.

Solomos' best friend was a Turkish Cypriot man by the name of Mustafa. "He was a great man," recalls Froso. "He never married but he really loved my

family. Would you believe that there were Turkish Cypriots in Archimandrita that were nicer to our family than some of our own relatives?" Unfortunately, in 1974, Mustafa was transported to the north of the island after the separation of the two communities. Mustafa was never seen or heard of again.

"Many Turkish Cypriots would visit our house in Mousere," exclaims Froso. "They were mostly passing traders from nearby villages. Although we couldn't speak their language, it didn't matter, they could all speak perfect Greek. My parents would always treat them with the same courtesy and respect as they would treat our own relatives."

Solomos had a black horse named *Mavrakis* (Blackie). He was often seen riding his beloved mare from village to village. On one occasion he rode at breakneck speed to fetch a doctor from the village of Pachna to help save a woman who was experiencing complications during childbirth. Both the woman and her baby survived.

"We had everything we ever needed in our village," Froso recalls. "We didn't need to buy anything, only lemons. That's all we had to buy." Froso's family had around 200 goats and about 100 sheep. The family also owned two large oxen that were paired up to pull a threshing board across their wheat field. The wheat was milled into flour and the flour was mixed with water to make bread.

Froso Neofytou at twenty-two years of age. 1956

Solomos and Eleni Charalambous and her brother Kleanthis (left) in Mousere. c.1930s

"My mother would get up early that morning and light the oven. She would slaughter a young goat or lamb (to cook). She would make a large pot of *koupepia* (stuffed vine leaves) and roasted potatoes and *stifado* (stew). We had everything. Christmas and Easter were the same for us. Everybody would feast at our house. Froso becomes overwhelmed with emotion as she recalls her fond memories of growing up in Mousere. "I will never forget those days," she cries. "The life I had with my parents back then, I will never forget it. Never!"

Froso attended school up until the fifth grade. "We were eager to learn as much as we could in those days," she tells me. "Even though most of the children in my village didn't finish primary school – we knew as much, if not more that the students who graduate from high school today. We valued our lessons and our education back then. We respected our teachers. My parents would tell us, don't be like us. We cannot even sign our name. I remember my mother would sign official documents by making a thumbprint." Froso is filled with emotion again, trying hard to hold back her tears.

"Everything was better back then. Especially the food. I remember the *trahana* (dried wheat soup) my mother would make from scratch using only home grown and home made ingredients. Even the yoghurt was all made at home. You didn't buy ingredients in those days. Everything you needed for a recipe came directly from an animal or from the earth. That is why I tell you that the food you eat today does not taste as good as the traditional food we cooked and ate in the village."

The people of Mousere would often exchange food with one another. Froso remembers her mother would exchange her homemade *haloumi* (cheese) with a

Froso remembers that her house was always full of people. Her parents were very hospitable and were always ready to welcome any guests or visitors. On the Holy day of Saint John the Baptist (the patron saint of Mousere), villagers from far and wide would attend the morning mass and then converge at the Charalambous house for the grand feast that followed.

relative for a basket of pomegranate fruit. Others might exchange freshly baked bread for a basket of figs or grapes.

Froso explains that as well as sharing food, the people in her village also helped each other with chores. "In the summer, my mother and I would help our neighbours to make the short sticks of sun-baked *trahana* and they in return, would help us to make ours. My father and brothers would help other farmers to thresh their wheat and the other farmers would help to thresh our wheat too. That's how it was. Everybody worked together and helped one another"

Frosa claims that when she was about fourteen or fifteen years old, she could make and bake around thirty-three loaves of bread on her own. "I remember the exact number because that was the capacity of our oven," she remarks proudly. "I use to chop wood and light the oven on my own. I would knead the dough on my own and I would bake the bread on my own: every fifteen days; that was my job. The smell was incredible and the taste was even better. You can't find bread like that anymore. My mother would make me stand on the side of the road outside our house to give fresh bread to whoever was passing by. I remember on hot days my mother would get me to fill a large pitcher with water to offer a drink to the thirsty farmers returning home from their fields as they passed by our house. She was such a thoughtful and caring woman."

On the topic of social life, Froso is again animated. "Our friends were our relatives and our relatives were our friends," she proclaims. "If we left the house to go anywhere it was to visit a relative or an aunt or grandparent. Don't forget I had lots of first cousins. I always had company. There was no need to leave the village. Everything I needed was in the village. Besides, the beach was too far away and we didn't have the time or the means to visit other villages or the main towns. Even our school excursions were conducted on foot." It wasn't until Froso's brother Humbi became a bus driver that she was able to leave the village and visit other places, though these excursions were limited.

When asked about the games she played as a child, Frosa laughs and shakes

Solomos Charalambous on his horse Mavrakis. Mousere, Paphos. c.1930s

Froso Neofytou at twenty-six years of age. 1960

her head. "What games?" she says. "Who had time for games? If we had any spare time, we might step outside to play with the neighbour's children. I remember we played a game called *Bigginou* where we had to kick a stone around on the ground. If someone in the village had a ball we

threat against her father Solomos, Froso's family were forced to leave the village and move to the town of Limassol. Froso was eighteen at the time and remembers these events well. "I don't want to reveal too much", she confides. "But my father knew about the immoral and unorthodox behaviours of a certain individual and had threatened to report him to the authorities. So, this man had planned to have my father killed and make it look like an accident. It was public knowledge that the arson attack in Mousere was also his doing. He was a very bad man indeed. Luckily my father was pre-warned about the threat on his life and he was able to move us all to Limassol in time."

In 1959, Froso aged twenty-five was introduced to a tall, good-looking man named Yianni Neofytou. Froso's uncle Kleovoulis was acting as the official matchmaker and had arranged the formal introductions.

Yianni was born in 1925 in the village of Filousa near Arsos. He had migrated to Queensland, Australia in 1950 and had now returned to Cyprus nine years later, hoping to find a wife. Yianni had owned and operated a *kafenion* (coffee house) in Filousa before he was inspired to migrate to Australia to purse the promise of steady work and good money. He went to work at the sugar plantations at Home Hill near Cairns. After working long days cutting sugar cane he would set-up a small *kafenion* at the barracks serving coffee to the migrant workers.

"I remember my parents asked me for my opinion about Yianni," says Froso. "What can I tell you I said to them? If you think he is good enough for me, then I

Yianni Neofytou hunting rabbits in Queensland. c.1953

will abide by your wishes. You have to understand that in those days I respected the wishes and opinions of my parents. In any case, it's all down to luck and fate sometimes. We were married in 1959."

In 1961, Yianni left his pregnant wife Frosa in Limassol to return to Australia before his British passport expired. He moved from Queensland to Melbourne

might pass or kick that around. Another game that we played indoors was called *Stroumulla*. You tied a cloth around a person's head to cover their eyes and they would have to try and catch you as your ran around the room. We used to laugh a lot playing this game. Especially when someone would crash into a wall or hit their head on something. Of course, we only ever played this game when our parents were not home."

In 1952, after an unexpected act of arson in Mousere and a distressing death

Froso and Yianni's wedding photo. 1959

Froso's parents Solomos and Eleni Charalambous. c.1960s

where he found a job at a Wool factory in Williamstown and rented a small house. A year later, Froso arrived with her nine-month old daughter Neofyta (Toula) and began her married life together with her husband and child.

"Soon after I arrived in Melbourne, my husband had an accident at his work He crushed his hand on a big machine and had to stay home for six months to recover. Thank God, his employer still paid him a wage. It was very difficult to pay rent and start a family. Praise God we managed to get by."

Frosa and Yianni bought their first house in Clifton Hill in 1963. That same year their second daughter Eleni (Helen) was born.

Yianni left the Wool factory and went to work at one of the large Repco factories in Melbourne manufacturing car parts and accessories. In 1969, Froso and Yianni welcomed the arrival of their son Solomon (Solo).

Life in Clifton Hill was good for the Neofytou family. Yianni was earning a decent wage at Repco and Froso even found time to babysit some of the neighbourhood kids to earn a few extra dollars. They now had plenty of friends and a few close relatives in Melbourne.

In 1972, a fellow Cypriot named Emilo Georgiou convinced Yianni to buy a milk bar in Essendon. Froso and Yianni would own and operate two more milk bars and a chicken shop over the next twenty years. They were forced to retire in 1988, to care for their son who was suddenly diagnosed with schizophrenia.

Just over ten years later, Froso's husband Yianni died of lung cancer in February 1999. Despite a number of health scares and warnings from his family he continued to drink and smoke throughout his married life. "My husband learned to smoke cigarettes when he came to Australia in 1950," Frosa shakes her head and

Froso's friend Christina. Year and location unknown.

chokes back tears. "He continued to smoke ever since he started to work on the sugar plantations in Home Hill."

When asked to compare the past with the present, Froso is quick to respond. "People were much more loving and caring when I was growing up. They were much more courteous and respectful; much more attentive than they are today. When Cyprus rushed to become this modern and westernised country, everything was forgotten."

ACKNOWLEDGEMENTS
Thank you Aunt Froso for your honesty and support over the years and for allowing me to document your life story in this book. I would also like to thank her daughter Helen Kappos for her assistance.

ABOVE: Yianni Neofytou. c.1963
RIGHT: The Neofytou family in Clifton Hill. c.1964

Grigoris
SAVVAS LOUPI

LIVADI-PAPHOS

Grigoris Savvas Loupis was born on the 1st of December 1921 in the tiny village of Livadi in the district of Paphos. The village was located within a dense pine forest between two mountains. In the 1920s, only fifty families lived in Livadi and they all worked as goat herders.

"We used to leave our goats to roam free throughout the forest," says Grigoris. "One *chobani* (goatherd) might have a herd of fifty goats, another might have two hundred animals. The goats all mixed freely together and somehow they knew their way home and who was their master. The goat herders would whistle and each goat knew which whistle to follow. No one worried about declaring the exact number of goats in their herd. They might have one hundred goats listed on their official title but in actual fact, they owned five hundred goats or a thousand. Who was going to check?"

During the hot summer months many goat herders would cook their meat *souvla* in the forest while their goats wandered nearby. Many bushfires were started this way. In the winter, the goat herders would bring the goats down into *mandres* (pens) near the coast. A *mandra* is usually enclosed with a fence made from interlocking branches and contains a roofed area for the animals to shelter under from the rain. During February,

the goats would all give birth to kids and the villagers would take turns milking the nanny goats. "They used to make cheeses, and *haloumia*. They would sell these at the village festivals in Paphos. They made their money. People were poor but they survived. The *mandres* were located about two miles from the village. Two English miles that is."

Grigoris states proudly that the river that ran through the village provided the families with an endless supply of fresh drinking water, as well as irrigating their vegetables and fruit trees.

His father, Savvas Stylianou Loupis was a goat herder too. Despite being illiterate, he was appointed as the village headman or *mukhtari* by the village inhabitants. "My father was illiterate so he had to rely on his children to help him perform his duties," remarks Grigoris. "We had to record all the births and deaths in the village or write out receipts for the sale of animals and property. I was doing the job of the *mukhtari* at ten years old, since my father couldn't read or write."

Grigoris tells me that his father, who was born in 1880, wore a fez on his head. "Many Greeks in Cyprus wore the fez at that time," he states.

Grigoris remembers how all the men in the village wore the traditional baggy trouser called a *vraka* and how they also

Grigori's brother Christos Savvas Loupi. c.1948

carried a knife, tucked tightly into the sash that was wrapped around their waist. "The British forbade the carrying of knives but the men in our village all had them. They used the knives for work and sometimes to settle an argument."

Grigoris' mother Theopisti Elias was originally from Pyrgos, near Morphou.

Grigoris' daughter Androulla Savvidou (third from the left), aged thirteen at the Commercial Business School in Morphou. 1967

She gave birth to nine children: Menelaos, Maria, Anastasia, Neofytos, Theseus, Grigoris, Katerina, Christos and Stylianos. Alas, four of her children died quite young. "I was told that after my mother gave birth, the baby sometimes became quite ill after only a week. Whether it was an infection or some other reason, who knows. By the time my father would go by donkey to try and find a doctor, the baby died. That's how it was in those days."

When Grigoris was a young child, he attended elementary school. He remembers that a priest taught the lessons in a one-room building. "All the village children would sleep at the *mandra* with the goats and our parents would wake us up at daybreak to go to school. We would carry our *balaska* (shoulder bag) and walk the two miles back to the village to attend the school." Grigoris was a keen orator and amateur actor. He becomes rather animated as he describes his time in the Actors Guild. "The Guild was set up in the village during my late teens. Our small village was more advanced than so many others in the region. We put on plays and theatrical shows for all the locals to enjoy. People came from near and far to see the plays we put on. It was amazing. I had a leading role in many performances."

In the 1930s, British-appointed forest rangers began to fine any goat herder who was caught grazing their animals in the forest. More fines were issued if someone was caught owning more goats

than they had claimed on the official documents. Frustrated by the new rules, the goat herders eventually agreed to sell their goats to the government and give up their ancestral occupation.

In 1948, Grigoris sent his younger sister Katerina to meet with the mother of a young girl he had admired in the village for many years. Her name was Archondia Panaretou. Her father Panaretos had died when she was quite young and her poor mother Aglaia was left a widow to raise her six daughters. Grigoris' sister was given instructions to deliver and announce his intentions to marry Archondia. "We got engaged in 1948 and a year later we were married," says Grigoris smugly. "My wife got pregnant before we got married. These things happen I guess. I will tell you that from the day that we got married, I did not allow my wife to work out in the fields like all the other women. I was content for her to stay at home."

Archondia gave birth to her first child, a boy named Nestoras, in September 1950. In 1951, the inhabitants of Livadi were paid by the British Authorities to relocate to a new flat plain adjacent to the village of Prastio near Morphou in the district of Nicosia.

"The British Government had succeeded in convincing us all to leave old Livadi and go and live in Neo Livadi," Grigoris begins to explain. "Our goats were destroying the mountain landscape and the forests. I guess the government was intent on protecting

the trees. I remember some Cypriots would deliberately start a forest fire because the government would pay them to fight the fires they themselves had started. It did not help our cause when the Forest Rangers discovered that the fires were an act of arson."

Within a few years, old Livadi was abandoned and soon became derelict. Only the church and the school were spared. Every family that was relocated to the new village received up to 200 pounds compensation for their old house (depending on the size) and 50 pounds for each family member. The inhabitants would use the money to purchase land and build a new house. The new village was named Neo Livadi (New Livadi).

In 1953, Grigoris and Archondia and their young son Nestoras eventually moved from the old village of Livadi to Neo Livadi. Grigoris immediately busied himself preparing the barren fields he was given by the government to plant his orange grove. His fields, which were located opposite the monastery of Agios Nicholas, were littered with thousands of rocks and stones. Little by little he would dig the hard earth and collect all the stones one by one, using them to create a series of low walls. He would then plant row after row of orange trees, taking great care to ensure they were properly fertilised and well irrigated.

Four giant electric pumps were installed to supply Neo Livadi with underground water, as there were no rivers nearby. The displaced villagers slowly settled in and successfully grew orchards of lemon and orange trees. They had transformed themselves from goat herders to citrus growers and were now benefiting financially through the export of their fruit.

In 1954, the Loupis family welcomed the arrival of their daughter Androulla followed by Maro in 1957 and Aliki in 1962. As the children grew, so did the orange trees in Grigori's orchard. It would take around ten years for the trees to be fully grown and bear fruit suitable for the export market. Along the perimeters of his property, Grigoris planted pomegranate trees, pear trees and even grape vines. No patch of earth was left neglected or barren. He also cultivated a variety of summer and winter vegetables.

Grigoris admits that the move from old Livadi to Neo Livadi meant that many families could escape the harsh and impoverished conditions they had endured as peasant goat herders. They were able to break out of the shackles of debt and for the first time live more prosperous lives. Some former goat herders (like Grigoris) became quite wealthy as citrus fruit growers.

Grigoris was determined to succeed. While he waited for his orange grove to mature he took a job working for the American owned Cyprus Mines Corporation (CMC) where he earned around three shillings a week.

For ten years as his trees matured Grigoris existed with very little sleep. During the day he would tend to his fields and trees, then in the late afternoon he would go down to the pier to help load the ships with the copper ore that would arrive in wagon carts on narrow tracks out of the mine. At midnight Grigoris would return to his orchards to begin an all night ritual of watering, often catching a few moments of sleep amongst his beloved trees.

Eventually Grigoris was able to afford to buy his first car. Now he could travel to visit places like Kyrenia, Nicosia, Famagusta and Apostolos Andreas. "I hardly travelled anywhere before I owned a car," he says. "How far could you go with just a donkey? We knew about the geography and history of Cyprus from school, but in those days, people stayed in their villages."

In July 1974, Grigoris' family were forced to evacuate their home following the Turkish military invasion that was triggered by a *coup d'état* that threatened the safety of the local Muslim population on the island. Just six days earlier, Grigoris' eldest daughter Androulla had married her high school sweetheart Koulli Aristidou.

As they were fleeing Neo Livadi, Grigoris' family were suddenly stopped at a road block that was manned by Turkish soldiers. The situation looked very bleak. By chance, Grigoris' Turkish Cypriot friend Niyazi was also there and was able to convince the Turkish officers not to shoot Grigoris' family and let them escape. Niyazi was the *mukhtari* of the neighbouring village of Kazivera. Before the war, he would supply fruit pickers from his village to gather the oranges from Grigoris' orchards, ready for export.

Apart from a few personal belongings, the Loupis family had lost everything. Luckily, Grigoris had enough money saved to rent a house in Limassol for his traumatised family to live in. They were now refugees in their own country.

In 1975, a year after the invasion, Grigoris decided to shift his entire family to Australia where his sister Katerina lived. Katerina had migrated to Melbourne in the 1950s and now owned two houses in Collingwood. She kindly let her brother and his family live rent-free in one of her houses until they could afford to buy their own residence.

In 1979, Grigoris found work in a factory named Vinyl Clad in Collingwood, manufacturing ice cream containers. He was earning around a hundred dollars a week. His daughter Androulla and son-in-law Koulli also worked there. Factory life in Australia was a strange and foreign place for Grigoris. It was a world far removed from the picturesque mountains of Paphos in Cyprus where as a boy he would roam free with his herd of goats. It was certainly nowhere near as idyllic as his orange grove in Neo Livadi.

Uprooted twice in his lifetime, Grigoris was not one to give up or to lie down in defeat. Whatever the challenge, he was always determined to move forward and to conquer each obstacle in his path. He was determined to forge a new life for the sake of his family in Australia.

Grigoris worked at the Vinyl Clad factory for two years until he retired aged sixty in 1981. He would spend the remaining thirty-four years of his life helping to raise and care for his grandchildren and great grandchildren together with his wife Archondia. As always, his ruling passion was to provide and care for his family. Everything he had achieved in his life was for them. His selfless life exemplifies the true character of Cypriots from a bygone era: a time when family was everything.

ACKNOWLEDGEMENTS

I would like to thank Grigoris Savvas Loupis for sharing his wonderful story with me. Grigoris passed away in 2015. He was ninety-three years old. Special thanks to Androulla Koulli Aristidou for her assistance with her father's story. Sadly, her husband Koulli Aristidou passed away in 2014. His support with this project was much appreciated.

Grigoris (aged twenty) with his sister Katerina (aged seventeen) and their mother Theopisti Elias. Livadi. c.1941

Philippos IOANNOU

Philippos Ioannou was born on the 7th of March 1926 in the village of Neo Chorio in Paphos. His father was Ioanniou Styllianou and his mother was Elizaveth Ioannou. At the time, the village was home to around 1,200 residents (all Greek Cypriot).

Philippos was the second youngest of eight children (seven brothers and one sister). Each child was born in quick succession, a year apart in age. Apparently his oldest brother Stellios was the second strongest weight lifter in Cyprus in the 1930s. Only a first cousin, Neofytos, was deemed stronger. In fact, the Stylianou family has a long history of strongmen. There is even a famous local legend about Stylianos (Philippos' grandfather) who was six-foot tall and born with super human strength. The legend tells how during the Ottoman period, Stylianos from Neo Chorio was able to defeat the champion strongman of Cyprus and Turkey at that time named Arab-Ali. Apparently, Stylianos used the prize money to pay off a large debt.

Philippos did not like school. He preferred instead to roam around his village, exploring the countryside and catching little birds to bring home for his dinner. His working life began when he was only six years old. He was sent to work in a *bakaliko* (general store) in Ktima, about twenty miles from his village. One day while he was dusting the store's shelves, he accidentally hit and shattered some glassware. The angry shopkeeper's wife promptly escorted him onto a bus and sent him straight back home to his disappointed parents.

In the summer months, the children of Neo Chorio would spend their afternoons playing on the beach, which was only a mile from the village. At seven years of age, Philippos developed into a confident swimmer. He could dive and stay underwater for up to four and a half minutes. It was during one of these incredible dives when a local fisherman, Giorgios Frangos, spotted him. Frangos was so impressed that he immediately offered Philippos an apprenticeship as a junior fisherman.

With his father's consent, Philippos was sent away with Master Frangos, who taught the young boy all the tricks of his trade. This included how to repair nets, how to find and catch fish, and how to scale and prepare fish for the markets. Together they would row out after midnight to a spot about a mile from shore. There, they would cast their nets overboard and sit and wait in the cold darkness, with only the flickering of their lamps illuminating the water. Just before daybreak, they would haul their catch onto the boat and row back towards land. Baskets full of fish would be loaded onto donkeys and transported to the fish market in Ktima to be sold. Philippos worked seven days a week, practically living on the boat with Master Frangos. For all his time and labour, he was paid three pounds a year. "Our nets were always full," he boasts. "There was plenty of fish in the ocean in those days."

Philippos Ioannou's British passport photo. 1951

goat herders while the animals grazed nearby, eating everything in sight.

In 1942, seventeen-year-old Philippos decided to join the British army as a volunteer to assist the Allied war effort. Perhaps it was the lure of getting paid two shillings a day, or maybe it was the promise of free cigarettes that enticed him (each man received fifty per week). He recalls how during the Second World War, the local Cypriot women were paid three pence a day (or two piastres) to fill large army tins with sand. The tins were then loaded onto trucks and transported to Limassol where they were used as fortification against potential invaders.

Soon after he joined the Cypriot Volunteer Regiment, Philippos was sent to Syria, then to Palestine, Egypt, and finally, to the battlefront in Italy.

It was in Egypt, during a training exercise, when an English Corporal struck Philippos across the head for failing to perform a particular drill. Rather than cowering to his commanding officer, Philippos hit back. He was immediately court-martialed and sent by ship to Italy. On the ship he was locked in a small cabin and guarded day and night by two Cypriot soldiers. He remembers shouting at them from his cell. "You fools! How do you think I will escape? I'm on a ship for God's sake - in the middle of the ocean."

The young girl is Vasilia Chrysanthou Mene, (Philippos' wife) aged twelve in Neo Chorio together with her father (on the far right) and relatives. c.1940

Living on a fishing boat was difficult for a small child, but Philippos became accustomed to the job and learned to function with very little sleep. To this day he gets by with only three to four hours of sleep a night.

Because Philippos was always in the company of grown men (fishermen), he was taught to smoke from the age of nine. The cigarettes he preferred to smoke were the English brand Players. Before returning home, Philippos would sometimes stop by an orchard to eat some oranges or mandarins so that his parents would not be able to detect the smell of cigarettes on his breath. He knew that he would surely get a beating if his father found out he was smoking. Philippos was allowed to return home

to his village only on stormy nights, otherwise he was required to stay and live on Master Frangos' boat.

Philippos worked as a junior fisherman for almost five years. At age twelve, he left the sea and moved back to dry land. He found work tending to a large herd of goats that belonged to a wealthy landowner from Neo Chorio. Once again, the hours were long and the pay was minimal. He was expected to lead the herd out to pasture at 5am each morning and return them back to the village at sunset. He worked twelve hours a day, seven days a week and was again paid the princely sum of three pounds a year. For most of the day, however, he would relax in the shade of a tree, conversing and playing with other young

Philippos Ioannou in the Cypriot Volunteer Regiment. c.1942

The Cypriot Regiment consisted of muleteers (or pack transport units) whose main task was to transport food, supplies and ammunition to the British troops fighting on the front line of battle. According to Philippos, the front line colonial soldiers were mainly from India and Africa.

Philippos was not afraid of the horrors of war, and was often the first to volunteer to lead his two mules to the front line. Each Cypriot muleteer was often expected to lead two (and sometimes three) pack animals. On one occasion however, one of the mules that Philippos was leading stepped on a land mine and was instantly ripped to shreds. The shrapnel from the blast injured and wounded a number of the other animals and soldiers, including Philippos. Medical officers quickly bandaged his wound and after some rest, he was deemed fit to return to duty a few days later.

Philippos was one of the lucky ones. It is estimated that around six hundred Cypriots were killed in action during the Second World War. This was nothing compared to the casualties suffered by the colonial soldiers. According to Philippos, the Germans slaughtered so many African soldiers that their bayonet blades became blunted and bent. He also recalls how the English commanding officers would scare the African soldiers by telling them that the Cypriot volunteers were in fact cannibals. Philippos could never understand why the African soldiers would recoil back in fear whenever he approached them with fresh supplies.

An unexpected surprise

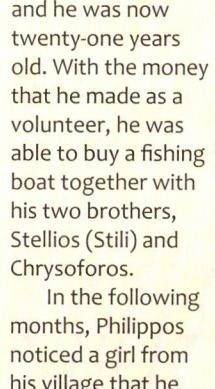
Philippos' sister-in-law Eisavou with her two sons Frixos and Kyriako. 1962

for the Cypriot volunteers was the abundance of food that they found in the abandoned towns and villages across Italy. Whenever they would enter a new village they would find all the houses deserted but fully stocked with all types of food and goods, including wine. The volunteers would then help themselves to whatever they wanted without retribution from their commanding officers. According to Philippos, not a single volunteer went hungry in Italy.

After the war, Philippos returned to Cyprus and back to the world of fishing. It was 1946 and he was now twenty-one years old. With the money that he made as a volunteer, he was able to buy a fishing boat together with his two brothers, Stellios (Stili) and Chrysoforos.

In the following months, Philippos noticed a girl from his village that he liked, and shortly after, expressed his intention to marry her. She was a shepherdess. Her mother agreed, but her father did not approve. "I will not allow my daughter to marry a fisherman," he shouted. Soon after, however, the wife of the village *mukhtar* (headman) introduced Philippos to another girl named Vasilia

Vasilia Ioannou's passport photo. c.1955

Chrysanthou Mene - who happened to live next door to the shepherdess. Vasilia was a self-taught weaver and spinner and would use her *voufa* (loom) to produce the most beautiful and intricate rugs and bed spreads in the village.

Philippos and Vasilia were happy. More importantly, their parents were happy, so the young couple were married on the 25th October 1946. Philippos remembers that at his wedding, some of the Turkish Cypriot guests from nearby Androlikou village arrived with seven slaughtered lambs to be served at the feast. Relations between the two communities had always been pleasant and harmonious.

Vasilia had a younger brother, Savvas Chrysathos, who adored Philippos and would follow him everywhere. So when Philippos and his father announced one cold wintry day that they were going to gather firewood in the nearby forest at Akamas, young Savvas begged to go with

Philippos Ioannou's Army Service and Pay book. c.1942

them. Reluctantly, Philippos agreed. He remembers it was one of the coldest days of the year and it began to snow quite heavily. The snowfall was so severe in fact, that they soon lost all sense of direction. The two men and the boy resorted to holding onto the tails of their donkeys and allowing the animals to lead them through the forest. Apparently, donkeys have a keen sense of direction, and these ones knew exactly where to go.

As they struggled through the snow, Savvas noticed a long branch in the distance and decided to walk towards it. The snowstorm worsened and the boy suddenly disappeared from view. Philippos and his father searched frantically but to no avail. They decided to return back to their village to call for help. The search lasted for hours until the boy was finally found crouching inside the crevice of a small cave. He had frozen to death. Philippos went into shock. The death of his young brother-in-law would haunt him for many years. To this day, he blames himself for not protecting the boy.

In 1951, Philippos decided to travel to Australia. He went alone, leaving his wife and two young children, (Savvaki and Panayiota) behind. Philippos planned to work abroad for five years and then return to Cyprus with enough funds to buy his own fishing boat and live a comfortable life. He set off from Limassol on the ship Corsica in early December 1951 and arrived in Sydney, fifty-two days later, in February 1952. The Corsica was very old and very slow and had to stop at many ports along the way for service and repairs. Also on board the ship was a consignment of potatoes and raw onions destined for Ceylon. Unfortunately, by the time the

Philippos' older brother, Stellios also known as Stili.

Philippos' mother (seated) holding her grandson, Savakki. Philippos' wife Vasilia (rear) holding her baby daughter Panayiota surrounded by her parents and in-laws. Neo Chorio. c.1953

Philippos with his children, Savvaki and Panayiota in the backyard of their Wollongong home. c.1957

Philippos (left) and his brother Harry posing with an English man who is holding a large crayfish. Latchi beach. c.1948

ship reached Colombo the onions and potatoes had turned to mush and were ruined. The stench was so overpowering that Philippos and the other passengers spent most of the day retching or gasping for air at the helm of the ship. To add to their misery, the captain of the ship ordered all the male passengers to empty the sacks of ruined potatoes and onions overboard, creating an even more nauseating experience.

Despite his lack of education, Philippos was a quick learner and was able to acquire skills in many areas after he reached Australia. During his first few years in Sydney, he found work in a number of factories, learning multiple trades all without any prior experience. He moved to Wollongong where he worked on a fishing trawler at nearby Port Kembla. Because he had learned Italian from his time in Italy during the war, he was able to communicate easily with the Italian trawler owner. Unfortunately, his lack of schooling meant that he was unable to send any letters to his wife and family back in Cyprus. Frustrated, he decided to buy a Greek and English dictionary and taught himself how to read and write in both languages – something else to add to his increasingly large list of skills.

Two and a half years after arriving in Australia, Philippos had made enough money to bring his wife and two young children from Cyprus to join him in Wollongong. He bought a house for four thousand pounds and taught himself how to cook. A few years later, in 1961, Philippos and Vasilia welcomed the arrival of twin daughters, Anna and Eleni (Helene).

Philippos and Vasilia opened their first fish and chip shop in Figtree, Wollongong. It was an instant success and regarded by many of the locals as the best fish and chips in the region.

In 1968, Philippos and Vasilia move to Melbourne with their twin daughters Anna and Helene to be reunited with their married children Panayiota (Donna) and Savvaki. They opened a fish and chip shop in West Sunshine which they ran for four years. Vasilia was in charge of the grill and hamburgers, helped by her daughter Anna. She developed a special gravy that was a real winner with the customers who would come from near and far to buy the hamburger with the special sauce.

Philippos refused to serve frozen fish. Twice a week he would wake up at 2am in the morning to go to the fish market for fresh fish that he would clean and cut himself. Upon his return home, his wife Vasilia would be there waiting for him with his morning coffee and toast.

In time, Philippos and Vasilia sold their house and shop in West Sunshine and bought a new fish and chip shop in Preston which they ran for ten years. They continued to work as a team, playing Greek music and singing together in the back room while they prepared the food for the lunch and dinner rush hours.

In 1985, Vasilia's health started to decline and Philippos was worried that the long hours in the shop were a contributing factor so he sold the shop. Vasilia was diagnosed with Leukaemia and given only months to live. Philippos was distraught but remained devoted to his wife until the very end.

Philippos turned ninety-two in 2018 surrounded by his growing family. He is loved by everyone and his smile has earned him the nickname 'smiley'.

ACKNOWLEDGEMENTS

I would like to thank Philippos Ioannou for sharing his incredible life story with me. Special thanks to Helene Polydorou for her support with her father's interview and for allowing me to scan their old family photographs.

Philippos strutting down Crown Street in Wollongong, NSW. 1952

Themis & Eleni
YIANNI

Themistocleos (Themis) Yianni was born in the village of Innia, Paphos on the 15th of August 1927. He lived together with his father Yiannis Themestocli, his older brother Efstathios, his younger sister Christina, and his stepmother.

Sadly, Themis' own mother had died soon after he was born and his father, (spurred on by the villagers) decided to remarry to have someone to look after his three young children so that he could tend to his harvesting and crops in the faraway fields. The woman he married (a widow herself with a nine-year-old daughter) was strict and cruel and had an evil plan to get rid of Themis and his siblings so that her own daughter would inherit the family property and fortune.

Apparently, one day as the wicked stepmother was walking along a stony path she accidentally dropped baby Christina onto the ground. Christina died. The stepmother's evil intentions did not end there. She constantly attempted to starve Themis and his brother Efstathios in the hope they too would perish.

Themis remembers how one day, his stepmother tried to feed him *pilafi* (burghul wheat) that was contaminated with *bitera* (wheat chaff). "When my father returned home earlier than usual, my stepmother ran and hid the *gatsarolla* (large pot). I was old enough to talk, so I ran and told my father where to find the pot. He saw the *pilafi* with the *bitera* and flew into a rage. He kicked my stepmother out of our house and out of our lives

forever." In 1937, when Themis was ten years old, an earthquake destroyed the school in his village. His father sent him to study at a Turkish Cypriot school in the neighbouring village of Arodes, where he stayed for nine months.

At age eleven, he was sent to Limassol to work at his cousin's *kafenion* (coffee house) which was coincidently named Themistokli. He was trained to make coffee and serve customers and became a very competent and popular *kafeghis* (coffee maker). "For the first nine months I was paid nothing," he remarks. "Not a single shilling. After my first year I was paid one pound. After my second year I was paid two pounds and after my third year I was paid three pounds."

Young Themis needed to stand on a wooden crate to reach the stove in order to make coffees. He could easily make around 150 coffees during the busiest nights from 6pm until 9pm. The café business was booming during the Second World War, as Limassol was home to many Greek refugees (from Rhodes, Crete, and elsewhere) who were drawn to the *kafenion* to listen for news about the war. It was the only place to have a wireless radio for miles around.

In 1943, Themis became unwell. A local doctor advised him to return to his village in Paphos where the better climate would help him recover. When Yiannis Themestocli realised that his son was a talented and experienced coffee maker he decided to rent a *kafenion* in the village for him to manage. The *kafenion* belonged

to a relative named Giorgios who had a weakness in his legs and could no longer stand for long periods of time.

Within a year, Themis' *kafenion* became so popular that many of the other nine *kafenia* in Innia were forced to close due to a lack of business. Though Themis was indeed a great coffee maker, another reason for his success could well have been the illegal gambling that took place in the back room. Men young and old, Christian and Muslim would gather there to play a popular card game called *Shemé*.

In the space of a few years, Themis' life had changed dramatically. He went from earning two pounds a year at the

Themis (right) and Efstathios Yianni with their cousin Eleni Aristidou. Ktima, Paphos. 1943

Eleni's uncle (her father's brother) Chrisotholos Pallas aged seventy. Innia village, Paphos. c.1940s

'Themistokli' *kafenion* in Limassol, to earning two pounds a night playing *Shemé*. One day a Turkish Cypriot *chaóush* (police sergeant) came to the café along with his constable. He wanted to buy something to eat and drink but did not have any money so he made a deal with the young Themis. "If you let us eat and drink at your *kafenion* for free," he said. "We will turn a blind eye to the illegal gambling that takes place here." Themis was dumbstruck. Was this Turkish official offering him protection? As it turned out, that is exactly what he was offering. Every time somebody went to the police station to report Themis for gambling, the police sergeant would telephone the *kafenion* to 'tip off' Themis. It helped that the only telephone in the village was located in Themis' *kafenion*.

For games that attracted high stakes, Themis would station a man on his roof as a look out. When the look-out would spot the authorities coming towards the village he would quickly pull a string that was attached to a bell. The ringing would warn the players below to abandon their game and to hide their cards and money. Themis' *kafenion* soon became known as the *'Kafenion tou Koudroupi'* after a well-known gambling house in Limassol by the same name. Cypriot men from all over Paphos would come to Innia to try their luck at Themis' *kafenion*. Some men

would gamble livestock or sacks of grain. Some would lose up to thirty pounds in one night, (the equivalent of their annual income). They would then return home to the fiery wrath of their wives or mothers.

Themis had a secret admirer in the village named Eleni. She was the daughter of a goat herder named Panayi Pallas. Themis and Eleni had spent years admiring each other from afar.

As she grew older, Eleni would often admire Themis as she walked past his *kafenion* with her cousin (also named Eleni) on their way home from the village well. Themis also noticed the two pretty girls as they walked past giggling to themselves. At the village festival, Themis would try to impress the girls by strutting past them and throwing coins at the feet of the young children gathered in the square - much to the amusement of any onlookers. Themis made sure his pockets were always full of coins *(piastres)*.

Eleni was born on the 15th of December 1929. As the daughter of a goat herder, she was not required (or expected) to attend school, and so did not learn to read or write. "I would regret this for the rest of my life," she tells me. Instead of an education, Eleni was expected to help her father Panayi look after his large herd of around two thousand goats. From a very young age she would spend days and nights away from her village with her mother and siblings. They would live in a small hut in the *mandra* (pen) where they would milk the goats and make fresh cheese *(haloumi and anari)*.

When the British introduced strict forestry laws banning the grazing of goats on crown land, many goat herders (including Eleni's father) had no choice but to sell their goats. The family decided to try their luck managing a sheep farm, which proved to be an unrewarding enterprise. Cypriots have always favoured goats over sheep simply because the

goats produce more milk than sheep and deliver twice as many offspring.

Eleni enjoyed the company of her five older brothers and younger sister. Despite her family's poverty, she was never bored, nor was she ever idle. There was always too much to do; washing clothes, ironing, preparing meals, cleaning the house, fetching water from the well, gathering pumpkins or zucchini, feeding the animals and so on.

Once all the housework was finished, Eleni would sit in the courtyard of her house with her mother and sister and a few of the other female neighbours laughing and chatting under the stars while they cracked walnuts or shelled

Thimos Pallas, (Eleni's brother) aged nineteen serving in the British Army. c.1941

peas. Her brothers were usually at the *kafenion* together with most of the other males in the village. By the time she reached her mid-teens, Eleni was an accomplished housekeeper and quite mature for her age. It's no wonder her parents considered her ready for marriage at just seventeen.

Themis and Eleni were married in the church of Panayia in Innia on the 18th of August 1946. Their respective fathers had met with the local priest nine months prior to discuss and sign the *prikosynfonon* (dowry agreement).

The wedding feast took place at Eleni's parents' courtyard, outdoors under the stars on a warm summer evening. The guests were treated to large pots of *resi* (wheat and lamb pilaf) and also *kolokasi* (taro and meat stew).

Unfortunately, Themis and Eleni do not have any photographs of their wedding day. Their *koumbaros* (best man) who was an amateur photographer, offered to take their wedding photos. When he went back his darkroom in Nicosia to develop the film, something went wrong. The film and the photos turned out all black. Themis believes that the film in the camera was accidentally exposed to daylight and thus ruined.

In early December 1951, Themis suddenly announced to his wife that he had made plans to travel to Australia. Eleni was shocked. They had three young children; Avgoulla who was almost four, Anna who was almost two and a baby boy Marius who was just a few days old. Themis decided not to tell his wife about his trip until days before he departed to save her the anguish. Despite her protests, he boarded the ship Ravelo and left Cyprus. His decision to leave was largely influenced by the desperate pleas of his older brother Efstathios who was living in Melbourne at the time and feeling quite homesick.

Eleni was heartbroken. Over the next two years she enlisted help from a cousin to write a series of letters to Themis asking him - begging him - to return to the village and back to his family. Themis always wrote back expressing a vague reluctance to return. His last letter to her was more definitive. "I'm sorry Eleni *mou*," he wrote. "But Australia is now my home and I do not plan to return to Cyprus. If you want to be with me, you must leave the village and come with the children to join me here." Eleni's mother Evthymia helped to convince her to sell her home and property and to abide by her husband's wishes.

In 1954, full of trepidation, Eleni reluctantly bundled together her belongings and her three young children and boarded a ship named Cyrenia, bound for Australia. Amongst her belongings were the children's cots and mattresses, six wooden chairs, a trunk full of linen and lace and every necessity that she could manage to bring onto the ship. She had plans to make her new home in Australia as habitable and as Cypriot as possible.

Being illiterate was one of Eleni's main concerns aboard the ship. How was she going to understand the paperwork or signage along the way if she couldn't read or write? As luck would have it (although Eleni credits divine intervention) when the ship anchored in Cairo, she bumped into a man named Haralambos who happened to be her cousin by marriage. Haralambos was also on his way to Australia with his wife and children and since he could read and write, was able to help Eleni

with all the necessary documentation along the way. He also played violin and in the evenings he would entertain the passengers and the crew with many familiar tunes. The ship's cook, a homesick father who was missing his son, took a liking to Eleni's children, especially the young Marius. He offered to babysit for Eleni, allowing the poor mother to have a rest every so often.

Forty days after leaving Cyprus, Eleni and her children were finally reunited with Themis on a crowded wharf at Port Melbourne. Themis drove his family to the western suburb of Sunshine to begin their new life together. Two and half year-old Marius looked suspiciously at the strange man sitting beside him in the car - he did not recognise his father.

Themis found work almost immediately after arriving in Melbourne. He was employed by the large British company, Imperial Chemical Industries (ICI) in Yarraville where his brother Efstathios also worked. Themis was trained as a plumber at ICI. His prior experience as a coffee shop owner or coffee maker did not affect his ability to learn a new trade. Within a few years Themis became quite a skilled labourer.

By the time his wife Eleni and children arrived from Cyprus, Themis had earned enough money to buy a block of land in Sunshine (for 100 pounds). The Yianni family lived with Efstathios and his family for two years until they could afford to build their own house. As the children grew older, Eleni also joined the workforce. She took on seasonal work at the Smorgon fruit-canning factory in Laverton. The factory was owned by a Russian Jewish immigrant and industrialist named Victor Smorgon.

After eight years working at ICI, Themis took a job as a sheet metal worker at Massey Ferguson in Sunshine. Approximately six years later he was enticed back to plumbing by a Cypriot friend named Philippos Philippou who had set up a domestic plumbing business in Sunshine. Themis eventually joined the Board of Works where he stayed until he retired in the early 1980s.

When asked about her life in Australia, Eleni does not express any regrets other than missing her parents. She is glad that her husband was able to find steady and continuous employment. She is grateful that they earned enough money to be

Eleni's older brother Haralambos Pallas. c.1942

able to educate their three children and provide for all their physical and emotional needs. "All I wanted was that my children would receive the education I myself was denied in Cyprus," she exclaims. "Australia has been very good to us. I have no regrets."

ACKNOWLEDGEMENTS
I would like to thank Themis and Eleni Yianni for sharing their story and making me feel so welcome in their home. Sadly, Themis passed away in February 2018 after a short illness. Special thanks to their son Marius Yianni for his kindness and support over the last few years. I would also like to acknowledge Khassandra Yianni for suggesting that I should interview her grandparents.

Achilleas DEMETRIOU

Achilleas Demetriou aged twenty. c.1948

Achilleas Demetriou was born in the town of Polis Chrysochous on the 2nd of February 1928. His parents Demetrios and Anastasia Haralambos were humble people who struggled to make a living against a backdrop of poverty, economic depression and an unfair government taxation system. Achilleas was the eldest of six children (five brothers and a sister). They all lived together in a mud and straw brick house.

Achilleas remembers attending junior school in Polis without any shoes and without a piece of bread to eat; such was the extent of his family's poverty. Fortunately, some of his teachers and a few locals decided to set up an outdoor soup kitchen in the courtyard of the 18th century church of Agia Kyriaki to feed the poorest students. He is still extremely grateful for the kindness of strangers who donated and prepared the food each day. It helped him and others in similar situations survive the school day, especially during the last three years of his education.

After the Second World War, the village of Polis experienced a rebirth and a sudden growth in population. This was the result of large numbers of Cypriot volunteers returning from the war, getting married and having children. According to Achilleas, the population of the town swelled to over two thousand inhabitants. In 1946 however, things took a turn for the worse. Unemployment was on the rise creating a bleak economic forecast for many inhabitants of rural Cyprus. Much of the population in Polis

moved to the larger townships of Ktima, Limassol and Nicosia. Even more departed the island completely, opting to migrate to faraway countries like England, South Africa, America and Australia.

Despite the poverty and hardships that existed at that time, Achilleas remembers that the love and support of his family was enough to sustain him and keep him hopeful for a better future. "We didn't have much in those days," he says. "We often went to bed without a meal - hungry. But we always felt loved and that is what kept us going."

Demetrios Haralambou (Achilleas' father) was a talented and popular carpenter who often made furniture based on the promise that his customers would pay him upon completion of the work. This was not always the case. According to Achilleas, his father lost a lot of money due to customers being unable to pay or even refusing to pay him. "I remember my father employed two Turkish Cypriots named Mustafa and Devrish and sometimes he didn't have enough money to pay them because he wasn't getting paid himself. It was terrible. I wanted to help him. As soon as I finished primary school I went to work with my father. I was twelve years old."

Achilleas and his father made furniture for various families in Polis as well as the surrounding villages: Droushia, Prodromos, Neo Chorio, Makounta, Peristerona, Pelathousa, Kato Yialia and Fasli. A popular commission was the wooden chest used to contain the dowry of a daughter about to be wed. Achilleas and his father Demetrios also made

violins. Because father and son would travel from village to village plying their trade it was commonplace for a customer to provide their food and lodgings for the night. Greek or Turkish alike they were embraced all the same.

In 1946, at age eighteen, Achilleas decided to abandon the life of a travelling carpenter and open his own small workshop in Polis. He specialised

Achileas and Eleni Demetriou. Polis. c.1949

in doors, chairs and other household items. He also made the wooden cradle (*samari*) that was fastened onto the back of a donkey, as well as the twin wooden arms that were attached to oxen for ploughing the fields. All the wooden furniture and farming tools were made by hand; Achilleas did not use any modern woodworking tools. As well as this, he employed a number of ancient and traditional techniques that had been used for centuries.

Like his father, Achilleas struggled to earn a living, as many customers were unable to pay him for his work.

"Can you believe that there are people who have died without paying me," he laments. He also remembers that some of his customers would arrive to collect furniture he had made for them with a bag of wheat as payment. They could only pay him with goods instead of coin.

The wood Achilleas preferred to use was called *rashi* and could be sourced from the nearby Akamas forest. This wood was very strong but malleable and could resist being burnt for a lot longer than other wood.

In 1948, Achilleas met Eleni. She would soon become his wife. Eleni was born on the 10th of June 1925 in nearby Neo Chorio. As the story goes, Eleni's parents Michalis and Marika (Maria) Alexiou had commissioned Achilleas and his father to come and build some furniture for them. When the two fathers met they discussed the making of the furniture as well as the making of a marriage between Eleni and Achilleas. Apparently, a debate ensued as to where the happy couple should live once they were married. Achilleas' mother wanted them to live in Polis while Eleni wanted to live in Neo Chorio close to her parents. Eleni's father settled the matter by agreeing to build his daughter a house in both villages.

After they were married, Achilleas could see that his business was not improving and that he simply was not earning enough money to raise a family. His daughter Maroulla (Mary) was born in 1950 and his wife Eleni was expecting their second child (Stasoulla, born in 1952). Their financial situation was becoming very difficult.

It was around this time that Achilleas saw an advertisement in the

local newspaper from the Australian government seeking qualified tradesmen and craftsmen. He decided to take a chance and try his luck in the so-called lucky country. He boarded an old and painfully slow container ship named the Corsica in December 1951, arriving in Melbourne two months later.

He remembers all too fondly that from the moment he stepped off the ship onto the wooden pier at Port Melbourne, he made the sign of the cross and thanked God for his good fortune in bringing him to such a country. "Can you imagine," he told me. "Coming from a village with mud brick huts and no electricity to this wonderful place full of grand buildings, big green parks, footpaths and wide asphalt roads."

Upon his arrival, he went to live with a Cypriot acquaintance named Andreas who was from the village of Peristerona. After three months the two men travelled together to the Victorian country town of Winchelsea located about thirty miles from Melbourne to work as 'rough carpenters' for a coal mining company called Roach Bros.

Achilleas spoke little English and had to rely on a Greek-to-English dictionary to translate key words and phrases. He remembers a sign at the Winchelsea railway station warning the locals to notify police if they saw a foreigner loitering in the area. By the time he could translate the sign a local policeman approached him on the suspicion that he was loitering. Thankfully, the coal mine manager Mr Ralph Shinas was able to verify that Achilleas was indeed an employee of Roach Bros. From that day forward, Mr Shinas looked after and protected Achilleas as he settled into his new life and trade in Winchelsea.

Achilleas enjoyed living and working in country Victoria. At Roach Bros he was earning around nine pounds a week and receiving three square meals a day, as well as free room and board. He had heard that some migrants became side-tracked once they arrived in Australia and were swept away with delusions of grandeur or seduced by their newfound freedom. Some married men ran off and had affairs with local Australian women, conveniently forgetting about their wives or fiancés waiting for them back in Cyprus.

Achilleas had planned to earn enough money in Winchelsea and then return to

Eleni's father Michalis Alexiou with a family friend in Neo Chorio. c.1960s

Cyprus to live a more comfortable life in Polis with his wife and two daughters. However, he received a stern letter from his father-in-law warning him not to return to Cyprus because the political and economic situation on the island had deteriorated. "Stay where you," his father-in-law warned. "Stay and arrange to bring your wife and children to live with you over there." Achilleas agreed and began to prepare the immigration papers for his family.

In 1953, Achilleas returned to Melbourne where he purchased two blocks of land for four hundred pounds in the leafy suburb of Essendon. His foreman friend Ralph Shinas had advised him to move back to Melbourne, as 'the bush' was no place to bring his family to live. By the time his wife Eleni and his daughters Mary and Stasoulla arrived in 1954, he had just finished building his first home on one of these properties.

Eleni and Achilleas would soon adopt (what would become) a lifelong practice of welcoming and inviting many new arrivals from Cyprus to stay in their home until they could be resettled. They also welcomed the arrival of two more children, Chrysa and Pheodon. Apparently when Pheodon started school he was teased by the other children about his Greek name so his sister Mary suggested that he should call himself Fred. The name stuck and he has been known as Fred ever since.

At first, Eleni found it very difficult to adapt to life in Australia. She would often sit outside her back door, combing her hair and singing sad homecoming songs about Cyprus.

Achilleas felt differently. He enjoyed building a carpenter and builder in the western suburbs of Melbourne. In the late 1950s he sold his house in Essendon and moved his family to a new home that he built in Sunshine. For the next decade he would build many homes in the area. In 1977, he was employed by the Ministry of Housing where he stayed and worked for sixteen years.

Achilleas was also actively involved with the Greek Cypriot community in Sunshine. He helped with the building of the Greek Orthodox Church dedicated to Apostolos Andreas, as well a community hall and Greek school.

He was secretary of the Apostolos Andreas Greek Orthodox Committee for twenty-two years and president for six years. His involvement with the church was recognised in both Melbourne and Cyprus. Even the President of the new Republic of Cyprus, Archbishop Makarios, had heard about his good deeds in Melbourne. So well known was his reputation that whenever Achilleas and his wife would return to Cyprus they were always offered free accommodation by the Archdiocese. Achilleas and Eleni in return, would invite many visiting priests, bishops and dignitaries from Cyprus to eat and stay at their home in Melbourne.

Achilleas was forever grateful for what Australia had given him. If any foreigners dared to criticise Australia, he would retort. "Listen mate, this country gave us our livelihood. It gave us food to eat. It made us wealthy and helped us to raise and educate our children."

Much to his great sadness, his wife Eleni passed away in 2017.

Achilleas still lives in the same house next to Apostolos Andreas church in Sunshine. He is well known and well respected in the area. Although many of his friends have since passed away, his house is never without visitors and guests, including his children and grandchildren. At ninety, he still drives, does odd jobs here and there and even undertakes the weekly shopping. He continues to enjoy being out and about meeting and talking to people. Australia has looked after him and so he continues to return the favour.

ACKNOWLEDGEMENTS
I would like to thank Achilleas Demetriou for sharing his story (and his home-made *Zivania*) with me. Special thanks to his daughter Mary Philippou for her kind assistance and support.

Achilleas' brother George with his wife. 1950

Charilaos
IOANNOU

harilaos Ioannou was born in the village of Polemi in Paphos on the 22nd of April 1931. His siblings were Giorgios (born in 1925), Kyriakos (born in 1928) and a sister Maria (born in 1933). Polemi at the time, was a large village with around 3,000 inhabitants and boasted a courthouse and two cinemas.

Charilaos attended primary school from 1936 until 1942. In his spare time, he helped his parents Yiannis Ioannou and Katerina Nikolaides with farm work and domestic duties.

There is a story about how his brother Giorgios earned himself the nickname *Komantos* (meaning someone in charge). Apparently, after many years watching his illiterate father trying to pay off a loan, he accused the moneylenders of taking advantage of his father by not deducting his repayments. Giorgios had correctly calculated that his father had already paid back his loan several months earlier. The moneylenders flew into a rage and started to call him *Komantos*. The name stuck and his father's debt was scratched from the books.

At the age of twelve, Charilaos was sent to live with a relative up in the mountains to look after his flock of goats. "I did not like being a goat herder," he says, shaking his head. "Too many fleas. And I was so bored. So, after six months I gave it up and returned back home. I was meant to get paid one and a half pounds

a year but because I only stayed for six months I wasn't paid at all."

After his failed experience as a goat herder, Charilaos was sent by his father to learn a trade. He became an apprentice shoemaker to Master Mavris, working in his workshop for four years with no payment. Master Mavris lived near Polemi and was married to Eleni (Charilaos' first cousin) who bore him twelve children. Charilaos, who was not yet a teenager, was required to look after their younger children from time to time, which was something he did not enjoy. He did, however, learn to become a shoemaker in exchange for board and food.

When his apprenticeship finished in 1945, fourteen year old Charilaos found steady work as a shoemaker in the neighbouring village of Psathi. He would walk two miles from Polis there and back every day except Sundays and was earning three shillings a week.

In 1946, he moved to Limassol and found temporary work at the Haralambos Coffee Company. After attempting various labouring jobs in and around Limassol (including working at the port), he decided to go and live in Nicosia.

Jobs were scarce in Cyprus after the Second World War. Charilaos was fortunate to find work at a building supplies company in Nicosia, where he earned five shillings a week filling trucks with sand and gravel. While his wages were minimal, Charilaos managed to earn

Charilaos Ioannou in Nicosia aged eighteen. 1949

enough money to rent a small room, pay a laundry person to wash and iron his clothes and buy food to eat.

Although he was born and raised a Greek Orthodox Christian, Charilaos had many Muslim friends. "There was never a problem," he states proudly. "I tell you, we all got along like brothers. I remember when it was Easter, our goat herders and shepherds would give their flocks to

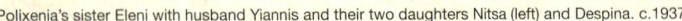
Polixenia's sister Eleni with husband Yiannis and their two daughters Nitsa (left) and Despina. c.1937

the Turks to look after and when it was their Bayram, they would give their flocks to us to look after. That was the way it was back then. There were no problems between us."

Charilaos went on to tell me another story. "I knew a Turkish barber once who was from Lefka. We called him Barber-Ahmet. He was married but his wife could not have any children so they adopted

a little orphaned Christian boy. When Ahmet died, he left all his wealth to his adopted son. He could have adopted a Muslim boy but Ahmet didn't distinguish one child from the next. All he knew was that he had adopted a Cypriot child. That's all that mattered. Religion did not enter into it."

In 1950, Charilaos was out of work again. Prompted by his friends, he joined

Charilaos Ioannou in Cairo, Egypt between 1950 and 1952

the British Armed Forces and was sent to serve in Ismailia in Egypt. In the early 1950s, Ismailia hosted the British Military HQ and the Civilian Administration Centre of the Canal Zone. Charilaos set up a shoe repair shop in the British camp fixing and repairing the shoes and boots of the military personnel. "Whoever knew a trade was automatically put to work to support the British Forces that were stationed there," he recalls. "I worked alongside tailors, blacksmiths and carpenters."

In 1952, Charilaos returned to Cyprus and opened a small shoe shop near Ledra Street in Nicosia. Two years later he would meet Polixenia Sarris. He was renting a small room in a building that was located across the road from the Kallithea Hotel and restaurant. The Kallithea was owned by Polixenia's adoptive parents, Yiannis and Eleni Sarris.

Charilaos would spot Polixenia mopping the floors or cleaning the tables at the restaurant and he soon developed an attraction towards her. One day, he noticed that Polixenia was mopping the floors barefoot. He mustered the courage to go and introduce himself. "You'll catch a cold," he said smoothly, pointing at her bare feet. His opening line was enough to grab her attention. Days later he found himself asking her parents for permission to marry their daughter.

Charilaos and Polixenia were married on the 30th March 1954. He was twenty-four and she was twenty-one.

He bought a block of land in Strovolos for 260 pounds and built his first home for himself and his young bride. Their first child Andreas was born the following year in 1955, followed by Marios in 1956, and Joanna in 1959.

In late 1959, Charilaos kissed his family good bye and left Cyprus, bound for England. The escalating civil unrest and the worsening unemployment crisis on the island saw thousands of Cypriot men emigrate abroad during the 1950s seeking a better future.

Soon after he arrived in London, Charilaos set up a cobbler shop on Plender Street in Camden Town where he would spend most of his time designing, making and repairing women's shoes. He rented a room at the Queen's Building in London's East End for one pound a week. In 1960, after six months apart, Charilaos was able to arrange for his wife and three children to join him in London. His daughter Joanna had just turned one.

In 1964, the Ioannou family welcomed the arrival of a fourth child, Nicholas.

Life in London was difficult for the Ioannou family. Despite the cheap East End accommodation and some mild success with his shoe shop business, Charilaos struggled to make ends meet.

In 1967, he decided to apply for an Australian Government scheme that invited people to emigrate from England to Australia for only ten pounds with their children travelling for free. Australia promised employment, housing, a more relaxed lifestyle and a better climate.

Charilaos and Polixenia's wedding photo. The bridesmaid is Nitsa (Polixenia's niece). Nicosia. 30th March 1954

Charilaos and Polixenia with their sons Andreas and Marios. Nicosia, 1957

ABOVE: Polixenia's mother Maritsa (seated). Her sister Eleni with husband Yiannis and their eldest daughter Despina (right). c.1950

BELOW: Charilaos working in his Camden Town shoe shop in London. June, 1967

suburb of Burwood. "I remember I was earning forty-nine dollars and fifty cents a week," he states. "Women workers were earning around thirty dollars. It was a lot less. I didn't mind the work at Footrest, although I had to travel two hours by tram to Preston and then two hours back home to Burwood."

In 1970, the Ioannou family moved into new accommodation in the northern suburbs of Melbourne. After Charilaos retired from Footrest Shoes, he continued to work as a shoemaker from home. His expertise as a master cobbler attracted many customers to his home-based workshop. In 2016, Charilaos died after a short illness surrounded by his family. "Live a decent and honest life and grow up to be honourable men," were his final words to his grandsons.

Charilaos lived an honest life and was indeed an honourable man.

ACKNOWLEDGEMENTS
I would like to thank Charilaos Ioannou for taking the time to share his living memories about the past with me. Special thanks to his daughter Joanna Georgiou for her kind support and for proof reading her father's life story.

The aim of the scheme was to increase Australia's population following the Second World War.

In 1968, Charilaos and his family travelled on the ship Fairstar from England to Australia to pursue the promise of a better life which would hopefully include steady employment and proper accommodation. However, when they arrived a month later, Charilaos struggled to find a job or even a place to live. His family had to settle for temporary migrant accommodation at the army barracks in Preston while he joined the long unemployment queues.

After three long months living at the army barracks, Charilaos found a job at the Footrest shoe factory in Preston. He also found a house to rent in the leafy

Agathi
CONSTANTINOU

Agathi Constantinou (nee Spyrou) was born in Stroumbi in the district of Paphos on the 1st of May 1924. Some family records, however, suggest that she was actually born in 1922. Her parents Giorgios (Yiorki) and Lambrou (Lambrini) had seven children - Eleni, Kosta, Theodoros, Elias, Agathi, Elizavete and Andonakis.

Agathi's father was a travelling salesman who sold Singer sewing machines around Cyprus. He was also a master shoemaker (cobbler) and owned a small shop in the heart of the village.

Agathi speaks fondly about her parents, in particular her father: "Even though he was barely educated, my father could communicate with every class of person, from the poorest peasant to the wealthiest aristocrat."

Master Giorgios (as he was often referred to) was respected and well loved by all who knew him. It was not uncommon for men in the *kafenion* (coffee house) to immediately stand up and offer Master Giorgios a chair as he entered. As a cobbler, he never took money from the poor. In gratitude, many poor people gave him baskets of oranges, *haloumi* (cheese) or a few loaves of bread.

Agathi recalls the night her father brought two strangers to their home. It was a wet, stormy night, close to midnight when her father came across two cold and hungry Turkish Cypriot travellers huddled together in a dark corner near the village square. They had become stranded in the village because of the storm and did not have anywhere to stay. Without hesitation, Master Giorgios invited the two men back to his house and summoned Agathi and her mother out of their beds to cook the strangers a meal and to fetch them some dry clothes to wear. The men were fed pork sausages and some soup, which they ate with much gusto and appreciation. Afterwards, Agathi's mother realised that she had made an error feeding them pork, as they were Muslim. A few days later, the two men returned to Agathi's house with two large baskets full of oranges and mandarins as a gift to thank her father for his kindness. This is an example of how the Muslim and Christian communities coexisted and lived together peacefully.

By the time Agathi was old enough to attend school, a few of her siblings had left the village. Her older brother Kosta was sent to Egypt to find work (he would later move to Sudan). Her brother Elias went to live in South Africa and her other brother Theodoros and her younger sister Elizaveth both moved to Limassol. Theodoros became a successful tailor and Elizaveth became a dressmaker.

It was common for younger people in Stroumbi to move away from home to seek a more prosperous life elsewhere. After all, the village was small, with only around three hundred inhabitants - most of whom were desperately poor and

Agathi (on the left) with her sister Elizaveth. c.1940s

trying to survive by working as farmers or goat herders.

As a young child, Agathi would find ways to amuse herself with other children in the village. They would play popular games like chasey, hide and seek and marbles. Agathi even made her own dolls. She would bind together thin branches from a tree to form a skeletal frame and then wrap strips of cloth around the sticks to form the body and the head of the doll. She would then use tree-sap to glue strands of her own hair onto the head of the doll. She would even use empty cicada shells as shoes.

Agathi admits that she was naïve and gullible as a young girl. Once, a gypsy woman came to her house and asked her if she wanted her fortune told. Agathi

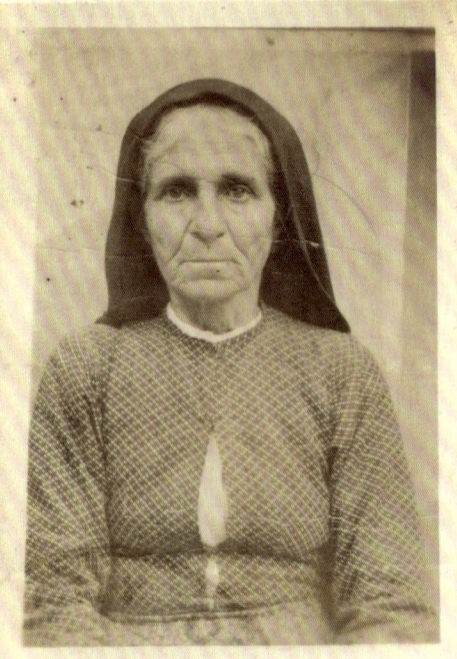

Agathi's aunt Kyriakou from Drimou. Year unknown.

agreed and so the gypsy told her a tale that someone had secretly taken hair from her head and placed a spell on her that she would never get married. As proof, the gypsy woman cracked open an egg to show Agathi that there was hair inside. Agathi was so frightened that she agreed to pay the gypsy woman the required fee to break the spell. At that moment, her father arrived home and banished the gypsy from his house with a slap across her face. He was very cross at his daughter's gullibility.

Agathi and her siblings were spared

the hard toil of working on the land. Their father earned enough as a cobbler to be able to employ a team of farmhands to plough and tend to his fields. Master Giorgios did not want his children to slave outdoors under the hot sun. He wanted them all to be educated and to pursue more practical crafts and trades. With this in mind, Agathi was trained by her aunt to embroider, sew and weave. By the time she turned sixteen, she had become an accomplished and skilful embroiderer.

"I had a good memory, so I was able to learn fast," she says proudly. "I was able to create intricate patterns in a short amount of time." At this point of the interview Agathi jumps out of her chair with astonishing agility and goes to fetch some remarkable woven fabrics from a nearby cabinet. "Did you make these?" I ask her upon her return. "Of course I did, who else?" she answers sharply. "I was sixteen years old and each one took me about three months to complete."

As a young teenage girl, Agathi enjoyed nothing more than sitting on the balcony of her house embroidering and basking in the fresh air. She would immediately run and hide, however, when the villagers were seen returning home from the fields. "I was afraid that if they saw me sitting there they may think that I was lazy or spoilt. You see, all the girls in my village worked in the fields. I was very lucky to be allowed to stay at home with my mother to sew and embroider."

Agathi remembers a blissful and innocent childhood. She would spend a lot of her spare time talking and playing with the other girls in the village, including her cousins. "I wasn't allowed to mix with the boys. It was forbidden. You have to understand, in those days if a girl was seen with a boy it could jeopardise her chances of getting married."

Many young men were interested in Agathi, from within and outside Stroumbi. Their interest was largely due to Agathi's good nature and sweet appearance, but also because of her family's good reputation. Master Giorgios was kept busy declining all the requests for her hand in marriage: "No, no," he would say adamantly to the would-be suitors. "My Agathi is not ready for marriage."

Agathi remembers a jealous cousin who would tell her horrible lies about some of her admirers to try and dissuade her from developing an interest in any of

Agathi's uncle Arestidi. Year unknown.

them. "People would gossip and make up stories all the time," Agathi remarked. "There was a lot of jealousy and envy going around." It turned out that her jealous cousin was trying to redirect the would-be-suitors towards herself.

There was one admirer, however, who was particularly persistent and eventually successful in gaining Agathi's attention. His name was Chrysanthos Constantinou, a popular young barber in the village. "We knew of each other from a young age since we lived in the same village," Agathi tells me. "However we were never allowed to meet in person. I found out that whenever Chrysanthos would go to the *kafenion*, all the men would gossip about the girls in the village. When my name was mentioned, the men would tell him that I was a good catch."

Apparently, Chrysanthos would send his aunt to Agathi's house on a weekly basis to try and arrange their marriage. Her father kept ignoring her requests until one day Agathi's frustrated mother pleaded with him, "just tell them yes or no and let the poor family rest." With that, Master Giorgios finally gave his consent for Chrysanthos to marry his daughter.

When Agathi discovered that Chrysanthos wanted to marry her, she wanted desperately to sneak a look at him. Unable to simply walk past his barbershop she decided to hatch a clever ruse. There happened to be a water trough located near his shop, so Agathi asked her mother if she could take their

A family from Pisouri who would sew for Agathi's family. They were visiting Stroumbi on the day this photo was taken, as they were friends of Agathi's father. Year unknown.

that every time he saw her walking her donkey past his shop he would run back inside clutching his head (as if in pain) and shout out, "I must have her. I must have her. I will go crazy if I don't marry this girl. She is the best-dressed girl in the village. I must have her," much to the amusement of his customers.

Once, when Agathi was walking to the water trough with her donkey, Chrysanthos decided to follow her. At one point, she bent over to adjust her stockings, causing her long skirt to rise up and reveal her long slender legs. "I thought I was going to die on the spot," Chrysanthos later told her. Agathi had no idea that he had been watching her.

There was also the story that before they were officially introduced, Chrysanthos would return home from work and immediately go and lie upon a large woodpile next to his family's mud brick oven. He would do this every day until his suspicious mother followed him there and discovered that her son had a perfect view of Agathi sitting on her balcony doing her embroidery. Once again, Agathi was unaware that she was being admired from afar.

Agathi's father promised to give Chrysanthos a house and a parcel of land as part of her agreed marriage dowry. Chrysanthos apparently responded by saying, "Master Giorgios – just give me Agathi, nothing else. All I want is Agathi."

Agathi and Chrysanthos were married on the 19th of October 1947. She was twenty-two years old and he was twenty-one. On their wedding day, they received a total of one hundred pounds from their guests, which was a considerable amount of money in those days. In an incredible act of kindness, Chrysanthos gave the money to his brother-in-law Elias so that he could fulfil his desire to travel to South Africa. Agathi was overwhelmed that her husband would care enough about her family to help out in this way. Her attraction to Chrysanthos grew even more. Her brother Elias went on to became a wealthy businessman in South Africa, owning his own restaurant and a number of successful petrol stations.

In 1948, Agathi gave birth to her son Christos (Taki). Just three years later in 1951, her husband Chrysanthos suddenly announced his intention to leave Stroumbi and travel abroad. "He had become increasingly annoyed by the

donkey to drink from it. "What are you talking about dear girl?" her mother exclaimed. "There is a water trough next to our house." Agathi told her mother that the donkey refused to drink from the trough next to the house. Unconvinced, the mother led the donkey straight to the nearby water trough. Sure enough, the donkey refused to drink. No matter how many times Agathi's mother tried, the animal refused. Agathi was finally allowed to walk the animal to the water trough opposite Chrysanthos' barbershop.

What Agathi's mother did not know was that her clever daughter had secretly trained their donkey to refuse the water from their water trough. Every time the poor animal would dunk its head for a drink she would smack it across the nose until the donkey gave up completely. Her clever ruse had worked. She was now free to walk past Chrysanthos' shop, sneaking shy glances at him as he stood there in his doorway smiling back at her. "We fell in love with our eyes," she recalls fondly.

Chrysanthos later confessed to Agathi

gossip and the narrow-mindedness of some of the men in our village," she told me. "He wanted to travel to Australia to set up a new life for us. I was very upset. I did not want him to leave. As far as I was concerned, we had a comfortable life in the village with plenty of friends and a beautiful three-year-old boy to cherish and look after."

Chrysanthos was so adamant to leave Cyprus that he lied to Agathi about being drafted as a soldier to fight in a fictitious war. "Would you rather see me die at the front?" he asked her. "Or should I travel to Australia where it is safe?" Having limited knowledge of the greater world, poor Agathi believed him and reluctantly agreed to let him leave.

After Chrysanthos left for Australia, she stayed in the village with her parents and young son. In September 1953, a devastating earthquake hit Cyprus in the district of Paphos. Thirty-eight people died and hundreds more were injured. Many villages suffered extensive damage, including Stroumbi, which was partly destroyed. Half of Agathi's house

collapsed in the earthquake including a room where her young son usually slept. Fortunately, young Taki was staying with his uncle Theodoros in Limassol at the time of the earthquake. "Who knows," Agathi says. "If my son was with me in the village that day, he may have died."

Agathi missed Chrysanthos terribly. So much so, that one day she decided to send him a letter in which she wrote a lie that their son was gravely ill. On receiving the letter, panic-stricken Chrysanthos sent a frantic telegram to his brother-in-law Theodoros in Limassol to find out what had happened. Theodoros immediately confronted his sister who confessed to her desperate lie. "What were you thinking?" Theodoros shouted at her. "Do you think Australia is forty miles away?"

Theodoros apologised to Chrysanthos in a hastily written telegram and explained that his sister had lied in the hope that he would return to Cyprus. From that day forward, every letter that Agathi wrote to Chrysanthos was read and checked by her father. Agathi could not hold back her tears. In fact, she would use the excuse

Wedding in Stroumbi. The bride is Agathi's second cousin Anastasia with her husband Nikolas. Agathi is standing next to the bride, as maid of honour. Year unknown.

that she needed to fetch grapes from the vineyard so she could hide amongst the vines to sob uncontrollably - away from the disapproving eyes of her parents and fellow villagers.

Chrysanthos struggled living abroad away from his wife and son. Work in Melbourne was surprisingly scarce. Because of his limited language skills and lack of formal qualifications as a barber, he had no choice but to accept work as a labourer.

Chrysanthos first job was digging ditches for a coal company in the country town of Yallourn. When in Melbourne, he would take on odd jobs in the hope of earning a few extra pennies. These included dealing cards at a local Greek *kafenion* and even cutting hair for some of the patrons.

It was not uncommon in the early 1950s for newly arrived migrants to struggle to find work. Chrysanthos was more fortunate than others. One of his friends was known to walk the length of Lygon Street (around eight miles), at least once a week knocking on factory doors looking for work. On his return trip home he would scan the sidewalks for stray pennies to buy himself something to eat.

In 1954, three years after he left Cyprus, Chrysanthos was able to finally arrange the paperwork for his wife and son to come and join him in Australia. After three years apart, Agathi was overjoyed at the prospect of being reunited with her husband. Her one regret was that her sister Elizavete was able to convince her to cut her long hair before she departed from Limassol. "My hair was my pride and joy," she laments. "It fell down the length of my back below my waist in two long dark plaits. My sister told me that it was uncouth to travel abroad with long hair and I believed her. My father was devastated when he saw my short hair."

Before Agathi left Cyprus, her father gave her some worldly advice. "When you arrive in Australia, you will meet many people; some nice and some not so nice. Whatever you do, never say a bad word about anyone. Keep your mouth shut and your opinions to yourself. If you do not like someone, just slowly disassociate yourself with them. Words are like bullets. Once they leave your mouth you can never get them back."

Agathi's second cousin Anastasia with her husband Nikolas. Agathi was the maid of honour. Year unknown.

Agathi and her son Taki boarded the Italian ship SS Soriento. They were placed into the lower-class (or steerage section) of the ship, despite having paid for second class. It turned out, an unscrupulous shipping agent in Limassol pocketed the money and gave the unsuspecting Agathi the lower-class tickets. She remembers rows of bunk beds all made of hessian cloth and that the food on the ship did not please many of the passengers, especially the daily serve of pasta and beans.

Soon after the ship departed, Agathi became extremely seasick and was often bedridden for days on end. Thankfully, she had met a few kind passengers who took turns to look after her son Taki.

Agathi's seafaring adventure was about to change for the better after she befriended a couple from the Greek island of Chios, who were also travelling to Australia with their son Dino.

Agathi's older sister Eleni holding her son Kosta. Agathi is on the right holding her niece Katerina. 1947

One day Agathi (no longer bedridden) caught sight of Dino's mother bent over in a corner and moaning. Agatha suspected the poor woman may have suffered a heart attack. Instinctively, she climbed a ladder to the upper deck and alerted Dino, who rushed to fetch the ship's doctor. The mother's life was saved.

In gratitude, the family from Chios invited Agathi and her son to share their First-Class cabin with them for the remainder of the trip. "Only God knows how I managed to find the strength to climb up that ladder to alert that boy," exclaimed Agathi. "I can tell you that some of the other passengers were not happy that I had moved into First Class. They even tried (unsuccessfully) to report me to the ship's authorities."

By the time the ship finally docked in Melbourne, Agathi was still quite weak and frail. Her reunion with her husband

Chrysanthos on the wharf was very emotional. Chrysanthos took his wife and son back to his small rented apartment on Exhibition Street in the city. Young Taki was not impressed when he discovered that he had to sleep in his own bed that night: a rude shock after sharing his mother's bed for the last three years.

The Constantinou family's first rental property, was in a large building opposite the Exhibition Buildings in Carlton. At any given time, there would be five or six families living together in the building, all sharing the kitchen and the outdoor toilet. The gas meter required three-pence to operate for a specified length of time. It was not uncommon to have a queue of people waiting in the corridor for their turn to cook a simple meal.

Although Agathi was glad to be reunited with her husband, she struggled to settle into this new and strange land.

Language and culture was a huge barrier and she was lonely when Chrysanthos was at work. Her attempt to speak English with her Australian neighbours was usually met with bouts of laughter.

Chrysanthos finally found steady work as a barber, working for a Greek man who owned a small shop under the iconic Flinder's Street station. Despite earning a decent wage, he still struggled to make ends meet, so Agathi made the difficult decision to also join the workforce. She had no choice but to leave her young son at home alone while she went off to work in a nearby factory. This was quite heart-breaking for her. "I used to go to work and cry every day," she says softly, fighting back tears. "It was very difficult for us in those early years."

Agathi and Chrysanthos had intended to stay and work in Australia for only a few years and then return back to Cyprus to live permanently. However, the brewing tensions and unstable political situation on the island delayed their return for good.

"You know, Costa *mou*," Agathi says with outstretched hands. "I believe that had we returned to Cyprus during that unstable time, perhaps my son Taki would have been drafted into the army or killed during the conflict in 1974. Perhaps my husband Chrysanthos - with his tendency to speak his mind – might have been shot and killed. It was probably just as well that we stayed in Australia, the way things turned out in Cyprus."

Agathi's siblings, Elizavete and Theodoros. c.1941

Chrysanthos, Agathi and young Christaki. c.1950

In 1957, with Taki now attending school, Agathi went to work in a nearby factory in Abbotsford called Ring Grip while Chrysanthos continued to work as a barber in a number of different establishments. They moved into a larger rental property before eventually purchasing their first Australian home in Carlton. Chrysanthos was earning thirteen pounds a month and Agathi was earning nine pounds. The mortgage for the house was around ten pounds a month. Agathi remembers how they struggled to have enough money leftover to pay the bills and buy food.

At Ring Grip, Agathi was stationed on the assembly line putting together American designed wall plugs. Ring Grip was one of the main electrical accessory manufacturers in Australia. Agathi could easily assemble 1200 plugs a day; 240 more than the required quota. She often received a salary bonus for her efforts.

In the late 1960s, Agathi's brother Kosta arrived in Melbourne with his young wife and family, after fleeing from the civil war in Sudan. Kosta and his family left Sudan with the clothes on their backs and few personal belongings. He had migrated to Sudan in the 1930s and after many years working for others, he set up his own successful grocery business employing half a dozen people. In 1956, he travelled to Athens where he met and married a Greek woman, twenty years his junior. He returned to Sudan with his wife where he continued to run a successful business - until he lost everything in the civil war. When Kosta arrived in Australia, he also struggled to find work, as he spoke no English and was now in his late fifties. Eventually, he found a job with General Motors. Agathi remembers seeing her brother one morning dressed in his work overalls and sitting on the edge of his bed sobbing and speaking to himself. "Forget Kosta from Sudan. You are Kosta from Australia now". It was an affecting moment for the siblings.

Agathi returned to Cyprus in 1969. It had been fifteen years since she last saw her parents. She closes her eyes and recites a poem. "Mother, this bitter life abroad has made me long to see you. But I have roots and branches here (Australia) that pull me back again."

Chrysanthos eventually bought his own barbershop in the suburb of Ivanhoe. He had a constant stream of customers, including many students from Ivanhoe Grammar School. That was until the Beatles toured Melbourne in 1964 and changed the hairstyles of young Australian boys forever. The new 'mop-top' style meant that haircuts for boys became less frequent.

With his business declining, Chrysanthos sold his Ivanhoe barbershop and bought another business in Heathmont in the mid-1970s. He worked there until 1986 when he retired and handed over the business to his son Taki. Chrysanthos passed away in 2009.

Agathi still lives in the family home and at age ninety-three (or ninety-five, depending on which birth record you believe), she still shows incredible vitality. She is astonishingly fit and nimble and her memory is largely intact. She claims that if it weren't for her large garden she would have died years ago. "My garden has kept me alive." Agathi has two grandchildren and three great grandchildren.

ACKNOWLEDGEMENTS
I would like to thank Agathi Constantinou for allowing me the privilege to interview her for this book. Her ability to recall facts about the past was truly impressive. Thanks also to Vicki Raffoul for inviting me to interview her grandmother and for all her assistance thereafter. Special thanks to Agathi's son Taki for his amazing generosity and support.

Chrysanthos Constantinou. c.1951

Andreas & Panayiota
NIKOLAOU

Andreas Nikolaou was born in the village of Kallepia in the district of Paphos on the 6th February 1931. His parents, Nicolas Georgiou and Nymfodora Alexandrou were simple farmers and spent most of their time growing crops and tending their vineyards. Andreas would often accompany his older siblings, Eleni and Christodoulos to the family farm to assist with the many tasks required throughout the four seasons. Andreas remembers collecting *rasha* (a special firewood) that he would sell to various bakeries in Ktima town. The ten-mile trip to Ktima by donkey would usually take a few hours but Andreas would deliver his wood whatever the weather.

Andreas spoke fondly of his time living in Paphos. "Whoever owned a vineyard in Cyprus managed to survive. Except if the weather turned bad or a drought occurred. Our family vineyard produced many edible delights. The leaves were used for cooking *koupepia* (stuffed vine leaves); and the grapes were eaten fresh off the vine, sold in bunches, or dried and sold as sultanas. The grape juice was used to make *soujouko* (sweets) or wine. The Cypriot village that did not have items or farm produce to sell usually suffered the most from poverty."

At the age of thirteen, Andreas was taken out of school by his father to learn a trade. He was sent to work as an apprentice with a chair maker in Ktima

Andreas Nikolaou aged twenty-four in Ballarat. 1955

named Yianni. After two years, however, he left and went to work with a master furniture maker named Nicholis *tou* Yatou.

Every Monday morning before sunrise, Andreas would meet up with other young apprentices on the outskirts of his village. Together they would walk across the fields and through neighbouring villages until they reached Ktima. They would work all week staying in rented rooms or at their master's house and return to their villages only on the weekends.

"There were five or six of us from Kallepia that would meet on the side of

the road," Andreas recalls. "One boy was a carpenter's apprentice; another was a tailor's apprentice; another was a cobbler's apprentice and so on. We each had a small basket of food to last us a few days. This might include grapes, a potato, a hard-boiled egg, a piece of haloumi cheese and some bread. My parents would sometimes deliver extra food to me by bus during the week."

During his apprenticeship in Ktima, Andreas would share a room at night with a cousin named Haralambos who also worked in the furniture-making trade. He remembers sleeping on a bench that was covered in fresh wood shavings. "It was such a pleasant smell to sleep on the shavings from a pine tree," said Andreas. A few years later his parents gave him a proper mattress for his bed that was stuffed with sheep's wool.

When they finished work every Saturday afternoon, Andreas and the other young apprentices would return to their villages on foot. If the boys did not feel like walking the ten miles home, they would scamper onto the back of a truck or bus to hitch a free ride. "We didn't have any money to afford the bus fare," remarks Andreas. "Don't forget, we did not get paid for the first two years of our apprenticeship."

One particular Saturday afternoon, Andreas fell awkwardly off the bus when it was his turn to jump off. "No one showed me the proper way to jump off a moving bus," he laughs. "I wasn't crying because my hands and feet were bleeding. I was crying because my one and only pair of trousers now had large holes in them."

After his two-year apprenticeship in Ktima, Andreas started to get paid one shilling a week. He worked for Master Nicholis for six years, from the age of thirteen until he turned nineteen. By the end of his apprenticeship, he was earning six shillings a day.

In 1950, Andreas decided to leave Cyprus and travel to Australia. He was now twenty years old and like so many other young men, he was drawn to the promise of a more prosperous life abroad. Cyprus, after the war, was suffering economically and jobs were scarce all over the island.

Andreas left Limassol in December 1950 on board the Egyptian-owned ship SS Misr, stopping at Port Said, Djibouti, Colombo and finally arriving in Melbourne in January 1951. Apparently the ship fare was 172 pounds and the entire trip took twenty-eight days.

A few weeks after arriving in Australia, Andreas found work as a carpenter for the State Electricity Commission (SEC) in the country town of Morwell. Many Cypriot migrants were forced to live and work in country Victoria because of job shortages in Melbourne. The paper mill in the country town of Traralgon, for example, was a large employer of Cypriots during the 1950s. For some migrants, however, Australia became the 'not-so-lucky country', due to the Government's credit squeeze in the 1950s. More than a few men decided to return to Cyprus.

Andreas stayed and worked in Morwell for two years. He was paid around fifteen pounds a fortnight with food and board provided. "I remember the hot summer days, trying to sleep in a tent at night and working during the heat of the day on tall wooden scaffolding. There were no health and safety precautions back then. We didn't even

FROM LEFT: Andreas Yiallouris, Rogges, Prodromos Neofytou, Nikos Frenaritis, unknown, Andreas Nikolaou, Yiorgos. Morwell, 1952

wear harnesses or hard hats. We slept in tents for six months until they eventually moved us into timber huts."

Andreas found plenty of work with the SEC in Victoria, moving from Morwell to Seymour, then on to Ballarat and Mildura and even back to Melbourne, on occasions. "I preferred to work in the country towns rather than the city," he told me. "In the country towns you received food and board, whereas in Melbourne you had to find your own food and accommodation - which was tough for us migrants. For instance, I used to rent and share a room in the city with a few other single Cypriot men. On my days off work, I would travel to Melbourne by bus and stay in a room on Mackenzie Street. My friends and I would eat all our meals at various Greek clubs and cafés in the city. It would cost us a bit of money. Our accommodation did not have any hot water, so we would go to the city baths to wash and have a shower."

Andreas was introduced to Panayiota Nikolaou in August 1957. He was working in the small country town of Alexandria and had come to Melbourne for the weekend. A friend who knew Panayiota invited him to visit her house. Andreas remembers undergoing a minor interrogation by a man named Giorgios who was married to Panayiota's sister Erasmia. Apparently, Giorgios interrogated all of Panayiota's suitors.

Panayiota remembers that Andreas was rather underweight and looking pale. Apparently, he was suffering with the potentially deadly Asian flu. Despite his poor condition, Andreas managed to impress twenty-two year old Panayiota and she agreed to marry him. They were engaged on the 15th of August 1957.

Panayiota Nikolaou was born in Alaminos, Larnaca on the 23rd November 1935. Her mother Chrystofora Styli and her father Nicholas Kosta had six other daughters and a son.

She remembers that her village had around three hundred inhabitants, including a few Turkish Cypriot families. A bridge in the middle of the village separated the communities, however both Muslims and Christians would mix

Andreas' father, Nicolas Georgiou. Kallepia village, Paphos. 1948

and interact freely with one another. The Greek Cypriots would spend most of their time tending their crops and olive trees, while the Turkish Cypriots spent most of their time making *anari* cheese, yogurt and other dairy-based products. Panayiota's father was a master bee keeper and he would often give his Turkish friends large jars of honey in exchange for fresh milk or cheese.

Although the village of Alaminos was only two miles from the beach, Panayiota was never allowed to go there. Besides, none of the girls in the village wore or owned a swimsuit. "We were bashful," she explains. "We would never dare to show our legs to anyone, not even our father. When we returned home from the fields, we would go and hide in a dark corner to wash our feet and change our stockings. Nor would we dare to wear short sleeve clothing." Panayiota remembers that all the girls in the village had long dark hair, which was a symbol of pride and honour. "It was shameful to cut your hair short in those days."

According to Panayiota there were only two families in her village that were not directly related to her. "Everybody in our village was somehow related. Marriages therefore had to be arranged with Cypriots from other villages."

When she turned twelve years old Panayiota was sent to nearby Scala to learn how to embroider *lefkaritika*. She was paid to create embroideries on napkins and tablecloths for a shop in Scala and earned enough money to no longer rely on the pocket money her parents gave her. She worked long hours (often until midnight) by the light of a paraffin lamp, anxious to complete each commission. In those days, it was not compulsory for parents to send their children to school, so many children stayed home to help their parents with domestic chores or to work on family farms. Some were sent away to learn a trade or craft while others were sent to work as servants for wealthy families.

Panayiota spent many years living with her maternal grandmother Panayiotou Stili. Her grandmother became a widow at the age of twenty-five, after her husband was crushed under his ox-drawn wagon. Apparently, *Pappou* Stili had a reputation as the village strongman and was known to have once lifted an ox-cart with seven men on board.

Andreas Nikolaou.
Shell Refinery, Newport, 1955

Panayiota would often assist her grandmother in her small village grocery store by serving customers, calculating purchases and managing various lines of credit. Panayiota's grandmother could not read or write but she created a pictorial system of symbols to help her calculate every purchase. For example, if someone owed her five *grosha*, she would draw her little symbol for the currency, then add five short lines next to it.

In 1955, Panayiota left Cyprus on the ship SS Cyrenia to join her sister Erasmia who lived in Melbourne with her husband Giorgios Stavrou. She was just shy of twenty years old.

Soon after she arrived Panayiota found work at the Jam Factory in South Yarra. Unfortunately, the refrigerated environment affected her health and she had to leave the factory. She then joined her brother Kosta at a knitting mill in Fitzroy. There were lots of Italian women at this factory and soon Panayiota and Kosta learnt to speak Italian.

Andreas and Panayiota Nikolaou were married on the 23rd of November in 1957 at the Greek Orthodox Church of Evangelismos in East Melbourne. For the first two years of their marriage they lived with Panayiota's sister Erasmia and her husband Giorgios.

In 1960 Andreas decided to open a hardware store in the seaside suburb of Albert Park. Panayiota supported her husband's decision to buy the shop, which they named Nichola's Hardware. In fact, her newly acquired Italian language skills proved invaluable when dealing with the many Italian customers who came into the store. Panayiota laughs as she recalls

the early days of the hardware store. "When we opened the store in January 1960 I couldn't speak any English. But I eventually managed to learn English and a great deal about builder's hardware."

In the years between 1960 and 1976, Andreas and Panayiota lived in the space above the store with their two children Dora and Nicholas. As the children grew older, they decided to buy a house in nearby Hampton and relocated the family there in 1976.

After more than three decades, Andreas decided to sell his hardware store and retire in 1993.

Panayiota and Andreas had often planned to return to Cyprus to live with their children. "All Cypriot migrants living abroad remember and love their country," explains Panayiota. "As it turned out we were better off staying in Australia, especially after what occurred in 1974. Who knows what would have become of us, had we returned?"

ACKNOWLEDGEMENTS
Thank you to Andreas and Panayiota Nicolaou for inviting me into their home and allowing me to write and share their life story. Thank you also to their daughter Dora Eracleous for her kind assistance.

Panayiota Nikolaou (on the right) with a friend Athenia Demetriou at the village festival in Anafotia, Larnaca. 1954

ΦΕΝΙΟΝ "Ο ΝΑΠΟ

SECUR

Napoleon PANTAZIS

Napoleon Pantazis was born in the town of Ktima, Paphos in 1931. His parents Neophytos and Paraskevou had six children. Their first son Dimitris was born in 1928 followed by a daughter Eleni in 1930 and Napoleon in 1931. Paraskevou gave birth to two more sons (Kostas and Yiangos) but tragically, they both died young after succumbing to an epidemic that was ravishing the region in the early 1930s. In 1936, another daughter, Agnes was born.

Napoleon's father Neophytos Pantazis was born in Petra *(tis Soleas)* in 1900. Petra was once a small mixed village in Cyprus in the district of Nicosia, but is now completely uninhabited.

During the First World War, Neophytos enlisted with the Cypriot Mule Corp. He was posted just outside Salonika in Northern Greece, where he was required to use a mule cart to deliver food and provisions to the British soldiers at the front who were fighting the Ottoman Turks. He would often return back to base with injured or dead soldiers which must have been both physically and emotionally taxing work. Napoleon's father was only seventeen when he joined the Mule Corp. He had experience with mules from his years helping out his father Pantazis Louka, who owned and used mules on their family farm.

When the war was over, Neophytos returned to Cyprus, where he trained to become a policeman. Napoleon remembers that his father had two white police horses. One was named Varvara and the other Bianca.

In 1927, Neophytos Pantazis married Paraskevou Demitriou Kouti. Paraskevou's mother was from Neo Chorio. Her family had lived in this village for generations working as shepherds and farmers. They had orchards full of olive, fig and carob trees. Paraskevou's father was from the village of Ineia, next to Droushia.

Napoleon Pantazis' love affair with food started from a young age when he would watch his mother preparing feasts with only a few ingredients, all sourced from local farms and orchards. At the time, people grew or farmed almost all the food they needed. Most villagers had chickens, turkeys, goats and rabbits and perhaps one pig that would be killed at Christmas (to make *souvla, sheftalia and sausages*). Thanks to Neophytos' comfortable salary, his family were able to eat fish twice a week – a luxury most people in Cyprus could not afford.

In the 1930s, refrigeration was non-existent. Cypriots kept their meat in fly-wire wooden boxes that were suspended off the ground from a rafter in the kitchen. People would also make their own cheese like *haloumi* and *anari* from goat's milk. In the winter, Napoleon remembers how his mother and grandmother would make stuffed figs or cook chestnuts in a furnace or roast skewered olives over the hot coals. Food was the heart and soul of village life growing up in Cyprus.

"My mother was a great cook," recalls Napoleon. "She also made all our clothes. She kept silkworms in a large cane basket that was hung from a rafter in the house. My job was to feed the silkworms mulberry leaves. I enjoyed listening to the noise they would make as they munched on the leaves. It was like music to me."

As a policeman, Napoleon's father Neophytos was often required to work long hours - sometimes up to eighteen hours a day, seven days a week. He was also required to travel very long distances in order to settle disputes throughout the district of Paphos. Napoleon remembers that his father was always clean-shaven and immaculately dressed in his policeman's uniform.

Every few years, Neophytos would be transferred to a different village - so Napoleon and his family were constantly moving from house to house. They moved from Droushia, to Amargeti, back to Polis then on to Kouklia, Panayia, Kelokedara and Lyssos.

Napoleon started primary school at age seven, when his family were living in Droushia. He was taught Greek for the first four years. English was introduced later. His primary school education shifted from village to village depending on where his father was stationed.

"Every three years we would load our horse and cart and move to another village in Paphos," recalls Napoleon. "For me, Lyssos was my favourite village. I was a teenager by then and I remember how beautiful the village was. I met boys in that village who would become my life-long friends. Paul Savvas was my best friend and one day I would be the best man at his wedding in Darwin, Australia."

Napoleon attended high school in Ktima. His parents rented a room for him to live with Andronikos Komodromou and his family for around one pound a month.

Once a week, his mother would send him food and provisions.

After completing high school in 1948, Napoleon had the intention of becoming a policeman just like his father. In those days his father was earning around forty pounds a month, which Napoleon remembers was paid in gold coins. It was a good occupation.

Just before Napoleon could enrol with the Police Academy – a letter arrived from Australia. It completely altered his plans, changing his life forever. The letter was sent from Darwin by a man named Kleopas Stylianou, who was a family acquaintance. The letter expressed Kleopas' desire to marry Napoleon's older sister Eleni. Kleopas was amongst the first Greek-Cypriots who flew out to Darwin after the Second World War.

Napoleon decided to accompany his sister to Darwin. In January 1951, they flew from Cyprus to Cairo in a small-chartered airplane before boarding a larger passenger plane called the Constellation arriving in Darwin three days later.

The cost of the flight was 150 pounds, which his father had to borrow from a relative in Cyprus.

Napoleon decided to stay in Darwin until his sister was married. His plan was to find work and earn enough money to pay back his father's debt before returning to Cyprus to commence his studies at the Police Academy in Nicosia. But life, once again, had other plans for the nineteen year old.

Darwin in the early 1950s was a remote and intimidating place for new arrivals from Europe. After the war, some of the locals in Darwin were racist towards immigrants. The hot and dusty frontier town already had a small population of Greek-Cypriots who arrived after the Second World War - in somewhat bizarre circumstances.

Kleopas (Steve) Stylianou, Peter Syrimi and Savvas Christodolou were among a dozen men who left Cyprus by plane, bound (they thought) for South Australia. When they landed in Darwin the passengers were asked to disembark so the plane could be refueled. When the plane was ready to take off, the Greek Cypriots were not allowed back on board. An airport official apparently said to them: "This is Australia, mate, and this is as far as you go. If you want to go to Adelaide it will cost you another thirty quid." None of

Napoleon's father Neophytos Pantazis in his policeman's uniform. Paphos, Cyprus. c.1935

these men of course had thirty pounds, so Darwin became their final destination and future home.

At his sister's wedding, Napoleon noticed a young Greek girl who was the daughter of the best man, Paul Kanaris. Her name was Irene and in a few years she would become Napoleon's wife.

Napoleon found work as a handy man and yardsman at the Darwin Hospital. The fact that he could read and write English was certainly an advantage. His boss, an Englishman named Tom Flynn, decided to call him Paul because he thought the name Napoleon sounded too 'woggy' (a racist term that was used to describe foreigners). The name stuck and Napoleon came to be known as Paul.

Tom Flynn used to tease and play pranks on Paul (Napoleon) and the other migrant workers. One hot day Tom asked Paul to fetch a few cold beers from a freezer that was located in a tin shed. When Paul opened the freezer door he was shocked to find a dead body inside along with some cold bottles of beer. Tom had tricked Paul and sent him to the hospital morgue. 'You bastard!' thought Paul. His boss just laughed and offered him a cold beer. Paul refused.

Paul and about a dozen other workers all lived in huts at the back of the Darwin Hospital. They were fed three meals a day and were also able to do laundry. After a while, Paul's boss Tom assigned a group of Aboriginal people to work with him. Paul was fascinated as he had never seen or met Indigenous Australians before. They were very dark skinned and had thick raised scars on their chests. He tried to teach them to speak Greek - with little success.

Paul was earning around nine pounds a week at the Darwin hospital. It still wasn't enough money to pay off his father's debt, so he decided to take on a second job working at a friend's panel beating shop. He would leave the hospital job at 5.30pm and go to work at the panel workshop until midnight. Paul was often known to work around eighteen hours a day with very little sleep or rest. Within a year, he had earned enough money to pay off his father's debt.

During the summer of 1952, Paul and three friends (Costas Gabriel, Anastasios (Tommy) Stylianou, and Dimitris Cleanthou), decided to tour Australia after receiving their generous holiday pay. They travelled on a Pioneer bus from the Northern Territory (through the red centre) to Alice Springs and then by train to Adelaide and finally Melbourne. It was the longest road trip of their lives. In fact, the journey took as long as the flight from Cyprus to Australia.

They could not believe the vastness of Australia and how much uninhabited land there was. It was mostly flat and barren, but the contrast from tropics to desert to dense forest to bush was remarkable.

In Melbourne, Paul found temporary work at the Rosella factory, making tomato sauce and jams. When he returned to Darwin he found a job at the Belsen Camp where he stayed and worked for a year. The camp consisted of sixty little fibro huts that accommodated workers and tradesmen who were employed to rebuild the township of Darwin following its destruction by Japanese bombers during the Second World War.

In 1953, inspired by his friend Tommy, Paul decided to buy himself a taxi. Darwin had a population of around seven thousand residents at that time and most of them did not own a car. There was scarcely any public transport, only a few buses, so many locals depended on taxis to get around. Paul and Tom were part of a team of ten Cypriot taxi drivers known as Independent Taxis.

Many local residents would often book Paul and his taxi to bring them into

town so they could go to the pub or visit the pictures. They would then book him again for the return trip home. Some of Paul's customers lived in far-away places such as Batchelor, located about sixty miles out of Darwin. A round trip would cost them around fifteen pounds. Paul even took passengers to the races in Katherine - a distance of almost two hundred miles. One of Paul's best-known and regular customers was a man named John 'Jack' White, who, in 1949, discovered uranium in an area known as the Rum Jungle.

Not one to rest, Paul took on a part-time job washing dishes at the Darwin Hotel. He was often responsible for waking up the drunks at closing time and sending them home.

In those early years in Darwin, Paul spent his leisure time with his friends,

Paul (Napoleon) and Rene Pantazis on their wedding day in Darwin. 2nd March 1957

playing cards and *tavli* (backgammon) at a Greek club located on Smith Street next to Independent Taxis. They would visit the few cafés and pubs in town or go fishing and hunting and organise picnics together. Thanks to his good friends, Paul never felt lonely.

In 1955, he began work as a waiter at the Rendezvous Café located in the heart of Darwin. The café was owned by Paul and Lambrini (Libby) Kanaris in partnership with George Fortiades. Paul was a frequent patron of the Rendezvous. Now he was working alongside the owner's seventeen-year-old daughter, Irene. He had first noticed Irene when she accompanied her father to the Darwin airport to greet him and his sister Eleni in January 1951.

Irene Kanaris was born in Perth, Western Australia in February 1939. Her father Paul Kanaris had immigrated there in 1936 from the Greek island of Astipalaia in the southern Aegean. According to Irene, in 1937 her father was shown a photo of her mother, Lambrini Anictomatis by one of his friends. Paul agreed to marry her. Lambrini who was living in Athens, was then placed on a ship and sent from Piraeus to Perth, thus becoming yet another, so-called 'mail-order' bride. Irene's brother was born in 1940 and her sister Mena in 1945.

In 1946, directly after the Second World War, Irene's parents were convinced by a family friend to move from Perth to Darwin to take over the popular Rendezvous Café, which was owned by Lambrini's first cousin Leo Fotiadis. The Rendezvous Café was originally established by Mick and Chrissie Paspalis in the late 1930s.

Irene was known by the locals as Rene (pronounced Rennie). She remembers that chocolates, sweets and ice creams had to be delivered from Western Australia. "To make the milkshakes we used powdered milk (Sunshine Milk). There was no fresh milk. We also made ice cream sodas called 'spiders' and we had a variety of ice cream sundaes."

Darwin, in the 1950s, had one picture theatre called The Star and many of the patrons would visit the Rendezvous Café at interval time or after a show. In 1957, the Rendezvous was the first café and restaurant in Darwin to install an air conditioner. A year later, a jukebox was introduced, which played rock and roll music to a mostly younger crowd.

According to local historian Leonard Janiszewski, Greek-run food-catering businesses in Darwin began during the 1940s and 1950s, the Rendezvous Café being a feature of this – along with the Star Milk Bar and the Continental Milk Bar.

They all wanted to express a sophisticated style in their design, aiming to offer 'a bit of Hollywood-style glamour' in what was then a frontier town. In 1921, there were only seven Greek-Cypriots recorded as residents of Darwin. After the Second World War, more Greek-Cypriots arrived. In 1948, three Dakota planes landed in Darwin with about sixty-five Greek-Cypriots on board each one.

Paul and Rene were married on the 2nd of March 1957 in the newly built (though unfinished), Saint Nicholas Greek Orthodox Church. They were married by Father Jones, a vicar from the Church of England (Darwin did not have an Orthodox priest at that time). Over five hundred people attended the wedding. After they were married, Paul went to work at Victoria Hotel's Dining Room and Snack Bar.

In 1959, Paul and Rene welcomed the arrival of their son Neophytos (known as Neville).

A year later, Paul received word from Cyprus that his older brother Dimitris, who was a successful schoolteacher in

the cliff and exploded into flames. Dimitris suffered extensive burns and was rushed to hospital where he died eight days later. He was only thirty-two years old.

The death of his brother had a profound effect on Paul. He now realised that by migrating to Australia he was forever disconnected from his siblings and parents in Cyprus.

In 1966, Paul and Rene welcomed the arrival of a daughter, Paula Christina. When Paula was two years old, Paul and Rene came up with the idea that the suburb of Parap needed a fruit and vegetable shop and so in July that year they opened the Parap Fruit and Vegetable Supplies.

By 1973, the business was well enough established that the Pantazis family decided to take a trip back to Cyprus leaving Rene's brother Peter and his wife Muriel (Micki) to run the business. Because of this trip, Paul was able to see his parents again one last time. His father Neophytos died in 1977, aged seventy-seven. His mother died fifteen years later, aged ninety-three.

Rene Pantazis at the Rendezvous Café. Darwin, 1956

Polis, had been killed in a car accident. He was driving home from Ktima with his two sisters and his aunt when a large truck collided with his Volkswagen - sending the small car over a cliff. The women managed to crawl out of the car just before it fell off

Back in Parap, things were going very well for Paul and Rene's fruit shop. That was until Christmas Eve in 1974 when the devastating Cyclone Tracy hit Darwin.

On the night of the cyclone, Paul closed his shop around 9.30pm and went

Paul and Rene's house in Darwin where they have been living since 1957

home to celebrate Christmas Eve with his family. There had been extensive radio warnings all day, but the residents of Darwin did not truly understand the destructive nature and force of a cyclone.

When the storm eased up around midnight, Paul decided to go with his nephew Angelo Angeli (his first cousin's son) to check his shop. Angelo had arrived from Neo Chorio in Cyprus. He was staying at the Pantazis family home with his young pregnant wife, Hariklia. Paul and Angelo had to navigate their car around many fallen trees and power poles to reach the shop. Ten minutes later, the eye of the cyclone passed over the area, and the wind became extremely fierce. The two men were trapped inside the shop, unable to leave.

Back at the house, Paul's wife Rene had decided to shelter in the bathroom with her children, two nieces and a very distressed Hariklia. Initially, the frightened family took shelter in the main bedroom of the house because it had air-conditioning. But as the house started to collapse around them, Rene's young son Neville suggested quite firmly that they should all make a dash for the bathroom. Neville had heard on the radio that the bathroom was the safest place to

take shelter during a severe storm. Rene believes that her son's quick-thinking may have actually saved their lives.

When Paul and his nephew returned home the next morning they found the house badly damaged and without electricity. Thankfully, everyone was safe. They were soaked and in shock, but alive. Cyclone Tracey was one of the most destructive cyclones in Australian history. Miraculously, the phone at the Pantazis house still worked and soon all the neighbours formed an orderly queue to ring their loved ones. In another act of generosity, Paul donated all the undamaged food from the shop to a nearby evacuation centre in order to feed the survivors. A few months after Cyclone Tracey, the Pantazis shop was back in business.

For most residents of Darwin, one of the tragic outcomes of the cyclone was the loss of personal property. For the Pantazis family, their precious old family photos from Cyprus were now destroyed.

In 1976, Paul and Rene decided to purchase a larger property on nearby Parap Road and four years later, they relocated and expanded their business to include a large continental delicatessen and supermarket.

They renamed the shop Parap Food Centre. In the early nineties, Paul's children Neville and Paula took over the management of the business and the store was renamed Parap Fine Foods.

Paul and Rene Pantazis (although officially retired) still play an active role within Parap Fine Foods ensuring that their legacy continues with the next generation. They still enjoy the fruits of their labour (pun intended) but are now spoilt by their children and grandchildren.

ACKNOWLEDGEMENTS

Thank you to Napoleon (Paul) and Rene Pantazis for allowing me to interview them and publish their life story in this book. A special thank you to their son Neville Pantazis for his kind support and assistance and for proof-reading my draft translations. Thanks also to Demetria Foka for suggesting that I interview her uncle back in 2017.

Special thanks to Peter and Sheila Forrest for allowing me to paraphrase a few sections from their book *Forty Fine Years* and to Wayne Lennox Miles for his permission to use his black and white photograph of Paul (page 86).

Ellou
NICHOLAIDOU

Ellou (on the right) aged five with her first cousin Chrissi Konnaris. 1944

Ellou Nikolaidou (nee Konnaris) was born in the small village of Trozena in the district of Limassol in 1939. She was the youngest of eight children born to Nikoli and Augusta Konnaris. Her siblings were Ioanna, Thouklis, Panayiotis, Yiankos, Arestis and Humbis. When Ellou turned seven, her family moved to the tiny mountainous village of Mousere (her father's birthplace) where she attended school for two years. She also went to a school in the nearby village of Vasa for four years.

Although many families lived in debt, or faced a life of poverty, Ellou's family were comfortably self-sufficient. This was due to the fact that they had their own vineyards, wheat fields and orchards. "Whoever owned arable and fertile land in Cyprus during the 1930s and was also debt-free could actually live a decent life," Ellou says. Her family also had goats, which provided them with fresh milk for drinking and for turning into cheese.

Ellou remembers her father Nikoli had little wooden drawers full of every type of seed that were arranged in neat, straight rows according to the seasons. "Because our father would plant and grow our food all year round we always had plenty to eat. I remember he would spread dozens of potatoes and onions across reed mats on the ground to keep them fresh and to stop them from germinating."

As a young girl, Ellou spent most evenings at home either reading her Bible or embroidering by the soft light of a paraffin lamp. "Things are so different today Costa," she says. "People barely bother to talk to one other. They sit and use their phones all day or send each other phone messages. In my time, we would all gather outside in our doorways and spend the evenings talking and laughing and telling each other stories. Hours and hours would go by. We were never bored. Nowadays you see so many people staring at their phones and they hardly have the energy or desire to talk to you. It is very sad."

Ellou recalls her Turkish friends Novalita and Esmiti, daughters of the *mukhtari* (headman) from the nearby village of Gerovasa. They would meet on the bridge that separated their two villages and spend the day exchanging stories or playing together.

On the 8th November 1959, Ellou married Giorgios Nikolaidou (also known as Kokos). They moved into a newly constructed house in Arsos village where their three children were born; Panagiotis in 1960, Augi in 1962, and Rena in 1966.

My own recollections of Arsos have continued to inspire me since my first visit in April, 1974. I remember as a young boy wandering up and down the steep and narrow pathways visiting my relatives and making new friends at every turn. I even attended school in Arsos along with my cousins Panagiotis and Augi. In those days, the village was full of people and activity. There were farmers with their pack animals, shepherds with their flocks, women sitting and conversing with neighbours in doorways and

Ellou's father Nikoli Konnaris. c.1983

children playing outdoors with sticks and stones and leather balls. Today, the roads and pathways are less crowded. Gone are the donkeys and goats. Many of the inhabitants have left too. Even my grandfather's old house at the top of the hill, which has long been abandoned, is now invaded by weeds and mostly obscured by an overgrown fig tree.

When I last visited Arsos in 2016, my first stop (as always) was the *kafenion* (coffee house). Upon entering the *kafenion*, I was greeted warmly by the elderly men who have been gathering there every day for the last fifty or sixty years. Someone asks, "Who are you?" I answer that I am Constantinos, the son of Panayiota *tou* Konnari. My uncle Giorgios jumps out of his seat to hug me. "Yiasou Kostaki *mou*! (welcome!)," he shouts and within seconds I am surrounded and shaking hands with all the men and a fresh round of coffee is ordered. Everybody in Arsos knows my mother's family. Word quickly spreads in the age-old manner (word of mouth) and soon all my relatives

Kostas (Parperis) and his wife Eleni from Anarita village, Paphos. He is the Godson of Ellou's father-in-law Panayiotis.

in Arsos are informed about my arrival.

The next morning my uncle Giorgios invites me to watch him make his annual batch of *zivania* (alcoholic home brew). At 6am I find myself in the courtyard of his house surrounded by an assortment of man-made contraptions. I stand next to his wood fire furnace and allow myself

to sample a few glasses of the fine stuff. I watch in amazement as my uncle chops firewood while telling me about his recent heart surgery. "Shouldn't you be resting and avoiding all this strenuous and physical work?" I ask naively. "What are you talking about?" he laughs loudly. "I'm fine now. That was a few weeks ago."

That evening, Ellou invites my family to her house for dinner. On the table is an assortment of dishes representing the typical Cypriot fare enjoyed by the villagers of Arsos for generations. We sit, eat and drink home-made wine for many hours into the night.

Despite being born in Australia, my Aunt Ellou and Uncle Giorgios have always treated me as one of their own. Their deep respect for my mother has always been expressed with humble and genuine hospitality. I have always felt privileged to be the son of Panayiota *tou* Konnari.

ACKNOWLEDGEMENTS

I would like to thank my Aunt Ellou and Uncle Giorgios for making me feel so welcome whenever I visit them in Arsos and for allowing me to publish their story in this book. Thanks also to their daughter Rena Nikolaidou for her kind support and assistance.

I look forward to sampling another batch of my uncle's homemade *zivania* very soon.

Ellou and Giorgios Nicholaidou with their young son Panagiotis. c.1962

TOP TO BOTTOM:
Ellou's cousin Andreas and her brother Humbis.

Andreas & Panayiota
ARISTOVOULOU

Andreas Aristovoulou aged twenty. Melbourne, 1961

Andreas Aristovoulou was born on the 6th of February 1941, In the village of Agios Athanasios in the district of Limassol. Andrea's father Georgios Hagi Christofi was born in 1913 and was one of four siblings. His parents Aristovoulos Hagi Christofi and Anthousa Aristovoulou (nee Charalambous) were a very well-known and respected family in Agios Athanasios. Georgios was also a popular and charismatic man in the village. He married Kyriakou Stavrianou Christodoulou in 1932. She was the daughter of Stavrianos Christodoulou from Statos in Paphos and was almost two years older than Georgios.

Before his son Andreas was born, Georgios decided to enlist with the Cypriot Volunteer Regiment (CVR), leaving his pregnant wife Kyriakou in Agios Athanasios with his two sisters Harithea and Eleni. Like his father Aristovoulos, who had served as a muleteer in the Great War, Georgios left behind a young family and enlisted for the financial rewards offered by the British Government. After a few weeks training at the military camp in Polemidia he was shipped over to Greece.

Sometime in 1941, Georgios and his unit were captured by the Germans while they were defending the port of Kalamata. After a brief internment in Thessaloniki, the Cypriot prisoners were transferred to the Aussig concentration camp in Sudetenland (now Dubí in the Czech Republic). Georgios knew to behave himself to avoid the swift and deadly retribution often inflicted by the prison guards. "My father did what he was told," exclaims Andreas. "There was this one Cypriot prisoner who refused to salute a German Officer and he was shot dead on the spot."

Kyriakou Georgios (nee Stavrianou) with her children Eleni aged four (on left), Andreas aged two and Harithea aged six. Agios Athanasios, 1943

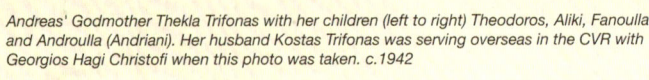
Andreas' Godmother Thekla Trifonas with her children (left to right) Theodoros, Aliki, Fanoulla and Androulla (Andriani). Her husband Kostas Trifonas was serving overseas in the CVR with Georgios Hagi Christofi when this photo was taken. c.1942

officials. As such, he was allowed to mix and socialise with the local population.

"My mother Kyriakou knew that my father was a Prisoner of War," adds Andreas. "The British High Command notified her immediately. First, she received a letter by registered mail from London stating that Georgios Haji Christofi was missing. A month later she received another letter stating that he was a prisoner in Aussig. You can't imagine her grief at the time."

The wives of Cypriot volunteers during the war were paid and given special privileges by the British Government. Every fifteen days, Kyriakou would go to the English food store at the Navy, Army and Air Force Institutes (NAAFI) in Limassol to buy bags of rice, sugar, coffee, biscuits and chocolate.

The NAAFI was an organisation created by the British government in 1921 to run recreational establishments needed by the British Armed Forces, and to sell goods to servicemen and their families. There were clubs, bars, craft shops, grocery stores, launderettes, restaurants, cafés and other facilities.

"My mother would often exchange a cup full of sugar or rice with the other women in the village for food that she did not have." Andreas went on to explain that the married men who joined the CVR received a special bonus that was given to their wives back in Cyprus. His mother would use this money to do her shopping at the NAAFI.

Aussig was liberated by the Russian army in May 1945 and the remaining prisoners were all freed. Georgios was sent to England for a number of months to recuperate. He didn't arrive back in Cyprus until the latter part of 1945, where he was reunited with his wife and family.

Andreas did not recognise his father when he returned from the war and

berated his mother for allowing a stranger to occupy her bed. "'You should be ashamed of yourself mother," I told her. "How dare you let this strange man sleep with you in your bed?" Andreas laughs loudly as he recalls the moment from his childhood.

Upon his discharge from the British army, Georgios received 900 pounds for his services as a soldier. Coupled with the allowance his family received in his

Georgios Aristovoulou Hagi Christofi as a Prisoner of War in Sudetenland. c.1943

absence, his family were able to escape the hardship they once endured before the war. Georgios found steady work in the stone quarries around Limassol where he was required to transport stones by truck to surrounding villages for the construction of roads and homes.

In 1950, Georgios immigrated to Australia where he paved the way for the rest of his family to join him in 1955. When he arrived in Melbourne, his first stop was the Cyprus Club located on Lonsdale Street. There he met many of his Cypriot compatriots and in no time they found him work at the Jolimont Railway Yard where his first job was fitting brakes onto the trains.

Andreas arrived in Melbourne from Cyprus with his mother and two sisters Harithea and Eleni, in the Australian winter of 1955. He was fourteen and a half

In Aussig, Georgios witnessed the horrors associated with the extermination of the Jewish people. "My father told me that the poor Jews were stripped naked and marched off to the gas chambers - men, women and children.

By comparison, the British prisoners were looked after very well. In fact, Britain would ship over crates of food to them through the Red Cross. My father put on weight while the Jews were starved and exterminated. It was horrible."

Georgios worked at a factory in Aussig and he managed to learn German by interacting with the local workers. "There were lots of young pretty German girls who worked there," says Andreas. "Oh boy. These girls were very flirtatious and they taught my father how to speak German. He was kept very busy in that factory - if you know what I mean?" Supplies of food, general goods and alcohol were packaged and prepared in the factory where Georgios worked. He managed to coax his way out of working in the factory by assisting the German guards with their deliveries to German

Georgios Hagi Christofi (seated left), Kostas Trifonas (seated right), Theodoros Xythontis and Kosta Hagi Christofi standing at back.

This photo was taken a few weeks before the four friends were shipped out from Limassol to Greece as part of the Cypriot Volunteer Regiment with the British Army. Theodoros Xythontis was killed during an Italian air strike in Syria. Limassol, 1940

BELOW: The German work pass that was issued to Georgios Hagi Christofi by the Germans at Aussig two months before the end of the war.

Ausgestellt am: 6.3.45

H.CHRISTOFI GADRCHIOS
Unterschrift des Inhabers.

Betriebsführer: Norbert Dürschmidt, Aussig, Bismarckstraße 2, Fernruf 3140.
Betriebsobmann: Wilhelm Rossin, Aussig, Turmitzer Straße 19.
Werkluftschutz: Leiter Oskar Löbel.
Werkfeuerwehr: Führer Ing. O. Ulbrich.

Aufenthalt bei Tagesfliegeralarm:
Stollen

Nicht übertragbar!
Auf Verlangen des Werkschutzes vorweisen!

Nr. Kgf 14

95053/32

Kriegsgefangener

Werkausweis

Name: Haji-Christofi
         Georgios
Vorname: Aussig
Wohnort: Kommando Dürschmidt
Straße:

Der Ausweisinhaber ist Gefolgschaftsmitglied der Firma

Carl Dürschmidt
Lack- und Farbenfabriken
Aussig/Elbe, Tel. Nr. 2105—2107.

Beschäftigt in Abt.:

als:

Im Werkluftschutz eingeteilt als:

years old; too old to attend school but old enough to start work. He was sent to work at an automotive spare parts factory in Abbotsford named A. Linard and Son Pty Ltd, which was later bought by the Wilmot Breeden Company. As a youngster Andreas was surprised to be earning six pounds a week. In Cyprus, he was earning only one pound a week working as an apprentice carpenter for his Godfather Kostas Trifonas, who was a builder.

As well as working full time at the factory, Andreas was also required to attend night school, to learn how to speak English. "How else could I communicate with the other workers?" He exclaims

Panayiota Panteli at the port of Limassol in 1960 saying farewell to her family before departing by ship for Australia.

Panayiota Panteli aged nineteen. Cyprus. 1959

loudly. "It was an embarrassment for us Cypriots. Our passports stated that we were British subjects and yet we couldn't speak a word of English. Other British subjects who arrived from India could all speak English."

Andreas did not have far to walk to get to his workplace. His father bought a house on the same street as the factory in Abbotsford. "He told me he paid 1,200 pounds for that house," says Andreas. "Before that, we used to rent a house in Collingwood for four pounds a week."

After arriving in Melbourne, Kyriakou had three more children: Nikos, Aristos and Stavros. "My brothers all received the education I was deprived," laments Andreas. "In any case, it was against the law in Australia to keep children

home from school. We weren't in Cyprus anymore."

By the time Andreas turned twenty-one he was ready to move out of the family home. "It was a tough time for me," he recalls. "My father was very strict. I was earning fifteen pounds a week and I had to hand over fourteen pounds to him. I was left with one pound. I couldn't save any money so I left home and went to live with my sister Eleni in the suburb of Brunswick."

Andreas enjoyed living with his sister and began to save his wages for the first time in his life. "I was very ambitious and quick to learn on the job. My boss Alfie did

not like me however. No matter how hard I worked he refused to increase my salary. I used to tell him, one day Alf - I will sit in your chair."

Andreas' prophecy came true. Within a few years, he was promoted to the position of Leading Hand and he later became the Foreman at the factory with over twenty-five workers under his supervision. Despite a lack of education, Andreas was able to achieve considerable success at Wilmot Breeden - which had since relocated to Preston.

In 1963, after two years living at his sister's house, Andreas was introduced to Panayiota Panteli. They were both twenty-

Panayiota Panteli and friends on the ship Patris on route to Australia in 1960.
From left to right: Panayiota, Toula, Rebecca and Vasiliki.

three years of age. Panayiota had arrived from Cyprus in 1960 to join her siblings who were already living in Melbourne.

Panayiota was born on the 14th of December 1940 in the village of Gaidouras (Famagusta district). She was the youngest of ten children (five girls and five boys). "When I was born, my eldest sister was already twenty-five years old and engaged to be married," declares Panayiota. With such a large family, her parents Panteli Antoni and Flourou Yianni struggled to make a living as simple peasant farmers. Despite this, they were caring, generous and very thankful to God for what they grew on their farm. After feeding her own large family, Flourou would often send Panayiota on errands around the village with baskets of spare food to give to other families who were less fortunate.

The call for a better life in Australia soon enticed Panayiota's siblings to leave Cyprus. "One by one they left. From 1946 onwards, six of my siblings had immigrated to Melbourne. Then in 1960 it was my turn. I was twenty years old. I remember sharing a cabin on the ship Patris with three other girls. Two years after I left Cyprus, my father Panteli died. I was devastated. How could I know that I would never see him again? We were always together; in the fields and at home; always together. I can still see him, remember him, standing on the pier with his little handkerchief, wiping away his tears."

When Panayiota met Andreas Aristovoulou in 1963, she was living with her sister Maria in Brunswick. "My older sister Eleni knew his mother," she explains. "Kyriakou would often visit my sister's mixed business shop in Carlton. My mother-in-law really liked me and wanted me to marry her son." Panayiota looks at Andreas and he nods his head in acknowledgement of this.

Andreas and Panayiota's engagement photo. Melbourne 1963

"Let me tell you another thing I liked about the British," Andreas suddenly says, changing the topic. "My mother was getting paid by the Australian Government. It was called Social Security. The Greek and Jewish migrants did not receive Social Security. Only migrants who were British subjects were paid. I think my mother was getting seven pounds a month. It didn't matter that we weren't Australian citizens."

Andreas and Panayiota were married in January 1965. They moved into a brand new brick-veneer house in the newly developed northern suburb of Thomastown. "I bought the house a year earlier," Andreas exclaims, "after we got engaged. I had my driver's licence but I didn't own a car so I wanted to buy a house that was close to the railway station in Thomastown."

In October 1965, Panayiota gave birth to her first child Pantelia (Leah) followed by Koula in 1968, Georgina in 1972, Tony in 1975 and George in 1981.

In 1979, Andreas' father Georgios retired from the railways. He died a year later, aged sixty-six.

Andreas and Panayiota have now celebrated fifty-three years of marriage. They have been living happily in the same house in the northern suburbs. Their house is easily distinguishable as a Cypriot dwelling by the abundance of well-grafted and full-grown fruit trees in both the front and back yards. To this end, Andreas and his wife have successfully managed to recreate a bit of Cyprus in Australia.

ACKNOWLEDGEMENTS
I would like to thank Andreas and Panayiota Aristovoulou for always making me feel welcome in their family home and for sharing their life story so passionately with me. Special thanks to their daughter Leah Georgiadis for her kind support and assistance over the last few years.

Nineteen year old Andreas Aristovoulou on his way to watch a soccer match at Olympic Park in Melbourne. c.1960

Chloe and George
GABRIEL

Chloe Gabriel (nee Pavlou) was born on the 19th of February 1932 in the village of Anogyra. The village at the time had around a thousand inhabitants, including around fifty Turkish-Cypriot families. Chloe thought it was remarkable that all the Turkish inhabitants could speak fluent Greek, when only a few Greek-Cypriot inhabitants could speak Turkish.

Chloe's parents Pavlos and Maria Evripides were fortunate to be able to afford an education for their four children. Chloe remembers that the school day would begin with the students reciting a morning prayer followed by a chorus of *God Save the King* (King George VI). The walls of the classroom were adorned with the portraits of various British and Greek Kings. After school, she would run home to help her mother with the domestic chores of the day. In her spare time, Chloe would visit her friends in the village to skip rope or play a game of volleyball, hopscotch or hide and seek.

When I ask Chloe about her childhood she remarks that she was never alone and had many friends to pass the time with. She made a point to say that she was never bored and the days passed all too quickly. "I thought it was strange how the little Turkish Cypriot children were allowed to come and visit our homes and play in our courtyards," she would say. "But we were never allowed to play in their courtyards unless of course we were accompanied by our mothers or

grandmothers. I thought that was odd."

In her younger years, Chloe spent the summer months playing outdoors with her siblings Dimitrios (Takis), Evripides (Bibi) and Zoe as well as a small swarm of Greek and Turkish Cypriot village children. She remembers that during the Bayrami festival the Muslim mothers would bake *kataifi* and *baklava* sweets and share them with their Christian neighbours. In return, the Greeks would bake *flaounes* (cheese pies) and *koulourakia* (biscuits) during the Orthodox Easter and share them with their Muslim neighbours.

When asked about male and female relationships in the village, Chloe remarked how it was socially unacceptable (forbidden even) for boys and girls to mix or go out together once they became teenagers. It was common, however for a boy to sneak a sly glance at a pretty girl. If the girl happened to glance back to show that perhaps she liked him, then her friends and family members would all mobilise to arrange a formal home visit. This would hopefully prompt the young couple to announce their intentions to get married.

Chloe's family were better off than most. Her father Pavlos owned a grand two-story house (one of the biggest in the village) where, on the ground level he operated a *kafenion* (coffee house) as well as a general store.

In 1940, Pavlos decided to join the Cypriot Volunteer Regiment (CVR). His decision was prompted largely by a

popular misconception circulating around the island at that time that if Cypriots joined the Volunteer Regiment and supported the Allied Forces in the Second World War then Britain would eventually cede Cyprus to Greece.

After a few weeks training in Limassol, Pavlos was sent to serve in Egypt and then Italy before ending up in Greece.

Chloe does not know exactly what her father's role was during the war but she was able to recall quite an extraordinary story. As the story goes, when Pavlos was stationed in Crete, he was ambushed and captured by the invading Germans and became their prisoner of war. Remarkably, after only five days in a prison camp, Pavlos and a friend named Gallikas hatched a plan to escape. One dark night, they dug a large hole under the barbed wire fence and crawled out.

The two friends fled all night through the rugged Cretan countryside, fearful that the Germans would soon be on their heels. As the sun rose at daybreak, they found themselves near a small Cretan village and decided to take refuge in a large tree next to a natural spring.

Throughout the morning a steady procession of Cretan women came to fill their clay jars with water from the spring. Suddenly, one of the women noticed the two men hiding in the tree. When she discovered they spoke Greek, she invited them to take refuge in her family home.

"I wish I had the foresight to write down the name of this family when my

George Gabriel's pappou Andreas Nicolaitis (seated), his parents Aristodithmos and Christalla Gavrielides and his uncle Omiros. Location unknown. c.1916

man returned for a third time, the two Cypriots decided it was safe to reveal their true identities and stepped forward to introduce themselves. The man invited them to stay at his house until he could organise a boat for their escape.

Pavlos and Gallikas were shocked to discover that the man's wife had asked their three young children to eat only carobs and chestnuts from local trees so that she could feed the guests eggs and cheese and the food of the house. After five days, Pavlos and Gallikas could not bear it anymore. It troubled them deeply to see the three young children deprived of proper meals just so they could be fed. They decided to sneak away in the middle of the night and seek refuge elsewhere. Luckily they came across some men who led them to a boat bound for Egypt. They were surprised to find other fugitives and refugees in the boat seeking a safe passage. There were scores of men, two women and one young child. There were also large tins full of fresh water and around thirty cans of condensed milk.

And so, it came to pass that on a moonless night, sometime in early 1943, the little wooden boat with its grateful human cargo, rowed away from a dark beach in Crete bound for a distant shore in Egypt.

Pavlos was told that the trip would take only a few days - but as he soon discovered, this was far from the truth. During the long journey, the little boat was rocked by treacherous seas and lashed by stormy winds, threatening to capsize the crowded vessel. The milk and water supplies were almost depleted and still there was no sign of land. The situation was becoming very bleak indeed.

Miraculously, after eighteen harrowing days at sea, Pavlos and the exhausted crew stumbled, dishevelled and half-dead, onto the shore of a remote and desolate Egyptian beach.

Far from safe, the survivors suddenly found themselves surrounded by a large group of soldiers wearing German uniforms and aiming their guns at them. Pavlos cursed his rotten luck and prepared for the worst. Thankfully, the men with guns turned out to be Greek soldiers who were dressed as German soldiers in order to fool their enemy. The uniforms they were wearing were in fact those of German soldiers that they had killed in battle.

father first told me this story," laments Chloe. "I can't even tell you the name of the village."

The Cretan family fed and clothed Pavlos and his friend and issued them with fake identity cards along with fake Cretan names. They were also provided with labouring jobs at a nearby factory.

Pavlos and Gallikas went along with everything their Cretan hosts had advised. Soon they met other men (and women) who were also hiding from the Germans. One day, a large Cretan man came into the factory and announced that he was looking for Cypriot soldiers disguised as Cretans whom he could help escape from Crete and allow a safe return home. Pavlos and Gallikas were very suspicious of this stranger and therefore chose to remain silent. The man returned the next day and made the same speech. Still Pavlos and Gallikas were silent. When the

Pavlos and Gallikas were transported to a Greek Army camp somewhere in Egypt where they were fed, clothed and allowed to recuperate. Pavlos was later issued with a special pass allowing him to return to Cyprus. It had been almost four years since he last set eyes on his family. His youngest daughter Zoe was only a baby and Chloe was eight years old when he had left in 1940.

Once his ship had docked at Limassol harbour, Pavlos went straight to *Solomi's Kafenion* located opposite the dock. This coffee house was a popular meeting place for Cypriots coming and going to and from Limassol. Pavlos was immediately recognised by men from his village and the word quickly spread that Pavlos *tou* Kourtelos from the village of Anogyra

had come home. It was his first cousin Dimitraki who won the coin toss to drive him back to his village. Another friend led the procession of trucks back into the village, sounding their horns as they entered to announce the return of their favourite son. One by one, the villagers came out of their homes and followed the motorcade towards the town centre.

Chloe who was twelve at the time, remembers the day when her father returned to the village. "I was in school when I received a message that I was to come home at once to see my father. I will never forget how fast I was able to run that day. My strides were so wide that it seemed that I was floating on air. When I approached my house I could see a large crowd gathering in the courtyard. To me it seemed that the entire village was there. When my father saw me, he beamed his largest smile and then rushed to lift me up high into the air. To this day, I can still remember the way I felt to be lifted up so high. It was so amazing. Unbelievable."

In 1945, Pavlos found a very well-paid job working as a sentry at the Customs House in Limassol. He earned an astonishing thirty-three Cyprus pounds a month. A few years later, he moved his family from Anogyra to Limassol.

When Chloe's older brother Dimitrios (Takis) finished high school in 1949, he decided he wanted to travel abroad so he could study electrical engineering. He was sent to Australia where he attended the Royal Melbourne Institute of Technology and later secured work at the General Motors Automotive Company.

In 1950, Pavlos made plans to move the rest of his family to Australia so that they could all be reunited with Takis. Many people (including Chloe) thought it to be a bad idea. A family friend tried to intervene by telling Chloe's father, "If you leave Cyprus now, you won't

Chloe's grandfather Evripides Pavlou Kourtelos and grandmother Pelayia from the village Anogyra. c.1952

just be cutting down your family tree, you'll be uprooting it for good. Let your sons go to Australia and remain here with your wife and daughters." Despite his friend's advice, Pavlos was determined that his children, and especially his two daughters, would have a better life and future in Australia.

And so in 1951, Chloe left Cyprus with her father and younger brother Evripides (Bibi). They were followed by her mother Maria and sister Zoe a year later. The total cost of the journey by ship for the whole family was nine hundred pounds. Many migrants arrived in Australia with perhaps two or three pounds in their wallets, but Chloe's father had a remarkable three hundred pounds, which was enough to place a deposit on a house.

Even though nineteen-year-old Chloe was sad to leave her beloved homeland, she knew better than to complain to her father. "What could I say?" she exclaims with outstretched arms. "What could I say? He was my father and he knew best." Her mother Maria also knew best to keep her feelings and opinions to herself and was determined to make the most of it. "I never heard my mother complain to my father – not once. In fact, not ever in her life," Chloe remarks.

Unknown children. From the Gabriel family album.

Chloe arriving at the church on her wedding day with her father Pavlos. 1954

Despite her father receiving no complaints from his family, Chloe wasn't entirely happy about leaving her country. "I remember feeling very sad when we left Cyprus. There was no reason for us to leave. My father had a good job, we lived in a nice house and we had hope for a good and secure future."

Life in Melbourne was not as easy or affordable as Chloe's father had hoped. He did manage to find a job at the railways, where he earned around twenty-eight pounds a month (about six pounds less than the job he had left behind in Cyprus). Pavlos worked at the railways for many years until he retired in 1970 aged sixty-five.

When Pavlos heard about the political and social unrest that had gripped Cyprus in the 1950s and 60s he was often heard to mutter, "Thank God for giving me the foresight to take my family away from these troubles. Perhaps I have spared the life of my sons."

In 1952, Chloe met George Gavrielides (later changed to Gabriel). George was good friends with Chloe's brothers and one weekend, they invited him over to have dinner at their house. That was how he met their sister.

Chloe and George were engaged in 1953 and a year later they were married. Chloe was twenty-one and George was twenty-three. "I told myself, that if I didn't meet a nice girl in Australia, I would return back to Cyprus," George says and smiles at his wife. "Thankfully, I met the best girl of them all and I decided to stay and marry her." Chloe blushes at this comment, then laughs out loud.

George was born in 1929 in the village of Malia, Limassol. At the time, the village boasted around two hundred Greek Cypriots and over a thousand Turkish Cypriots. George talks proudly about the relationship his father had with the Turkish Cypriots in the village. He remembers that every time a Muslim family was celebrating a wedding, the parents of the bride or groom would come to buy his father's homemade wine. His father would gladly give them wine but would always refuse any payment. Such was the love and respect between the Christian and Muslims in the village.

George's parents Aristodithimos and Chrystalla Gavrielides were married in 1916. She was only 16 years old and he was 21. Like so many Cypriots at that time, Aristodithimos worked as a farmer

tending to vineyards and orchards and looking after livestock.

Chrystalla's father Andreas Nicolaitis was an educated man. He was the first teacher from his village of Vasa Koilaniou to be trained in Athens, which was a

George Gavrielides aged twenty two. Limassol, 1951

sound accomplishment in those days. Devastatingly, his wife Areta (Chrystalla's mother) died during childbirth. This was depressingly common in those days. It was often impossible for pregnant women to receive medical help if a complication occurred. This was due to the remoteness of villages, the absence of roads and any reliable transport.

George's mother Chrystalla died when he was only eleven years old. According to George, she was rushed to a hospital in Limassol after complaining of severe abdominal pains. Was it food poisoning or appendicitis? No one knew. She died on the operating table. It was a tragedy and most likely something that would nowadays be preventable.

Chrystalla left behind four children. Her husband Aristodithmos was heart-broken; so much so that he vowed to never marry again. Whenever he was asked why he did not remarry he would simply reply, "How could I remarry? What would I tell my Chrystalla when we meet up in heaven?"

Being the youngest of four siblings living with their widowed father, it was perhaps inevitable that George would decide to leave Cyprus to seek his fortune in Australia. He arrived in Melbourne in 1950, alone and virtually penniless. In time though, he made friends, found work and his spoken English improved. His life would continue to improve, especially after meeting Chloe Pavlou.

Soon after Chloe and George were married, George bought a taxi. He worked long hours and drove around the streets of Melbourne earning enough money to buy a house in Blackburn. The family later moved to Templestowe where they were able to comfortably raise and educate their two daughters Lina and Maria and their son Aristodemos.

After twenty years of driving a taxi, George was persuaded by his daughters to apply for a job that was advertised by the School of Medicine at University of Melbourne. George the immigrant from a small village in Cyprus who drove a taxi in Melbourne was successful in getting the job as a technical assistant. Australia had finally proved to be a land of opportunity where anything was possible. George worked at the

university for twenty-five years until he retired in 1994.

Chloe and George still live in their house in Templestowe and are visited frequently by their three children and their extended families. They have seven grandchildren and eight great grandchildren, with another on the way.

Their house is never empty.

ACKNOWLEDGEMENTS

I would like to thank Chloe and George Gabriel for taking the time to share their wonderful stories with me. Whenever I would visit their house Chloe always had a table full of home-baked delights. Thanks also to their daughter Lina Pandeli for her support and for helping to arrange my interviews with her beautiful parents.

Chloe's aunt Electra with her husband Diomostenis and daughters Loula (on the right) and Dimitra. c.1956

Theodoros
KYRIACOU

Passport photo of Theodoros Kyriacos. 1969

Theodoros Kyriacou was born in the village of Monagroulli near Limassol on the 18th of June 1925. He was the third eldest of nine children (eight boys and one girl). His parents Kyriacos and Anna Christoforou struggled to earn a living from the back breaking and never-ending task of fieldwork as well as grazing sheep.

Theodoros attended school until the fifth grade. After a short stint as a shepherd he was sent away to Limassol to be trained as a *pablomatas* (quilt-maker) with a master craftsman. The quilt maker agreed to train and look after him for five years. It was a common practice in Cyprus for a junior apprentice to live and work with their master for a few years without receiving any payment.

Theodoros was sometimes required to accompany his master as they travelled to various village fairs to sell a selection of their hand made quilts.

At age seventeen, he decided to abandon the trade of quilt-making and instead went to work in the mines at Kalavasos. During the outbreak of the Second World War, he spent many hours working underground in hazardous conditions with only a lamp to guide him.

In 1943, work at the mines slowed down, so Theodoros decided to join the Cypriot Volunteer Regiment (CVR) for the British Army. He was paid two pounds a week and received a carton of cigarettes as a bonus. Sometimes the lure of receiving free cigarettes was enough incentive for a young Cypriot man to join the CVR. Theodoros had been smoking since the age of five. "A packet of cigarettes would cost me one *grosi*," he tells me. "I was now smoking around two cartons of cigarettes a week."

After the war ended in 1945, Theodoros, (now twenty) went to work for the Zacharides Company in Limassol. "I was being paid around six pounds a week," he says with a grin. "I spent my money on cigarettes, alcohol and women." Theodoros would often visit the cabarets and brothels located near the seaports of Limassol, Scala and Varosi. Many young men in Cyprus who felt trapped by the strict moral codes that existed at the time, sought to release their frustration by visiting prostitutes rather than committing the sin of interfering with a homely and pure Cypriot girl. Theodoros knew better than to take such a risk and potentially ruin a young girl's reputation.

From 1945 until the early 1950s, he enjoyed a blissful bachelor's life. He found steady work with the British Electricity Board digging holes along the roadside for the poles that would connect electricity between Larnaca and Limassol. After work and on weekends he would visit the beach with his many friends and at night he would stay up late visiting cabarets and brothels, often stumbling home drunk but happy. During this period,

Theodoros in his early-twenties posing for the camera. Monagroulli. c.1949

from afar when on rare occasions she and her girlfriends were allowed to watch the village boys compete in local football matches. It was actually Theodoros' uncle Sofronis, acting as the official matchmaker, who went to meet and talk to Fotini's mother Fanou to try and arrange the marriage. At first Fanou did not give her consent. She felt that Theodoros had a bad reputation as a womaniser and night owl. "I am sorry, Sofronis *mou*," she lamented. "But my daughter is still missing her father. It would surely crush her if she married a man who could not care and look after her properly."

Sofronis replied "Theodoros is older and wiser now. Please say yes and I promise they will live very well together."

Fotini was hiding in the next room and had heard the conversation. Poor Uncle Sofronis was forced to leave the house without an agreement. Instead of giving up, he went straight to the village *kafenion* (coffee house) to fetch Theodoros who was there, eagerly awaiting the verdict. "You have to come back with me," Sofronis pleaded. "Fotini's mother is concerned that you won't look after her daughter. You have to convince her that you are prepared to give up your wayward lifestyle and that you are ready to settle down." Theodoros agreed to go and plead his case to Fotini's mother. Fanou finally agreed and the date was set for the official wedding. Everybody was pleased. Unfortunately, Theodoros and Fotini could not afford the few shillings to pay for any wedding photography.

Once married, they lived with Fotini's Godmother for a year until their matrimonial home was built.

Fotini had given birth to four children within six years. Anna was born in 1953, Fay in 1955, Christakis in 1957 and Kyriakos in 1959.

Theodoros went to work for a company in Limassol that specialised in cement sheeting. His wages were low and he could barely afford to provide for his growing family.

Theodoros earned a reputation amongst the locals in Monagroulli as a free-spirited adventurer, showing very little interest in settling down. He was certainly regarded as the most outgoing and mischievous of the eight Kyriacou brothers. "I was a young man who loved life and I enjoyed myself. I did not quarrel with anyone. I had many friends. I loved to smoke and drink and I loved to sing and dance at the cabaret. We used to go there often to listen to our favourite Greek bands."

In 1953, an earthquake struck Cyprus. This event prompted a harsh end to the wandering and carefree life enjoyed by Theodoros. He rushed from Limassol to his village to see if his parents were okay. They were unaffected by the earthquake but many locals started to gossip and speculate that Theodoros had actually returned to the village to find a wife. He was, after all, twenty-eight years of age.

Theodoros decided to humour the village gossipers and agreed to meet a young girl that he had often admired from afar. The girl was Fotini Christoforou who was six years younger than him. She lived in Monagroulli together with her siblings and mother Fanou. Fotini's father, who was the village barber, had died when she was only twelve years old.

Fotini too had admired Theodoros

As his daughters grew older, they became increasingly concerned that their father would not be able to afford their marriage dowries as was the tradition. Anna in particular was also concerned about the financial hardships her family would continue to endure in Cyprus. She had known many Cypriots who had travelled abroad to seek a better and more prosperous life. Her uncle Demitri was one of them.

Anna wrote to her uncle outlining her concerns and explaining her desire to become a hairdresser. Her uncle agreed to pay for her apprenticeship in Australia. In February 1970, he arranged for his brother Theodoros and his family to travel to Melbourne where he lived. Anna's wish had been granted.

Uncle Demitri certainly played an instrumental role is altering the fate and lives of Theodoros and his family. First of all, he let them live in his family home for a year until they could afford to buy their own house. Secondly, he was able to secure work for his brother at the Sidchrome tool factory where he worked. Theodoros worked there for fifteen years.

Demitri's generosity is a testament to brotherly love that extended beyond the boundaries of their country of origin. Theodoros too played a pivotal role in keeping the family united and living in a harmonious environment. It wasn't just the family barbeques and dinners that he organised once a week: he welcomed everybody into his humble home - It didn't matter who they were. His children's friends were especially made to feel welcome. Together with his devoted wife

Fotini, they embodied all the wonderful qualities that true Cypriot hospitality had to offer.

What is truly remarkable about Theodoros *'Pablomatas'* Kyriacou, with regards to his role as a husband and father, was his immediate and unwavering devotion to his wife and children once he became a family man. He remained true to his word and became the devoted, kind and caring husband, father and grandfather that he was destined to be. His kindness towards all people regardless of their sex, race, age or status will remain his greatest legacy.

ACKNOWLEDGEMENTS
I would like to thank Theodoros Kyriacou and his wife Fotini for extending their hospitality towards me and sharing their stories in such an honest and sincere manner. Sadly Theodoros passed away in January, 2018. He was ninety-two.

Special thanks to Theodoros' daughter Fay Anastasiou and granddaughter Denise Markou for all their support and assistance with his interview and for checking the accuracy of his life story.

ABOVE: Theodoros and Fotini's engagement photo. Limassol, 1953
RIGHT: Theodoros dressed for hunting in Monagroulli. c.1962

Christos & Antigone
APEITOS

Christodoulos (Christos) Ioannou Apeitos was born on the 24th of January 1924 in the village of Agros (Limassol). He was the youngest of seven children (Artemis, Sophia, Nicholas, Christina, George and Kostis). His mother Angeliki actually bore twelve children but lost five to illness and disease when they were still infants. According to Christos his mother gave birth to her first child (Artemis) in 1900 when she was just sixteen years old. His father Yiannis, who was born in 1864, was twenty years older than her.

The village of Agros had over one thousand inhabitants during the 1930s and boasted a hospital and a police station - which was rare for rural villages in those days. Most people got around either by walking or by donkey; automobiles being very scarce.

Christos' father Yiannis and a few of his brothers worked at the nearby Amiantos Asbestos Mine during the 1930s. At one point Christos also spent a few months working there. The English-owned company employed over 5000 people at one time, attracting workers from many mountainous villages around Troodos. These workers also included

BACK ROW FROM LEFT TO RIGHT: Dimostenis (Antigone's uncle), Christos' sister Christina and brother Kostis Apeitos and his wife Efstathia. The man with the large moustache in the middle is Efstathia's father. The man crouching up front on the right with the cigarette in his mouth is Mr Kashafiri. Year unknown.

Wedding in Agros. The groom Stavros Kathis is standing next to his father Yiannis. The short man with the cap is the bride's father nicknamed Gountos (shorty). Christos Apeitos was the best man at this wedding and also took this photograph. c.1947

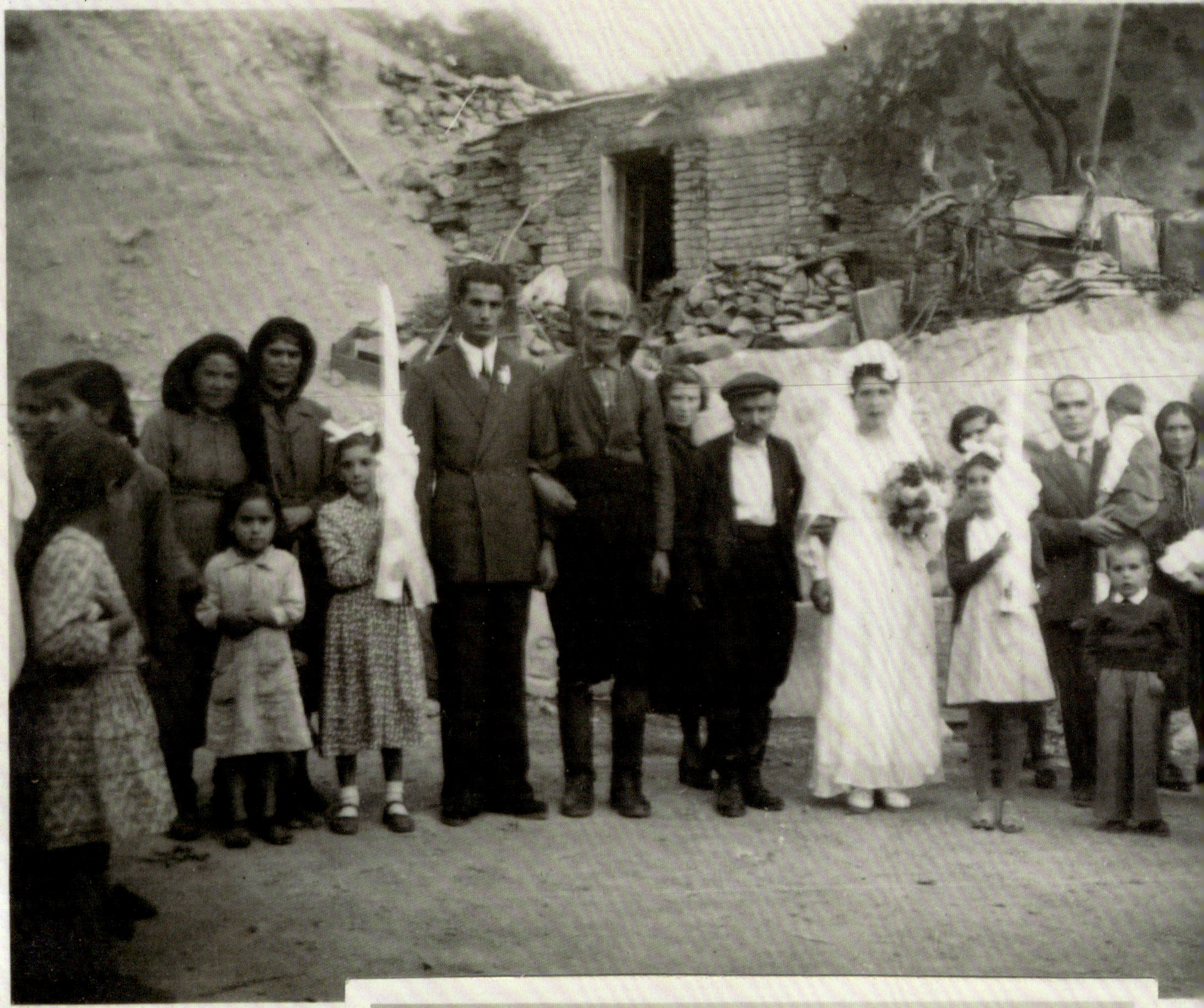

women and children as well as men. The working conditions in the mine were appalling. Asbestos mining during the first few decades of the 20th century was carried out by hand using primitive and simple tools. Many of the workers contracted lifelong respiratory and lung-related illnesses caused by the asbestos fibres and dust which greatly affected the quality of their lives.

"People were never idle in those days," Christos tells me. "Everybody worked; from six years old to eighty. My parents would take me out into the fields to help them to water or to tend to their crops and vegetables. My job was to

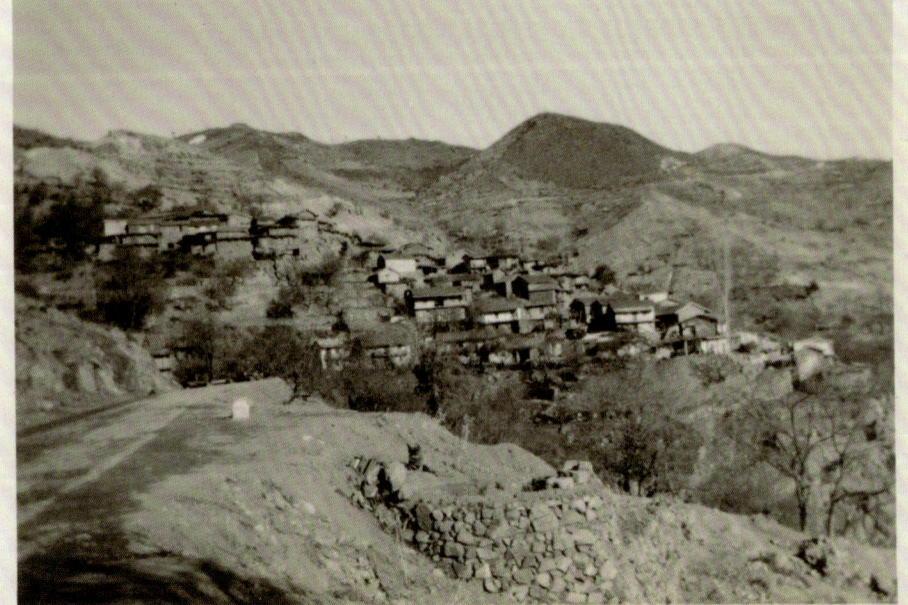

Agros village. c.1947

collect small rocks to help build low walls."

Christos also remembers scampering along the riverbeds with his friends when he was about seven or eight years old, looking for freshwater crabs to catch and eat. "They hid under the rocks," he says. "You had to be very careful not to splash or make the water cloudy with your feet otherwise you wouldn't be able to see anything." Another favourite past-time was hunting birds from the trees with a slingshot. Apparently, Christos was quite a successful marksman.

Christos attended primary school up to grade four. Unfortunately, his schooling was interrupted every winter as a result of an undiagnosed illness. "Every winter I was always sick and missed many months of school. I had to repeat grade two as a result of this."

In 1938, when Christos turned twelve, he was sent to live with his older brother Nicholas who was working in Nicosia. He found work at a *pantopoleio* (grocery store) in the main marketplace. "I remember there was a *jami* (mosque) next to the shop where I worked and every day the *hodja* would come to our shop to buy various things." Christos lived in Nicosia for five years and not once did he venture back to his village to see his parents. Nor did they come to Nicosia to visit him. Although distances were not that great, many inhabitants on the island were often left stranded where they lived by the sheer lack of transport (or money to pay for transport).

Christos eventually taught himself how to ride a bicycle (a green Rayleigh) and in time became the shop's main delivery boy, delivering food products to customers all over Nicosia. Although his boss provided accommodation and all

of his meals, Christos did not receive a wage. He worked for five years, all unpaid. On the day that he left the *pantopoleio* his boss handed him an envelope with a small sum of money in it. "I remember he gave me eight pounds," Christos recalls. "Can you believe it? After five years of service I was paid only eight pounds."

In 1942, Christos and two friends (Marinos and Giorgios) agreed to join the Cypriot Volunteer Regiment (CVR) for the British Armed Forces. His friends, however, went ahead and enlisted without him. Feeling abandoned, Christos decided to visit his parents in Agros; it being five years since he last saw them. Following the visit, he returned to Nicosia where he found work as a waiter in a tavern on Ermou Street. It would be another eight years before Christos would meet his future wife, Antigone Symeou.

Antigone Symeou was born on the 24th of September 1931 in the village of Lagoudera (Nicosia district). The village of Lagoudera was much smaller than Agros, with an estimated population of

Chris Apeitos on a rented motorcycle with his friend riding around the streets of Nicosia. c.1947

around 300 inhabitants at that time. Every year, on the 21st of November, Antigone and her family would make the four-mile trek over the mountains to visit the church festival in Agros in honour of the Virgin Mary. Legend states that the icon of the Virgin Mary in Agros was painted by

Saint Luke himself and is therefore one of the most revered icons in Cyprus.

When she was young, Antigone and the other village children would meet in the main square of their church to play games like chasey. The churchyard was usually the only large, flat space in a Cypriot village where children had enough room to play games. Once the sun had set and darkness had engulfed the village, the paraffin lamps would be lit and the children ushered indoors for their evening meals. Antigone's father, like most men in the village, would always set off for the *kafenion* (coffee house) after dinner. Her mother would be left to wash up and prepare the meals for the next day.

During the winter months, Antigone would huddle together with her siblings (Lefki, Loukia, and twins Savvas and Adrianna) around the fireplace singing songs or telling each other stories.

For girls like Antigone, any future prospects for marriage had to be sought and found in other neighbouring villages. The boys in Lagoudera would leave when they were quite young, often to pursue work or education in larger towns.

When I ask Antigone how she met Christos she replies. "Wait a minute," and begins flicking through a large notepad that had been sitting on the kitchen table. "I want to read you something I wrote down a few years ago to remind myself of the *panayiri* (festival) in Agros."

was my mother Polixeni, sitting amongst her friends and relatives. They had all made the trek from Lagoudera separately.

I went to join my mother and together with our large contingent we went to have lunch at somebody's house. We ate our fill with gusto, nursing huge appetites. Quite a lot of wine was also consumed. We then made our way home on foot singing along the way until we arrived back in our village, just as the sun was setting on such a glorious day.

Many years later on the 21st of November I would find myself once again getting dressed in my finest clothes to go back to Agros; this time however, I was going to meet my future father-in-law and mother-in-law."

Antigone places the notebook down and looks at me with wet eyes.

"That was beautiful," I tell her. "But you still haven't told me how you met each other."

I was impressed. Here was a woman from my mother's generation who had the foresight (and the inclination) to write down her memoirs and to record the special moments in her life. I could see that the notepad contained at least eighty pages of beautiful hand-written Greek. Antigone begins to read.

"It was the 21st of November: the Virgin Mary's holy day. My *pappou* (grandfather) and *yiayia* (grandmother) woke up earlier that day and got dressed in their finest clothes to go to the neighbouring village of Agros for the *panayiri*. My *yiayia* helped me to get dressed in my good clothes and she placed me on a donkey ready for the journey to Agros. I was still quite young. Once outside the village we met many other villagers, all dressed in their finest clothes and with happy expressions on their faces. We followed each other in single file along the narrow dirt track up the mountain, descending slowly on the other side towards the village of Agros. When we arrived, there was already a large crowd gathered in the centre of the village with many people holding onto their animals with a rope. We entered the crowded courtyard of the church and slowly squeezed our way into the church to kiss the icon of the Virgin Mary.

When we emerged out of the church and back into the courtyard my eyes could not believe the colourful sights all around

me. Everywhere I looked were beautiful stalls with every kind of Cypriot delicacy on display and for sale. Next to me were some women frying *loukoumades* (Greek doughnuts) in a large copper pot. I did not want anything. It was enough for me to simply behold the sights. I was happy.

I walked with my grandparents down the main road until we came across a crowd of people sitting, eating and conversing under some trees. There too

Best friends Christos Polycarpou (left) and Christos Apietos. Melbourne, c.1954

"Let me tell him," interjects Christos.

"No, no," Antigone remarks dismissively. "You'll take forever. I'll tell him." And so she does.

In 1948, when Antigone had turned seventeen, she was sent by her mother to Nicosia to look after her sick uncle, Antonis Dimitriou (her grandfather's brother). She recalls that her uncle seemed to be suffering from a deliberating disease, perhaps Parkinson's. Antigone's job was to wash and feed her uncle and push him in his wheelchair.

One fine Sunday evening in late October 1950, her second cousin Christos Polycarpou invited her to the cinema. On their way home, they bumped into young Christos (Apeitos), who happened to be a close friend of Antigone's cousin. Once the formal introductions were made, Antigone and Christos (Apeitos) managed to strike up a conversation. Antigone discovered that the two friends were getting ready to leave Cyprus. "It was a very quick meeting," said Christos. "We talked for a little while and then I told her I was leaving for Australia in two months. 'Take me with you', she said all of a sudden. I was surprised to hear her say that. I'm not sure why she said it but I can tell you, it left a lasting impression on me."

"I'm not sure why I said it either?" Antigone added, blushing slightly. "It just sort of blurted out."

And so on the 12th of December 1950, Christos Apeitos left Cyprus on an old renovated and converted battleship called the Corsica. He remembers there were about one thousand Cypriots on board, as well as a few hundred men and women from various Greek islands. The journey to Australia took fifty-four days.

Even after arriving in Melbourne, Christos could not forget Antigone. That fateful meeting on a dark street in Nicosia kept playing over and over in his head. He began to pester his friend (Polycarpou) to write to Antigone with a proposal of marriage. For some unknown reason, it would take Polycarpou three years before he finally sent Antigone the letter with the stated proposal of marriage.

Antigone remembers receiving her cousin's letter as if it was yesterday. With a coy smile and glancing upwards towards the ceiling, she begins to recite the letter from memory (word for word). "Dear Antigone, I don't know if you remember that young man I introduced you to outside the cinema in Nicosia? Anyway, he is here in Australia with me and has asked me to write to you to see if you would be interested in coming over here so he can marry you? Please write back soon and tell me your answer. If you ask me, I will tell you that he is a very good man and you will live very well together."

Once Antigone had received the letter she immediately sought her father's approval. No young respectful Cypriot woman would dare to agree to marry a stranger without her father's consent. At first, her father Symeos was not very happy at the prospect of his sending his daughter to the other side of the world to get married.

Antigone Symeou (left), her sister Andriana and their mother Polixeni after a trip to Apostlos Andreas in 1954

He did, however, know that the Apeitos family from Agros were well respected and this was enough for him to give his consent. The next day, a notice was placed in the newspaper announcing that 'Mr Christodoulos Ioannis Apeitos who lives in Australia and Miss Antigone Semeou who lives in Nicosia have announced their intention to get married'.

"Oh Costas, you should have heard all the yelping and well wishing that went on when people read that I was getting married," Antigone remarks with a broad smile across her face. Before the wedding announcement was placed in the newspaper, Antigone had written directly to Christos in Melbourne stating that she would indeed agree to marry him. He was working for the Country Road Board at the time and once he received her answer he decided to move back to Melbourne to look for a house to buy. "I had to find a house," he tells me. "I couldn't let her come and meet me in the bush." Migrants in Melbourne often referred to country Victoria as the bush.

"What if she had said no?" I ask him.

They both laugh. "Well, I would have no choice but to find another woman," he replies. "I suppose my brother Nicholas would have to go and find me a girl from my village."

On the 6th of January 1955, Antigone arrived in Port Melbourne on a ship called Neptune. She was twenty-three years old. She immediately moved into her fiancé's newly acquired home in the south-eastern suburb of Oakleigh. Christos remembers that the house was sold to him for 3,300 pounds. The deposit for the house was 1,000 pounds, and he only had 700 pounds. Once again, Antigone's cousin Christos Polycarpou came to his rescue and loaned him the remaining three hundred pounds.

Christos Apeitos aged twenty-two. 1943

"If it wasn't for my cousin," remarks Antigone. "Nothing would have happened. He was like a brother to me. He introduced us; he arranged our marriage and he help us to buy this house." Antigone picks up her notebook again, and after shuffling through a few pages, says: "Listen to this. I want to read to you what I wrote about my arrival to Australia." She adjusts her reading glasses and in a loud confident voice begins to read. "It was the sixth of January 1955. Our ship arrived on the day of Theophania at the dock of Port Melbourne bringing me for the first time from our faraway country of birth. A new country; new people; a new life awaits…. and now after all this time, the grey hairs on my head have witnessed another truth."

Christos and Antigone were married on the 1st of May 1955 at Evangelismos Church in East Melbourne. The wedding

reception was held at their house in Oakleigh where over two hundred guests were invited.

A year later in 1956, their son Yiannis (John) was born. That same year Christos received word from Cyprus that his own father Yiannis had died aged ninety-two. In 1957, a daughter Polixeni (Pauline) was born, followed by another son Giorgios (George) in 1960.

As Antigone serves me a plate of her famous *galaktoboureko* dessert, Christos confides in me his deep sorrow of never seeing his parents again after having left Cyprus. When he did return in 1989, only two of his siblings were still alive. He becomes quite emotional recalling the heartbreak he felt of not seeing his sister Christina ever again. "She really loved me a lot," he sobs quietly, covering his mouth with his hand.

Antigone worked at the same factory as her husband in the suburb of Carnegie. The factory (named Elmaco) manufactured plastic electrical parts and was owned by two Jewish brothers. Antigone was astonished to discover that she had earned ten pounds and four shillings for only five days' work. "I couldn't believe it!" she exclaims. "Back in Cyprus when I was caring for my sick uncle, I was paid six pounds a month and that was considered a lot of money in those days." Antigone was also shocked to discover that in Australia she was only

Christos Apeitos (far left) with friends from Agros. c.1947

required to work forty hours a week and her weekends were free to do as she pleased.

Christos and Antigone still live in the same house where they celebrated their wedding back in 1955. Their house is full of keepsakes and mementoes that are testament to a life well-lived; a life full of love and adventure. They are surrounded by their loving family and many friends who pop in frequently for a cup of coffee or one of Antigone's special home cooked treats.

ACKNOWLEDGEMENTS
I would like to thank Christos and Antigone Apeitos for allowing me to write their life story. I would also like to thank their two sons John and George Apeitos for all their support.

Chris Apeitos in Nicosia. c.1946

Wedding in Agros. Year unknown.

Gulten
ERDOGAN

Gülten Erdoğan (nee İrfan Yıldırım), was born in the village of Amiantos on the 10th January 1929. Her father Irfan Hasan was a Turkish Cypriot policeman and was married to Ayşe Mükerrem Halil. He was stationed in Amiantos when Gülten was born. Amiantos was the site of a large asbestos mine controlled by the Cyprus Mines Corporation (CMC). At the height of production the company employed thousands of local peasants to work at the mine in rather harsh and unsafe conditions. Some families even decided to settle in the area.

When Gülten was almost two, she moved to Nicosia with her parents after her father was transferred to a police station in the capital. In 1931, her sister Ayten was born. A few years later, Irfan Hassan left the police force to go and manage a small cafeteria for the Brotherhood Society *(Kardeş Ocağı)*.

In Nicosia, Gülten and her sister Ayten attended the Shakespeare School, located near Yeni Jami close to Agios Loukas church. Not much is known about the Shakespeare School or its founder and principal, Necmi Sağip Bodamyalızade. Apparently, he was an Oxford-trained scholar who never married and devoted all of his time and energy to the promotion of a classical-style education for the Turkish Cypriot children of Nicosia and surrounding areas.

Gülten's mother Ayşe spent many months of the year living in Lefke (Lefka) looking after the family vineyards and

orange groves in Xeros while her young daughters stayed in Nicosia with their father to attend the Shakespeare School.

Gülten's sister Altan was born in 1936 followed by her brother Saffet in 1938. When Gülten turned nine years old she was required to stay home and look after her younger siblings. Her education was halted for good. It was common practice at that time for the eldest daughter to stay at home to raise her younger siblings.

Gülten and her young siblings spent a lot of their time moving between Nicosia and Gemikonağı, Lefke. Their mother had a house and property in Karavostasi - a small mixed village located about four miles from Lefke. The port at Karavostasi was historically used by the Cyprus Mines Corporation to export copper and asbestos from the island. Its name means 'boat stop' in both Greek and Turkish.

After the Second World War, Gülten's father left his job at the Brotherhood cafeteria and opened a grocery store in the Arab Ahmet *mahalla* (neighbourhood) of Nicosia.

During the summer months, Irfan Hasan would sell blocks of ice to his customers for a few shillings each. Sometimes he would earn up to five pounds a day. He purchased the ice from a factory located on the main road between Nicosia and Kyrenia. His young son Saffet would deliver the ice to customers all over the capital on his bicycle. The small blocks of ice were placed inside specially constructed wooden boxes that were lined with tin. Saffet would start his

Gülten (holding the doll) and her sister Ayten with their parents Mükerrem and Irfan Yildirim. Nicosia, 1932

SHAKESPEARE SCHOOL
1936

Shakespeare School, Nicosia, 1936. Gülten is seated third from the right (front row) and her sister Ayten is second from the left (front row). The principal (centre) is Necmi Sağip Bodamyalizade.

rounds at 7am and finish by 11am before the heat of the day. People who could afford to buy ice in Nicosia had the benefit of ice-cold drinks and crude but effective refrigeration for their food. As the ice melted during the day, a little tap at the bottom of the wooden icebox would provide ice-cold water to drink.

When Gülten turned fifteen she was sent to an experienced dressmaker in Nicosia to learn how to sew and crochet. Her siblings on the other hand, were allowed to complete their schooling. In fact, her two sisters would eventually go on to become qualified teachers.

Although Gülten never worked as a professional dressmaker or seamstress, she did spend all her spare time making clothes and blankets for her family, relatives and neighbourhood friends.

In 1951, twenty-two year old Gülten

was introduced to a handsome man named Erdoğan Hasan Karabardak, who was ten years her senior.

Erdoğan Hasan was born in the village of Polis in Paphos in 1919 and was one of seven children born to Hasan Karabardak Haji Ramadan and Salise Mehmet Halofta Ağa. The Karabardak family were very prosperous landowners in Polis.

Erdoğan's early childhood in Polis was no different to most children growing up in rural 1920s Cyprus. Every summer he was required to help his family with the harvesting and threshing of the wheat. He was also required to gather grapes from the family-owned vineyard and load them into large baskets mounted onto donkeys to be delivered to drying sheds in the village. It was very hot and difficult work.

By the time he was fifteen, young Erdoğan had had enough of the rural

*Erdoğan Hasan aged eighteen.
Paphos, 1935*

Gülten (left) and her sister Ayten with their parents Mükerrem and Irfan Yildirim. Nicosia. c.1932

life. He left Polis and went to work in the copper mine in Karadağ, Lefke which was managed by CMC. He worked in the mine for approximately four years.

In 1940, after the outbreak of World War II, Erdoğan, aged twenty-one, decided to join the Cypriot Volunteer Regiment (CVR), which was a military unit for the British Army. He was stationed at the Polemidia army base in Limassol and then sent to Lebanon to be trained as a muleteer. He was soon promoted to Corporal and spent almost four years in Italy, in a camp near Naples and Rome. Erdoğan was able to learn English and Italian during his time served overseas. As well as speaking his native Turkish language, Erdoğan was also fluent in Greek, which he claimed to have learnt on the streets of Polis, interacting with his Greek friends and neighbours.

When the war ended, Erdoğan returned to Cyprus and opened up a nightclub in Polis with his friend and fellow CVR buddy, Mustafa Şükrü. The nightclub was very popular with the local men, especially since scantily clad female dancers were brought over from Italy to perform there. One of the dancers was a woman named Valenzuela Guerriero. Apparently, Erdoğan and Valenzuela had met when he was stationed in Naples

Gülten's parents Mükerrem and Irfan Yildirim. Nicosia. c.1925

during the war. For unknown reasons, Erdoğan abandoned his nightclub business in Polis and went to work as a team leader at the Limni copper mine.

In 1948, he moved to Nicosia where he trained to become a professional agriculturalist and apiarist.

His reputation as a gifted gardener soon attracted the attention of the then

British Governor, Sir Andrew Barkworth Wright. Erdoğan was studying at the Agriculture Department in Athalassa when his English superior recommended him for the job of Head Gardener at Government House in Strovolos. His starting salary was soon increased from fifteen Cyprus pounds a month to forty-five Cyprus pounds a month.

Life at Government House changed forever once Cyprus gained its independence in 1959 and became a Republic in 1960. Tensions on the island reached boiling point in the early 1960s.

Erdoğan and all the other Turkish Cypriot workers were expelled from Government House by President Makarios in 1962 and replaced with Greek Cypriot staff.

Gülten and Erdoğan had no choice but to move into a Turkish Cypriot quarter (and safe haven) in the Arab Ahmet *mahalla* of Nicosia, along with their three terrified children. Their house was located on Mahmut Paşa Street. Their world would never be the same again. Erdoğan was employed to maintain the Public Gardens in North Nicosıa where he stayed for eighteen years.

In 1970, Gülten's eldest son Sermen was sent to Australia after a family relative convinced his father that it would be safer for him to live abroad rather than stay in Cyprus during this most unstable and dangerous period. Once Sermen had settled in Melbourne, he arranged for his younger siblings to join him there.

In 1973, Gülten moved to Australia to be close to her children and grandchildren who were all living in Melbourne. She returned to Nicosia after her husband

begged her to come back. He resisted leaving Cyprus until he retired at sixty-three in 1982. That was when Erdoğan and his wife Gülten (aged fifty-three) decided to immigrate to Australia for good.

Erdoğan Hasan passed away in 2002,

29 Ekim, 1950 Pazar

Gülten İrfan Yıldırım (left) with her sister Ayten (middle) and their cousin Nezire Mehmet. Nicosia. October, 1950

aged eighty-three, following a long battle with dementia. After her husband died, Gülten became quite unwell herself. During the last decade of her life she suffered from hyperglycaemia, amongst other ailments. Independent until the end, she insisted on living on her own in her tiny unit in Saint Albans. It was only after her health deteriorated that she eventually had to be hospitalised. She passed away on the 19th of November 2015 aged eighty-six.

Gülten had lived a life serving others: first as a dutiful daughter and sister, then as a devoted wife and finally as a caring mother and grandmother. She always put the needs of others ahead of her own. Her life is testament to a time governed by patriarchal rules and a moral code that insisted that women existed to serve the men around them. To her credit, she managed to raise intelligent

Gülten married Erdoğan on the 10th of December 1951. Apparently, Erdoğan went with his mother Salise and his two sisters (Zalihe and Zehra) to Gülten's house in Yeni Jami and asked her father Irfan for permission to marry his daughter. Their wedding ceremony was held at the Haydar Pasha Mosque, the second most important Gothic building in Nicosia after Selimiye Mosque.

Once she was married, Gülten moved into her husband's two-roomed stone cottage at Government House. In August 1952, she gave birth to her son Sermen, followed by a daughter, Tülen in September 1953. In July 1955, her son Eren was born - completing her family of five.

Gülten's three children had a charmed upbringing growing up in the spectacular grounds of Government House. They were surrounded by acres of beautiful gardens that were carefully manicured and maintained by their father and his small team of Greek, Turkish and Armenian workers. Life under British Rule was idyllic for the young children. Their father had formed a close bond with many of the staff at Government House including Governor Sir Hugh Foot and his wife Florence Sylvia.

Erdogan Hasan. Nicosia, 1950

ABOVE: *Gülten İrfan Yıldırım. Nicosia, c.1949*
BELOW: *Gülten and Erdogan's engagement photo. Nicosia, 1951*

and open-minded children who in turn, always strived to respect and love her unconditionally. She is surely missed.

ACKNOWLEDGEMENTS
I would like to thank Gülten Erdoğan for sharing some of her life story with me in 2014. I would also like to thank her two sons Sermen and Eren Erdoğan for their kind support and assistance in helping me to document their mother's life story. Special thanks to Saffet Yildirim for providing additional information about his sister and his family.

ABOVE: *Gülten and Erdogan's wedding photo. Nicosia, 1951*

Jimmy TSINDOS

Jimmy Tsindos (baptised Thoucydides) was born on the 5th December 1938, in the village of Vasa Koilaniou. Soon after his brother Michalis was born in September 1940, their mother Irini contracted a serious infection. Tragically, she was unable to get the right medical assistance and she passed away. She had just turned twenty-eight years old.

Jimmy's father Charilaos was devastated by the premature death of his wife. He decided to return home to his village of Kathikas in Paphos, so his parents Efstathios and Victorou could help him look after his orphaned sons. Eventually, Charilaos made the decision to send his youngest son Michalis to live with his maternal grandmother Eleni Zachariadou in Nicosia. The two brothers would be separated for a few years until they were reunited again during their high school education.

Jimmy's maternal grandmother Eleni Zachariadou (nee Stavrinidis) was the principal of the girl's school in the village of Vasa. She was born in the village of Alona in 1884; six years after the British took ownership of Cyprus from the Ottomans. From a young age, Eleni was a devout Orthodox Christian and upheld its strict moral values. When she was still a teenager she went to study at the Teacher's College in Nicosia.

Upon her graduation in 1901, Eleni was sent to teach at the new school in

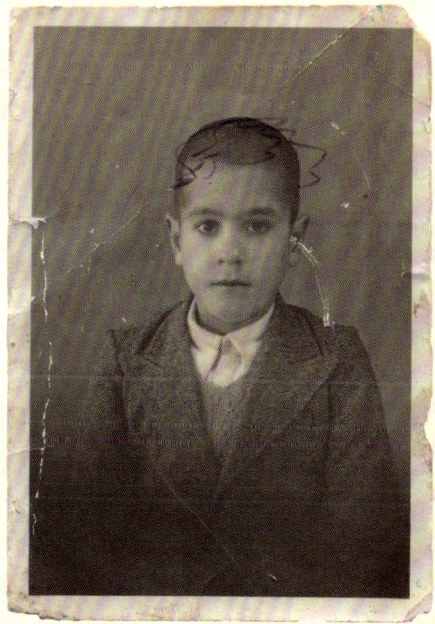

Jimmy Tsindos aged around seven. c.1945

Vasa. In 1903 she was married to the village *mukhtari* (headman) Thoucydides Zachariades. They had five daughters and a son. Olga was born in 1904, Antigone in 1906, Popi in 1908, Ismini in 1910 and Irini (Jimmy's mother) in 1912. Their son Costas was born in 1917.

Sometime in 1922, Eleni's husband was murdered at a wedding ceremony for unknown reasons. Poor Eleni was left a widow with six children to raise on her own. She decided to dedicate her life to God and to help those in need.

It was said that whoever came to visit her in the village would always find food to eat and a place to sleep. As well as being a schoolteacher, she also taught Christianity to the women in the village.

"My grandmother was very strict and very religious," Jimmy recalls. "She went to Jerusalem every Easter. I remember she would always bring us back little wooden crosses from the Holy Land and pin them to our undergarments."

Eleni demanded that her children follow her strict religious rituals. This included praying daily in a special room full of icons, giving thanks to God before every meal, adopting a strict fast during the holy months and doing the sign of the cross whenever in doubt or when passing significant religious monuments or buildings. She was a good mother who was anxious to teach her children the way to God. Being strict was the only way she knew to do that.

Eleni taught between 1901 and 1935. In 1948 she set up a philanthropic organisation called the Union (of the) Young Christian Orthodox (OXEN). She died on the 2nd September 1963, aged seventy-nine.

Jimmy explains how his parents first met. When his mother Irini was in her early twenties she went to live with her sister Popi who was a schoolteacher in the village of Phini near Troodos. One day, a young flourmill mechanic named Charilaos Tsindos arrived in the village to install a

Vasa Girl's School. The teacher Eleni Zachariadou (nee Stavrinidis) is seen in the middle of the photo surrounded by her five daughters. 1918

new engine for a wheat mill. When he laid eyes on Irini, he fell instantly in love with her. Apparently, school teacher Popi did not think Charilaos was a suitable candidate for her sister on the grounds that he was just a mill mechanic. At the time, teaching was regarded as a highly-esteemed profession and Popi and Irini belonged to a well-known and relatively aristocratic family.

Jimmy's father Charilaos was born in 1912 in the village of Kathikas in Paphos. His parents owned and operated a *kafenion* (coffee house) in the village and sold wine made from their own grapes.

His grandfather was the first man in the village to own a wallet *(tsendi)* and so he was nicknamed Tsindos thereafter. It was commonplace in Cyprus to give people nicknames which reflected their appearance, occupation, mannerisms or behaviour. In many cases the nickname replaced the actual patriarchal name.

When Charilaos was barely a teenager, he was trained by his father Efstathios to install diesel-powered engines to stone mills that would mechanically grind wheat into flour. Before the diesel engine, flourmills in Cyprus were hydro-powered using large man-made water wheels.

Despite her sister's protests, Irini Zachariadou went ahead and married Charilaos Tsindos in 1937. They were both aged twenty-five. The wedding was held in Vasa, which is also where they decided to live and raise their family.

Jimmy fondly remembers his younger years in Kathikas. "I was cared for by my grandmother Victorou while my father went to work all around Paphos as a flourmill mechanic. As I grew older, I would help my father sharpen the grinding stone used in the mills. This unfortunately meant that I was inhaling the black stone dust which was something that was unavoidable in those days."

In 1947, almost seven years after the death of his wife Irini, Jimmy's father married Eleni Sotiriou who was also from Kathikas. Jimmy and his brother Michalis were reunited for the wedding.

According to Jimmy, his aunts Olga, and Antigone also became teachers like their sister Popi and their mother Eleni.

Olga married Agathangelos Lapithiotis from Lapithos and together they opened a small tavern in Nicosia. Olga maintained an aristocratic lifestyle - even keeping a maid (named Fotini). Antigone married Michalis Kitromilides, a government worker. They settled in Nicosia together with their three children. She was fluent in French and an avid reader of novels.

Eleni Zachariadou. c.1927

Aunt Popi (Penelope) married a bookshop owner Niko Ioannidis, but had no children. She began to lose her eyesight towards the end of her life and died in the mid-1990s. Popi was famed for her philanthropic activities. Throughout her life she donated a vast amount of her wealth to the Blind Institute, the army, and the political party she supported.

Jimmy's other aunt Ismini became the first female chemist and the first female car owner in Limassol. Jimmy remembers writing letters to his aunt Ismini after he migrated to Australia. "All I would write on the front of the envelope was 'Ismini Zachariadou, Pharmacist, Limassol' and the letter would be delivered straight to her pharmacy."

Although she was married quite young, Ismini divorced her husband soon after the wedding. She was a popular young lady who enjoyed the high life and social scene at that time and was even crowned Queen of the Limassol Carnival in the 1960s.

A playgirl at heart, Ismini soon developed a taste for the nightlife and playing cards at her local *kafenion*. Sadly, her fast-paced life, which included rich food, alcohol and gambling, ruined her financially and she gained considerable weight. Her weight gain hampered her ability to walk and it is said that she died quite sad and alone. "When I saw her in the 1980s," Jimmy says softly. "She was living on bread and cheese; that's all – just bread and cheese. It was very sad."

Jimmy's uncle Costas lived with his older sister Olga in Nicosia as a teenager. He attended the PanCyprian Gymnasium for boys. After the third or fourth year he was forced (to his great disappointment) to leave school and work in his brother-in-law's shop to support his sisters. When he was in his late teens however, he began making his own money by dealing

FROM LEFT TO RIGHT: *Jimmy's aunt Nitza and aunt Theodora. Jimmy Tsindos is standing holding a cat. The others are unknown. Kathikas, Paphos. c.1940*

and selling scrap metal that he collected from the deserts of Libya. Not much is known about how he got involved in this business, only that he would travel back and forth from Cyprus to Libya.

In December 1945, Costas married the twenty-three year old Gabriela (Lella) Santi Rosa. Her father (Santi Rosa) was an Italian diplomat and her mother (Erminia Savvidou) was Greek Cypriot. They had met in Larnaca when Santi Rosa was posted there as the Italian ambassador.

During the 1940s and 50s, Costas and Gabriela embarked on what was to become a successful business career selling buttons and socks and eventually, all manner of haberdashery. Their first store, which they named ZAKO, was opened in Nicosia in 1946. In 1955, their daughter Eleni was born followed by Ermione in 1958.

made plans to leave Cyprus to study nautical navigation on the Greek island of Hydra. Unfortunately, his father could not afford the two hundred pounds required to pay for the expensive blue and white school uniform so his plans for further study were scrapped.

Feeling somewhat dejected and worried about the civil unrest that was brewing on the island, Jimmy left Cyprus. He decided to travel to Melbourne where his uncle George and uncle Kosta were living. He left Cyprus by plane in 1957 aged eighteen. The entire trip took seven days and five different aeroplanes.

Soon after Jimmy arrived in Melbourne he went to work with his uncle Kosta at his café in South Yarra. He lived with his uncle for six months before renting a room at a house nearby for one pound a week. Unfortunately, the house

Jimmy Tsindos aged around sixteen. Paphos. c.1954

Jimmy's parents Charilaos Tsindos and Irini Zachariadou on their wedding day in Vasa. 1937

the owner and her friend Mrs Mackenzie. Every morning Mrs Bullet would make me a cup of tea. When I went off to work at my uncle's café she would wash my clothes, iron my shirts, make my bed and clean my room. She was an incredible woman. When I came home at three in the morning she would get up to greet me with a cup of tea and some biscuits. She treated me like her son."

Mrs Bullet died suddenly from a heart attack and a distraught Jimmy was forced to find new accommodation.

Jimmy attended school in Kathikas, before moving to Nicosia where he completed his studies at the PanCyprian Gymnasium for boys. He lived with his aunt Antigone for a while, before moving into a boarding house that was associated with his school. Upon completing his fourth year at the Gymnasium, Jimmy

did not have hot water and frustrated with the task of having to burn wood logs to heat his water, Jimmy moved to another house that did have hot water and only cost ten shillings more.

"I was treated like a king at this house," Jimmy recalls. "There were two little old ladies living there; Mrs Bullet

Jimmy's uncle Kosta (Con) migrated to Australia in 1939. He initially worked at a clothing factory, before finding work in various hotels in the city. In 1957, he bought a small run-down milk bar in South

Yarra which he converted into a coffee lounge and named El Torro.

Jimmy began by cleaning the toilets, scrubbing down the kitchen and peeling potatoes at his uncle's café. After a few months he was promoted to chief dishwasher and then managed the coffee counter at the front of the café.

In 1961, the café was renovated and renamed Café Edouard. Jimmy was promoted to waiter, barman and finally manager. He worked with his uncle Kosta for ten years from 1957 to 1967.

"I guess I was always destined to enter the hospitality industry," he tells me. "When I was a young boy in Cyprus I used to work at my aunt Theodora's *kafenion* (coffee house) in Kathikas."

During the summer months Jimmy would stay with his uncle George and aunt Mabel at their guesthouse in Sorrento, where he would learn how to cook in their guesthouse kitchen.

George Tsindos has an even more remarkable migrant story. He was born in the village of Kathikas in the year 1903. When George was fifteen, he emigrated

to Australia to join his father Efstathios, who had arrived two years earlier in 1924. Both father and son worked together on the country farms near the town of Maffra.

In 1928, George's father Efstathios returned to Cyprus with the intention of bringing the rest of his family out to Australia. Unfortunately, the global depression intervened and he was forced to remain in Cyprus, leaving poor young George to fend for himself in Maffra.

Sadly, Efstathios died in a horrible car accident in Cyprus some years later. The patriarch of the Tsindos family would not live to see the dynasty his three sons and grandsons would create in Australia.

In 1930, George returned to Melbourne from Maffra, where, for a while, he was able to survive by selling chocolates on commission to the patrons at the Capital Theatre. He also found work as a barman at the newly established Marios restaurant in Exhibition Street. On Sundays (his day off) he would teach himself how to repair bicycles. It was clear to everyone who knew George Tsindos that he was not an idle person. He was always keen to seize every opportunity to work hard and to make money.

When George turned twenty-one, he was employed by Rinaldo Massoni to work as a drinks waiter at his prestigious Café Florentino on Bourke Street. In 1933, a three-course meal with a 135ml bottle of wine at Café Florentino would cost around three and a half shillings. In those days, six pence was considered an enormous tip. George made lots of tips. The Second World War,

however, completely interrupted his career. In 1941, a bout of rheumatic fever made George unfit to serve overseas, so instead, he was sent to work at a munitions factory in Footscray along with six thousand other Victorians. After the war, George was advised by his doctor to seek the fresh air of the country in order to improve his health. He bought

Charilaos Tsindos with his two sons, Jimmy aged about three and Michalis aged about fourteen months. c.1940

a guesthouse called the Monte Vista in Sorrento on the Mornington Peninsula. Each weekend, George and his wife Mabel would run a restaurant on the balcony of the guesthouse for the upper-class residents of Portsea where they would serve lasagne delivered exclusively from Café Florentino.

In 1950, George Tsindos and Leon Massoni (son of Rinaldo) agreed to become equal partners of Café Florentino.

George taught himself to speak fluent Italian during his time at the restuarant. When he acquired sole ownership in 1963, he insisted on pursuing the continental

Jimmy's cousin Andonis Lapithiotis (Olga's son). Year and location unknown.

cuisine the restaurant was famous for and employed both a French and an Italian chef. Café Florentino became one of the most popular restaurants in Melbourne. It was the place most frequented by the social elite and upper class aristocrats. The affordable prices also meant that people from other classes could also afford to eat there, providing they adhered to the formal dress code. With George at the helm, Café Florentino flourished and

Jimmy Tsindos. Melbourne. c.1958

became one of Australia's best known and well regarded Italian restaurants.

Jimmy met his wife Christina at a christening party in January 1960. Jimmy had been invited by his friend who just happened to be Christina's brother. "I was twenty years old and Christina was only sixteen," he recalls. "I told her that night that I was going to marry her. I am not sure if she believed me; but it happened." They were engaged eight months later and married in June 1961.

Christina was only twelve years old when she migrated from Cyprus (from the village of Alaminos) with her mother and four siblings. They were reunited with their father who had arrived in Melbourne to pave the way a few years earlier. Christina began work in a hat factory where she was trained as a milliner. According to Jimmy, when he met Christina in 1960, he was so impressed with her hat-making skills and creativity

that he convinced her to open her own millinery shop, which she did and called it Christina's Model Hats. The business was a huge success.

In 1963, Jimmy and Christina welcomed the arrival of their first son Harry. Two years later, their second son Andrew was born.

After a failed business venture with his uncle George in 1967, Jimmy had to (more or less) start over again. He remembers working three different jobs to make ends meet and to help pay off his debts.

In 1970, Jimmy arranged for his father Charilaos, stepmother Eleni, half-sister Irini and half-brother Fred to come to Melbourne. He borrowed $2000 from his uncle Kosta and together with his father they bought a modest Greek restaurant in Russell Street, which Jimmy renamed The Greeks. Apparently, the restaurant was the first in Melbourne aimed specifically at a non-Greek clientele. Up to that point, Greek restaurants catered mostly to Greek migrants and their families.

It wasn't until Jimmy decided to become a sole trader that things really took off and he became a successful restaurateur. Over the next twenty years, Jimmy and Christina Tsindos would open and operate a number of successful Greek restaurants in Melbourne, including the Greek Inn on Lonsdale Street and other Greek restaurants in South Melbourne and Richmond.

Jimmy would be one of the first restaurant owners to introduce plate smashing and Greek dancing to his clientele. During this exciting phase of his career, Jimmy would also break new ground by appearing on national television with a regular segment on a show called Grecian Scene introducing Greek cuisine to millions of Australian viewers. He would conduct cooking shows for the large Myer emporium on Bourke Street and educational cooking

workshops at a number of prestigious schools. In fact, when any Australian company or organisation wanted to introduce a Greek-based theme to their event, they would contact Jimmy.

Within thirty years of arriving from Cyprus he became a household name in Melbourne and was well respected by all who knew him.

Studio photo of Christina. East Melbourne, 1960

It is true that Jimmy Tsindos would not have been able to achieve so much without the support of his wife Christina and his uncle Kosta. "I owe my success to these two people," he says proudly.

Today the Tsindos legacy lives on in Melbourne with the next generation taking over and managing the family-owned restaurant businesses. Jimmy has long-since retired and is now enjoying a life full of activity and leisurely pursuits, including fishing, travel, and hosting

Jimmy and Christina Tsindos on their wedding day. Melbourne. June 1961

regular dinner parties for his family and friends. He lives with his wife Christina in a cosy beachside suburb of Melbourne where they enjoy the company of their sons, daughter-in-laws and grandchildren.

ACKNOWLEDGEMENTS

I would like to thank Jimmy Tsindos for agreeing to tell his story and have it published in this book. I would also like to thank his son Harry and nephew Antony (in London) for helping to double check some of the facts. Special thanks to Jimmy's cousin Ermioni Zachariadou (in Cyprus) for proof reading and correcting some of the information relating to her grandmother Eleni Zachariadou and her father Costas Zachariades.

Maria
FRANGOU

SKARINOU-LARNACA

Maria Frangou aged thirty four. 1957

Maria Frangou was born in Skarinou, Larnaca on the 30th of July 1923. Her parents Giorgios and Dimitra Frangou had seven children. Maria was the second eldest and the only girl. Due to the unfortunate lack of medical help available at the time, one of children died quite young. Maria's father Giorgios was a shoemaker and her mother Dimitra looked after the children and carried out a multitude of other domestic duties and rural tasks.

Dimitra was born in 1902 in Skarinou. At the young age of fifteen she was married to a man twice her age from the nearby village of Agios Theodoros. He was a mean and violent man and often starved Dimitra, allowing her to only eat bread and olives. The marriage lasted only fifteen months. Dimitra's husband died suddenly of what was suspected to be cancer. A widow at seventeen, Dimitra took her inheritance of 200 pounds and returned to her village and her mother's house. It was rumoured that many of the villagers chose to celebrate Dimitra's return, instead of grieving the death of her mean-spirited husband.

Giorgios Frangou's story is no less dramatic. He was born in 1897 in the village of Kornos. His father died when he was very young and his mother married another man who did not care about Giorgios and his older brother Christodoulos. In fact, when Giorgios turned ten he was thrown out of home

by his stepfather and told to fend for himself. The details are a little unclear, but apparently Giorgios decided to board a ship and travel to Egypt. Many Cypriot boys and men were living and working in Egypt at that time. He was taken in and looked after by a local family for ten years. During that time he was trained as a cobbler (a shoemaker). At 21 years of age, he decided to return to Cyprus. It was 1918 and the First World War had just ended. Giorgios opened a shoe shop in Skarinou and his business soon flourished. He was a master craftsman and news of his skill travelled fast.

On Sundays, he would travel by donkey to neighbouring villages to sell boots and shoes and take new orders. It was in Skarinou where Giorgios was introduced to the young widow Dimitra, whom he married in 1919.

From a young age, Maria was expected to help her mother with the daily chores. This included looking after her brothers. By watching her mother prepare the family meals everyday, Maria was able to learn how to cook.

Every Saturday, she had the thankless task of washing and ironing her brother's hand-made silk shirts. There were usually twenty-five shirts in total.

Embroidery was a past-time that Maria would enjoy in the evenings before dusk. The expectation of helping her mother with domestic chores meant that Maria could only attend five years of school.

Maria Frangou and Andreas Avraam. Larnaca, 1951

In October 1951, at the age of twenty-six, Maria was forced to marry Andreas Avraam, the somewhat despondent son of a neighbour in the village. "I was engaged in May 1951. I remember it was a very hot day. My father arranged my engagement without asking me if I wanted the groom or not. I agreed because I had no other choice. They had taught me to bow my head and take orders. My mother was harsh and authoritative. Many times I thought 'how did my father live with her for so many years?' He either hid his suffering or truly loved her."

As was the custom, Maria's father rewarded Andreas with a house for agreeing to marry his daughter. "My father also gave my husband a few fields and a property in Larnaca. He was lucky he only had one daughter. My mother was so proud she had sons; she did not consider me as important. Daughters were a burden because of the bridal price and dowry. I don't know how, but as things turned out I was engaged against my will. I would have preferred to have met and married someone I loved. My mother told me to be indifferent and that love will come later. I was a romantic and I had read many stories that spoke of undying love. I know I was engaged so

that I would not remain an old maid. I was not beautiful, but I had good manners and a lovely body. Make-up was forbidden in those days. The only thing you needed to know was good housekeeping and to obey your husband and respect your in-laws."

Maria was engaged in May and married in October. She was engaged for four months. "My fiancé was two-faced. When I was alone with my fiancé he tried to take advantage of me, to seduce me.

I resisted. One day, on the 6th of August at six in the evening the irreparable happened. I was his against my will. He insisted I was not a virgin to humiliate me. I was crying, telling him I knew no other man and had not slept with anyone. He was deceitful. He wrote to my brothers Harris and Minas, who were living in Australia, telling them that I was not a virgin. He told them that he was still willing to marry me but only if they agreed to send him a certain amount of money."

Maria and Andreas Avraam. Larnaca, May 1951

Dimitra Haralambou with her fiancé Giorgios Frangou. Her mother Eleni Haralambou is seated next to Dimitra's younger brother Michalis. Dimitra's mother is holding a photograph of her other son who died tragically on the operating table in America, aged thirty. Larnaca. 1918

Maria's brothers were very angry when they received her fiancé's demands. They sent an urgent telegram to their father Giorgios pleading with him to call the wedding off and to find their sister someone else to marry: someone capable of making her happy. Giorgios fearing the scandal that could occur in the village, agreed to give Andreas Avraam an additional 200 pounds so that he would marry his daughter.

"I cried and begged my father not to give him the money because I was not happy with him but my mother was shrewd. She gave me a lecture saying that I had to submit and accept his terms because there was no other solution. For three days I locked myself in my room and cried and thought of what I should do. My eyes were swollen from crying.

On the third day I made my decision. I called my father and declared that I would follow his wishes. I called my fiancé and we reconciled. From that day forward I put on an act. I obeyed convincingly. I tried to fix what was destroyed within me. We married in October and had a beautiful wedding day - despite my broken heart."

One month after their wedding however, Andreas, acting on a whim, left Maria with his mother in the village and migrated to Australia, apparently to start a new life. Once again Maria's father gave him money to pay for his ship fare.

"My husband promised me that he would work for five years in Australia and return so we could build a house in Skarinou and start a family," recalls Maria with a heavy sigh. "The first year I would receive two letters a month and I would write twice as many letters of which I am sure he did not read. Slowly the letters became fewer and fewer. I would wait anxiously in his mother's house, which had also become my prison.

My mother-in-law was acting as my bodyguard, following my every movement. I could not even go out to the balcony for fresh air. She was my shadow, following me everywhere."

It would take six years before Andreas finally succumbed to the pressure placed on him by Maria's family and arranged for his wife to join him in Melbourne in 1957. Reunited at last they moved in with Maria's brother Minas and his family in Richmond. Minas had migrated to Australia a few years earlier.

In 1958, their daughter Eleni (Helena)

was born followed by their son George in 1959. When Maria was six months pregnant with her youngest daughter Christina, she discovered that her husband Andreas was having an affair. "I remember it was the 2nd of February 1961. I found a photograph in his jacket pocket. It was a photograph of a woman leaning on a seat and smiling. There was also an address. I put the photograph back but kept the address. He came home and I told him it was over between us. He went pale. He saw the suitcase and asked why I am doing this to him? Why did I want to throw him out? How would I survive with three children? I told him, I did not care, and he should not be living a double life, it's either her or me. That was when he left for good."

Two years after Christina was born, Maria packed the rest of her husband's belongings and together with her two older children George and Eleni, she took a taxi to the address that she found in her husband's jacket. When Andreas came to the front door she spoke firmly and with incredible resolve. "Look at your children for the last time." She then turned around and left, never to lay eyes on him again. Maria was now determined and prepared to raise her three young children on her own.

When Maria's youngest daughter Christina was old enough to join her two siblings at school, Maria took the opportunity to look for full-time employment. By now, her parents had also immigrated to Melbourne and were living with her. She found a job at Stacks Pies in Blackburn that specialised in making cakes, sausage rolls and of course,

meat pies. Maria was required to work the evening shift, sometimes working up to ten hours straight. This allowed for only four hours of sleep each night. She still had to wake up early to dress and feed her children their breakfast and get them ready for school.

Maria and Andreas Avraam on their wedding day. Skarinou, 14th October, 1951

Thankfully, Maria's parents were able to look after the children when she was working at the pie factory.

Maria worked at Stack Pies for nine years. Shortly after leaving the factory, she found employment in Mena House, a hospital and nursing home located in East Melbourne, where she worked as a cleaner and tea lady.

In 1966, her brother Minas bought a new house in the nearby suburb or Prahran. Testament to his great generosity, Minas allowed his sister to live in his Richmond home rent free so that

ABOVE: Maria Avraam in Skarinou. 1953
BELOW: Maria's personal diary.

Maria's parents Dimitra and Giorgios Frangou. Skarinou, 1976

she could raise her children as a single mother without any additional financial burden. It was an act of kindness that Maria would never forget.

In 1973, after seven years of living in Australia, Maria's parents decided to return to Cyprus. Her father died ten years later. Following this, Maria's widowed mother returned to Melbourne.

In 1985, Maria had saved enough money to put a deposit on a small house in Brunswick. Her children agreed to help her with the mortgage repayments.

In 1993, she sold all her property assets in Cyprus (groves of olive and carob trees) and paid off her mortgage. For the first time in her life she was debt free.

When I first interviewed Maria Frangou in 2012 she was eighty-nine years old, living on her own and active. She was able to walk to the local shops, to church and to visit her many friends in the neighbourhood. When I last saw her in August 2018, she had just turned ninety-five and although less mobile, her mind was still sharp.

Maria is a survivor in every sense of the word. Her amazing story should serve as a testament to the strength and amazing resilience of the Cypriot women from her unique generation.

ACKNOWLEDGEMENTS
I would like to thank Maria Frangou for this very honest and frank account of her life and for sharing her living memories with me. Special thanks to Helena Kidd for her support over the years and for understanding the importance of documenting and preserving her mother's incredible life story.

Takis & Loulla
IOANNOU

Takis Ioannou's life began on the 12th of March 1934 in Kalavasos, Larnaca. He was the eldest child of Ioannis and Argyiri (Argyroula) Papamatheou along with his two younger sisters Athoulla and Athinoulla. "My parents were married in 1931," he tells me. "At that time, gatherings of more than four people were forbidden following the riots of 1931. That was after they burned down Government House in Nicosia. My parents had to get a special licence from the British in order to get married."

According to Takis, Kalavasos was home to a community of approximately 1000 Christians and 280 Muslims. The population would swell when men travelled from all over Cyprus to work in the mines located near the town.

From a young age, Takis was fascinated with his Orthodox religion. His father was a *psaltis* (cantor) for the church and his grandfather Papa Matheou was a priest. The church in the village was dedicated to the Virgin Mary and was located next to Takis' house. Takis was blessed with an incredible voice and was always seen in church singing the hymns together with his father.

When he was three years old Takis contracted typhoid fever. His father immediately rushed him to see a doctor in Larnaca. As a reward for his son's brave demeanour his father bought him a wind-up toy train for three shillings. It was the only toy Takis would ever own. At seven

years of age he fell out of a fruit tree and broke his wrist. This time, his father gave him a couple of slaps before he realised his son was injured.

Takis' parents were not the wealthiest people in the village, but they made sure that their children always wore shoes. It was well-known that barefoot children came from the poorest of families.

Takis' family produced their own olive oil. When the demand for their olive oil grew, his father would buy more land. In Cyprus, those who owned land were the luckiest people of all.

There was no running water in Kalavasos. It was Takis' responsibility to fetch water from the well three times a day for the farm animals to drink as well as for the family's domestic needs.

When Takis was eleven, he recalls getting drunk. "My father was the Church District Secretary in our village. One day he wanted to entertain some guests in our home. He handed me a few shillings and sent me on an errand to buy some brandy at our local *kafenion* (coffee house). I was curious so on my way home I had a little drink. Before I knew it I had drunk the whole bottle." Takis begins to laugh. "I drank the whole bottle of brandy and then I stumbled into a room at the school to hide. It wasn't long before a teacher discovered me there, sleeping in my own vomit and promptly sent me home. My father was not impressed."

As soon as Takis finished primary

school his father put him to work on the family farm. "I've been waiting for twelve years so that you could come and help me" his father would say. For the next five years Takis worked hard and was able to teach himself everything he needed to know by watching and learning from his parents. He was able to plough the fields, sow a variety of grains and take part in

Loulla Costantinou aged ten with her brother Costa and her mother Ermioni Costantinou. 1953

Takis Ioannou resting after cutting timber at the grape farm in Mildura. 1953

the annual threshing and harvesting of the wheat. He was even given the responsibly of operating the mill. "I was a man at twelve," Takis says. "Our mules were six-foot-tall and I was this little boy working amongst them."

When Takis turned seventeen he took a leap of faith and boarded a ship named the Corsica to travel to Australia with the single-minded intention of paying off his father's debt of 1000 pounds. The debt was for Mr Patishi, a carob factory owner from the nearby village of Zygi. As the ship departed, Takis saw his mother crying on the wharf. This was the first time he had ever seen her cry.

On board the Corsica that day were 850 Cypriots including six men and two girls from Kalavasos. The journey took an astonishing fifty-four days to reach Australia; twice as long as other ships at the time. The delay started in the Port of Limassol. Due to the rough weather, it took three days just to load the ship with a cargo of potatoes and onions, which were to be dropped off in the port of Colombo. Unfortunately, the December rains ruined the vegetables as they sat in their sacks on the open deck. The muddy mush created such a nauseating smell that many passengers became quite ill. As if the stench wasn't enough, the rough ocean between Limassol and Port Said caused nearly all the passengers

to become seasick. There was another seven-day delay in Colombo due to Ceylon's strict quarantine rules.

On board the Corsica was a man named Ioannis Costantinou who would one day become Takis' father-in-law – not that either had any idea at the time. Takis knew Ioannis from his childhood. "When I was a boy I would catch a ride on top of his bus as he transported carobs from Kalavasos to a factory in Zygi. I remember having to lie low on top of the carobs to avoid being struck by low-lying branches along the way."

On land in Port Said, Takis received an unusual welcome from the Arab beggars who had gathered at the port to pester the travellers for money. *Pakshish, pakshish,* (money, money) they would cry with their outstretched hands. Port Said was an impoverished town. Takis ignored the beggars, choosing instead to spend his money on ice cream and soft drink.

The ship Corsica was in a dilapidated state and badly understaffed. The captain would often pay passengers to work in the kitchen or to carry out menial tasks such as loading or unloading goods at various ports. It was in the ship's kitchen where Takis first met George Demetrios (nicknamed Tsimboukas). The two men would become lifelong friends.

Fifty-four days after departing from Limassol, the Corsica finally docked at Port Melbourne. Takis was both relieved and excited. Within a week, he was able to secure a steady job on the production line of a beer bottle factory in Spotswood. His job was to clink together freshly made bottles to ensure they didn't crack or shatter. A leather apron and gloves were the only protective clothing he wore. A few weeks into the job, a teenage friend named George Antoniou persuaded Takis to join the Rosella factory in Richmond. There, Takis was responsible for delivering cans of fruit and sauce by trolley to the steam cookers. The factory employed around two thousand women and only about a dozen men. Takis enjoyed the female attention he received. During this time, he was renting a small room with some other Cypriot migrants in a small house in Drummond Street, Carlton. He later moved into his uncle Alekos' house in Windsor, where he shared a room with his cousins. At one point, Takis lived in a house where each of the four bedrooms contained a different family. It would

seem that there were no housing regulations at that time, or perhaps they were simply ignored. Renting out rooms was an effective way for newly arrived migrants to find immediate and affordable housing.

In late 1952, Takis, (persuaded by his uncle Alekos) decided to move to Mildura for work. His job at the Rosella factory had only lasted three months. In Mildura, he went to work for a Greek farmer on his vineyard. "I bought myself a BSA Golden Flash motorcycle. In October 1953 I broke my leg after colliding with an FJ Holden. I remember the bone in my leg was sticking out. It was awful and very painful. I had to get twenty-four stitches." Before the accident, Takis spent his weekends at the local dance halls. He loved dancing. He lived in Mildura for two years before moving back to Melbourne in 1954.

Once again, through word of mouth, Takis found another job, this time at a bedding factory in the suburb of Prahran, where he worked as a machinist making mattresses. In the evenings he would catch a tram to Russell Street to visit his friends at a Cypriot clubhouse called Zenon.

Around this time, Takis befriended an Australian woman called Mary. It was common for young Greek and Cypriot bachelor men to meet and mingle with the local 'Aussies'. They saw it as the thrill of the chase or maybe some kind of exotic adventure. Takis had intentions to buy an engagement ring to give to Mary. He decided

Takis Ioannou (right) with a friend Themostiklis (middle) in a Djibouti taxi, French Somaliland. 1951

Takis Ioannou (middle) on his beloved Golden Flash motorcycle riding with friends Andrew (left) and Bill (right) and later fooling around on the St. Kilda Pier in Melbourne. 1954

to share his plan with his cousin Taso Evangelou. Taso immediately responded with a stern warning. "If you marry her, you will never be allowed to step foot in my house again." Yielding to his cousin's warning, Takis decided to end his relationship with Mary.

In 1956, Takis was conscripted into the Australian National Service. He was stationed in the army base at Puckapunyal for three months where he was quickly promoted to the rank of Corporal. He was then transferred to the Citizen's Military Force where he served on a part-time basis from 1956 until 1958. "We used to take part in parades in Melbourne and every year for two weeks we would go to the training camps," he recalls.

In 1959, Takis met Loulla Costantinou after the Greek Easter mass that was held at Evangelismos church in East Melbourne. He was invited to his uncle Alekos' house in Windsor for supper and Loulla was there with her family. They had travelled to Melbourne from Traralgon where they lived.

A few weeks after Easter, Takis travelled to Traralgon together with his uncle Alekos and aunt Stravroula to meet with Loulla's parents. Loulla admits that

it was love at first sight. "I just loved the way he looked."

Loulla was only eight years old when her father Ioannis left for Australia in 1951. She remained in her village of Pentakomo with her mother Ermioni and her older brother Costa. Loulla remembers crying in the school yard whenever she thought about her father so far away. She did not understand that he was seeking a better life and had planned to bring the family to Melbourne when the time was right. It would be five long years before they were all reunited. In 1956, Loulla, aged thirteen, arrived in Melbourne with her mother and went to live with her father and brother in the country town of Traralgon. Her brother Costa had arrived two years earlier.

Once engaged, Takis moved to Traralgon to be closer to his fiancé. He found work at the Australian Paper Mill (APM) where his future father-in-law also worked. Traralgon had many Cypriot residents. They moved there because of the promise of steady employment with companies such as the State Electricity Commission and the APM.

Takis finally paid off his father's debt and decided it was time to invest in property. He was about to purchase five blocks of land in the suburb of Sunshine for £200 each when he received a letter from his sister announcing that his father still owed £400. Always the dutiful son, Takis used the deposit for the land to pay off his father's debt. He then had to borrow around £200 pounds to pay for Loulla's wedding dress.

On the 19th of September 1959, Takis and Loulla were married in the Church of England in Traralgon. A few months later on the 17th of January 1960 they were married again, this time in the Greek Orthodox Church in East Melbourne.

In October 1960, their first child John was born, and three months later they moved to Melbourne to help manage a cousin's café at the Cyprion Brotherhood Zenon. They lived in shared accommodation in Windsor.

Takis remembers that after the mass migration from Greece and Cyprus, the queues to get into the Zenon restaurant would extend down the street and around the block.

Takis Ioannou (right) in the kitchen with Yianaki the kitchen hand at the Cyprian Brotherhood Zenon. Melbourne, 1955

The popularity of the restaurant was mainly due to the impressive culinary skills of the head chef, Mr Spyros Stasis.

Between 1962 and 1964, Takis worked on the construction of Boiler One and Boiler Two at the Hazelwood Power Station.

In 1963, Loulla gave birth to a daughter whom she named Emy (after her mother Ermioni). A year later, Takis built a new house for his growing family. He also went back to APM in Traralgon where he worked for twenty-seven years until he retired in 1991.

Between 1967 and 1971, Takis took on a second job delivering milk by horse and cart in the evenings. His milk rounds began at 5pm and would finish three hours later. If his horse was sick, his wife Loulla would be required to drive a milk truck while he delivered the milk on foot. Apparently, the horse would listen to instructions from Takis but had also memorised the route and knew where to go. For Takis, the horse was easier than using a truck to deliver milk.

In 1969, Takis and Loulla welcomed their third child; a daughter they named

Takis and Loulla Ioannou's wedding photo. January, 1960

Loulla's grandfather, Constantinos Ioannou. Year unknown.

Roulla after Takis' mother Argyroula.

In 1971, after twenty years abroad, Takis was able to finally return to Cyprus to see his sisters and parents. He stayed with them for two months.

Takis Ioannou has made a significant impact in the region of Gippsland. He always made time for his family, the church and the Greek community. He would organize Greek dances regularly throughout the year and helped to introduce a Greek School in Traralgon which operated for many years.

He joined the Greek Orthodox Church Committee in 1959. He soon became secretary, treasurer, vice president and eventually president. In the 1970s he was instrumental in helping to build the first (and only) Greek Orthodox Church in Gippsland, the Dormition of Our Lady located in Morwell.

Noted for his excellent singing voice he also became the chief *psalti* at the Greek church in Morwell. He laments that there are now more funeral services at the church than weddings or baptisms.

Takis and Loulla still live in Traralgon. They are blessed with three children and seven grandchildren. Takis still sings every Sunday in the Greek church he helped to build in Morwell.

ACKNOWLEDGEMENTS
I would like to thank Takis and Loulla Ioannou for sharing their story and for making me so welcome when I visited them in Traralgon in 2016. I would also like to thank their daughter Roulla Charilaou for all her support and assistance and Roulla's son Ari Charilaou for proofreading my initial translation of his grandparents' life story.

Andreas
PRASTITES

Andreas Prastites was born on the 24th of December 1929 in the village of Aradippou. Andreas was one of eight children (Kostas, Panayiotis, Pantelou, Eleni, Andreas, Chrystothea, Loukia and Louiza). His parents, Zacharias and Theodoula were actually blessed with fourteen children but tragically, six died soon after birth. Andreas cannot recall why so many of his siblings had died so young but suspects that poor nutrition, environmental factors and a lack of medicine may have been the cause.

His father Zacharias was a poor man who worked hard to feed his large family. He would travel each day by donkey selling fresh eggs and live chickens. Zacharias would purchase the eggs and chickens from local farmers and sell them, for a profit in the neighbouring villages and at the marketplace in Scala (Larnaca).

When Andreas was around eight or nine years of age he ran away from school after an incident with another student. "This student had head lice," he tells me. "He sat next to me in class and kept leaning towards me on purpose so I kept pushing him away. The teacher saw us and he grabs me by the shirt and starts to beat me quite hard. I managed to escape his grasp and I jumped through a window and ran away. After that I never went back to school."

Andreas never told his parents what had happened at his school. Instead, he would pretend to walk to school each morning and then hide out in the village all day until it was time to go home. He kept this rouse up for almost a year until his parents eventually found out and he suffered another beating for his trouble.

When he turned twelve, Andreas was sent to work in a nearby quarry where he was required to split large rocks to form square blocks that he would then shape and polish into floor tiles. "It was difficult work for a child," he says. "First, you grab a large slab of the flat rock and cut it with a *kouzma* (pick axe) or *pryoni* (saw). I could split one slab of rock into four tiles. Quite often I would find the fossils of ancient fish embedded in the rock."

At fourteen, Andreas went to work at a natural marble and mosaic factory near Scala. He would ride his bicycle ten miles every day, back and forth from his village to the factory. Once again, he was required to split stone and marble and prepare it for builders to use on floors, benches, building facades, hotel lobbies, stairs and courtyards. "We even made troughs out of the stuff. All by hand. We did not have any machines or special tools in those days. We had to polish the slabs using a stone. I remember that the skin on my hands used to peel and my palms would often blister or bleed. No one wore gloves back then."

Working in the quarry and at the marble factory was backbreaking work for young Andreas. He told me that his feet and hands became so tough that even a nail could not penetrate the skin.

Andreas Prastites' passport photo. c.1951

The Demetriou children with their mother Despina and grandfather (name unknown). From left to right: Nikos, Kyriakoula seated on her mother's lap, Katerina (Katina) and Eleni. Leonarisso, Famagusta. c.1929

In the beginning, he was paid one shilling a day but eventually after a few years, he started earning around ten shillings a day.

Andreas worked at the marble factory for six years until he turned twenty. Then in 1951, he was invited to leave Cyprus by his uncle Kostas Zacharoullas (his mother's brother) who was living in Melbourne, Australia.

On the 12th of July 1951, Andreas bid his family farewell and boarded the ship Hellenic Prince. He arrived in Melbourne almost a month later on the 8th of August. "I remember there were no cabins on the ship," he recalls. "There were around two hundred men in one large room and we all slept in bunk beds. The men had their sleeping quarters and the women had theirs."

Akis Peridis. Nicosia, 1927. Eleni Demetriou worked as a nanny caring for this boy in the 1940s

In his first year abroad, Andreas worked at a glass factory in Spotswood. He remembers being paid around eight pounds a week. During this time, he lived with his uncle (Kostas Zacharoullas) who had a fish and chip shop in Williamstown. His bedroom was located above the shop.

Every weekend Andreas would catch the train from Williamstown into the city to meet up with his friends. Together they would frequent the few Greek cafés, bars and clubs in the city. "I was very fortunate to have six or seven friends who were from my village and had migrated to Australia around the same time as me. I had known these guys since I was a young boy. We would often spend time together at the Cypriot Club on Lonsdale Street or catch a tram to St Kilda beach. We had a good time together. I can't complain."

In December 1952, Andreas and hundreds of co-workers lost their jobs at the glass factory due to the economic downturn and the government's credit squeeze. Andreas was fortunate however, to find work with the Country Road Board (CRB) and was sent to work in the country town of Sale, approximately 132 miles from Melbourne. Once there, he helped to lay the concrete driveways for the aeroplane hangers at the West Sale airport. He remembers that all the migrant workers lived in huts and were paid around twenty-four pounds a fortnight.

In March 1954, Queen Elizabeth landed at the West Sale airport during

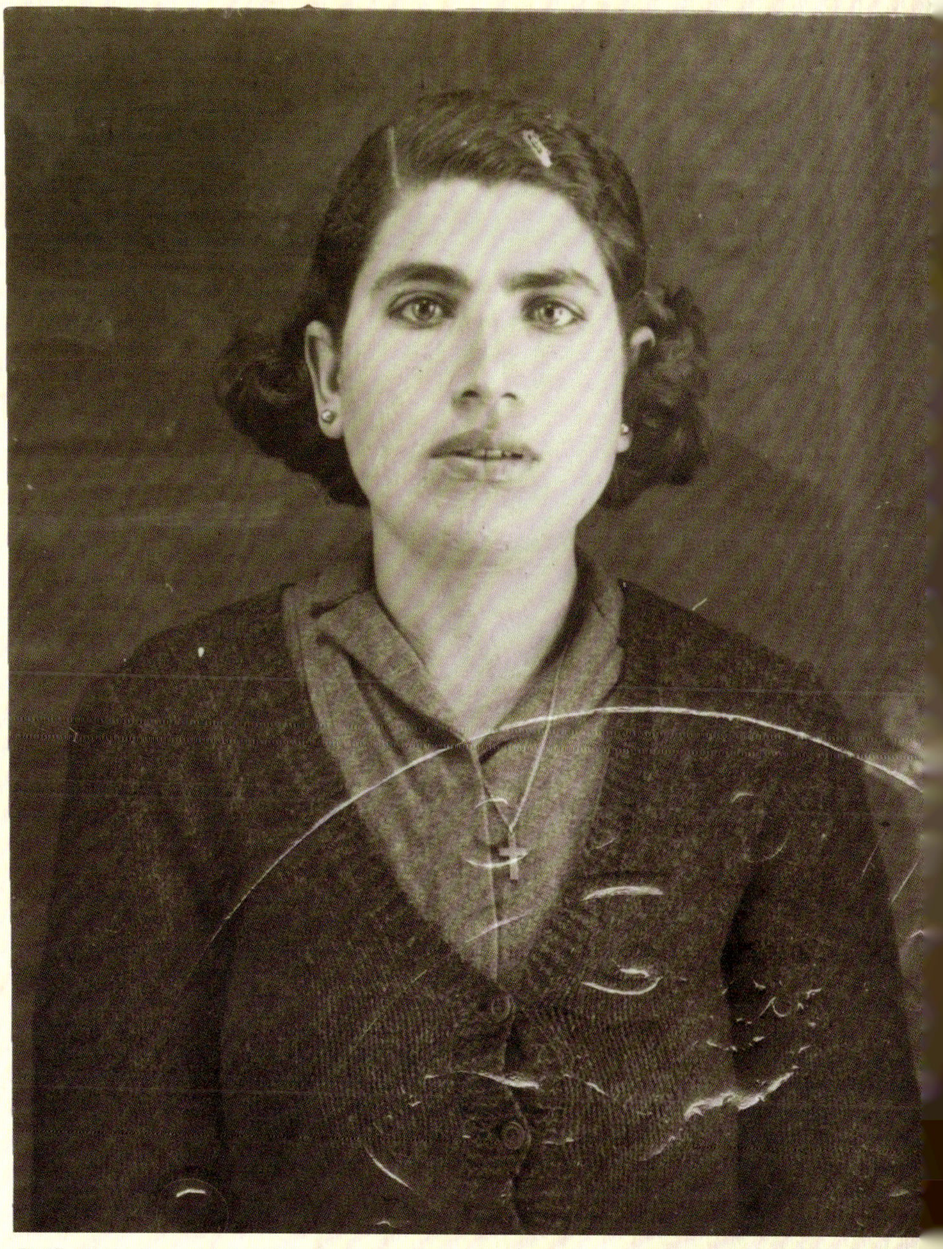

Eleni Demetriou's passport photo. c.1949

Katerina (Katina) Demetriou (left) with a friend. Leonarisso, Famagusta. c.1938

Unknown couple. Leonarisso, Famagusta. 1940s

According to Andreas, Eleni had had a difficult childhood largely due to severe poverty. She was born on the 10th of October 1923 in the village of Leonarisso, Famagusta. From the age of nine, she was sent to work as a servant for various wealthy Greek families in and around Famagusta, and later, Nicosia. With her father living in Australia, Eleni's mother Despina was desperately poor (with no source of income) and had no choice but to send her daughter into the all-too-common world of child labour.

Apparently, the experience for Eleni was horrible. In Famagusta, she was constantly beaten by the man of the house and at times was left unfed and unpaid. Unfortunately, nothing is known about her teenage years or young adult life in Cyprus. What is known is that at seventeen, Eleni was sent to work as a nanny for the Peridis family in Nicosia to care for their young son Akis. Apparently, she worked there for ten years and was at last treated fairly and with respect.

Eleni was a stunningly beautiful woman and Andreas was immediately smitten with her. Despite a few protests from his mother back in the village, he went ahead and married her anyway. When I ask Andreas why his mother objected he replies: "What mother is happy with

her first Australian tour. Andreas and the other workers stood along the runway to try and get a glimpse of the young Royal.

Later that year, Andreas was sent back to Melbourne by the CRB to build new roads and bridges in the inner and outer suburbs. One day when he was working on the Johnston Street bridge, he fell twenty-seven feet into the Yarra River. Miraculously, he survived without sustaining any serious injuries.

In late 1954, a family friend introduced Andreas to Eleni Demetriou.

Eleni had migrated to Melbourne in 1950 with her mother Despina and two sisters Katerina (Katina) and Kyriakoula. Eleni was working at an ice-cream cone factory in Prahran at the time when she was introduced to Andreas. As the story goes, her father Demetris Charnakas was already living in Australia, having migrated in the 1930s. For reasons unknown, it had taken him almost twenty years to finally arrange to bring his family to Australia.

Eleni's older sister Katerina (Katina) aged around seventeen. Famagusta, Cyprus. c.1938

the woman her son wants to marry? My mother wanted me to marry a girl from our village. It wasn't Eleni's age that bothered her. She didn't know that Eleni was six years older then me."

Eleni and Andreas were married on the 23rd of January 1955. For the first three years of their marriage, they lived together with Eleni's family in Prahran until Andreas was able to afford to buy his own house in the same suburb for three thousand pounds.

In February 1958, Andreas and Eleni welcomed the arrival of their daughter Despina. In October 1959, their daughter Zacharoula (Lula) was born.

Andreas worked for the CRB for twenty-seven years until he retired in 1990 at the age of sixty. By the time he retired he was riddled with severe shoulder and back pain due to arthritis and the strain caused by his occupation. The backbreaking work he had endured from a young age had finally taken a toll on his ageing body.

With wet eyes, Andreas tells me that his fondest memories were back in Cyprus when he was playing and being foolish with his loyal group of friends. "All of my friends are now gone," he says sadly. "Lazaros, Andreas, Andonis, Christos; all gone." He remembers with fondness the hot summer days when, as skinny, tanned teenagers they would all ride their bicycles to the beach in Larnaca and spend the day sitting together on the sand joking and teasing one another.

"I regret not going back to school when I was young," he suddenly remarks. "For most of my young life I couldn't read or write. When I came to Australia I could barely scratch together enough words to write my mother a letter. Thankfully, as I got older I became determined to teach myself to read and write Greek. Then after I found work at the Country Road Board, I managed to teach myself English. I had proven to myself that I was smart enough to learn how to read and write."

Eleni died in 2001 after suffering a major stroke. She was seventy-seven years old. Her death would have a profound effect on Andreas but thankfully he was comforted and supported by his children, grandchildren and many neighbourhood friends.

ACKNOWLEDGEMENTS

I would like to thank Andreas Prastites for allowing me to write his life story. Like so many Cypriots whom I have met and interviewed for *Tales of Cyprus*, the hospitality and kindness extended towards me is without equal. I would also like to extend my thanks and gratitude to Andreas' daughter Lula and granddaughter Elizabeth for their kind support and assistance.

Andreas Prastites on the Johnston Street bridge in Collingwood with the Country Road Board. Melbourne. c.1956

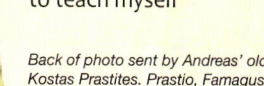

Back of photo sent by Andreas' older brother Kostas Prastites. Prastio, Famagusta. 1950s

Michalakis & Nina
CHRISTOU

Michalakis Christou was born in 1950 and raised in the beautiful village of Pano Lefkara. Although he successfully completed primary school he only lasted three months at the Lefkara Gymnasium-Lyceum (High School). He told his father he wanted to pursue other interests and education was not one of them. His father Efthimiou, who was one of nine children (eight sisters), insisted that his three sons receive the education that he himself was deprived. Michalakis however, persuaded his father to let him work with him in the fields instead of attending school. At eleven and a half he was allowed to work in the family orchard and vineyard and to look after the farm animals. By the age of twelve, Michalakis was even ploughing the wheat fields by himself with two large mules.

"We were boys - but we were men," he bellows with pride. "We grew up fast in those days. The hardship of our lifestyle forced us to grow up fast."

At thirteen, Michalakis bought himself a mule with the pocket money he had saved over the last twelve months. He would use his mule to deliver *katzara* (wood kindling) to the inhabitants of Lefkara to light their outdoor ovens.

"We didn't have supermarkets back then," he announces. "You couldn't just go out and buy whatever you wanted. No, no, no. The women of the village would bake in their ovens (usually on a Saturday) enough bread and *koulouria* (sesame bread rings) to last two weeks. There was a lot of work involved in making the bread, you know. First you have to harvest the wheat, then comes the threshing followed by the grinding of the wheat into flour. Then you have to make the dough, light the fire and bake the bread. It all took time and effort. It is not like it is today. For me, I had to find the right type of wood from the right type of bush. All I had was a small axe. It was a very physical job but I became strong and very good at this job."

I nod my agreement and tell Michalakis that one of my fondest memories is coming home from school and finding freshly baked bread in a basket on the table. I still believe it was the best bread I have ever tasted. We spend the next few minutes discussing the merits of village oven-baked bread.

I ask Michalakis to tell me what he remembers about the old *Agora* (market) in the village. His eyes gleam as he speaks. "It was wonderful," he replies. "The *Agora* was the largest and most popular market in the region. People from all around Lefkara would come with their donkeys and mules laden with their produce and all sorts of goods to sell."

Before Michalakis had turned fourteen, he was persuaded by a close friend to become an apprentice for a local master silversmith known as Nicos. Michalakis would complete his farm duties at 1pm then rush home to change clothes and eat a simple lunch, before going to work at the silversmith from 2pm until 6pm. It was a gruelling day. He earned five shillings during his first week. Eventually he would earn two pounds a week at the silversmith shop and he

Nina's adoptive parents Panayiota and Stelli Yialloniti. Pano Lefkara, Cyprus. Year unknown.

Michalakis Christou's parents. Pano Lefkara, Cyprus. 1946

worked there for three years. The master craftsman taught Michalakis how to make many wonderful items out of the precious metal. "We made icons, candlestick holders, chalices, cups, trays, whatever you want," he boasts.

At eighteen, like all young Cypriot men Michalakis was conscripted to serve in the army. Three months before his service had ended he was engaged to Nina Yialoniti.

Michalakis had known Nina since he was a young boy. Their love for one another had grown over time. They would meet in secret and exchange love letters. Nina recalls how he would pass by the dressmaker's house where she worked and he would whistle a special tune to try and attract her attention. He was a poor boy struggling to make a living while she came from a relatively wealthy family. Her parents Panayiota and Stelli Yialoniti wanted their only child to marry someone wealthy from the village. Nina, however, protested and insisted that the only man she would marry was Michalakis. She knew that many men in the village wanted

to marry her but her love and bond with Michalakis was unbreakable. Her parents knew that Michalakis was a good and proper man. Her mother especially had warmed to the boy years earlier and knew Michalakis was hardworking, obedient, respectful and ambitious. She knew that her daughter had found a good match and would live a good life with him.

Nina's parents were not her biological parents. The Yialoniti couple adopted her when she was nine years of age. They were childless and had sent word through the village grapevine that they were seeking to adopt a child. Nina's biological father responded and brought his middle daughter from the mountainous village of Pedoulas to Lefkara where he left her with the Yialoniti family to raise as their own child. Although she is grateful that her adopted parents were kind and good to her, Nina remains tortured by the thought that she was given away so easily by the parents she was born to, without any explanation.

"I remember the day I left my village," she says softly fighting back tears. "My parents never told me that I was to be given away. I had no idea. My mother found an old suitcase and bundled together some of my clothes and belongings. There was no good-bye or tears. Not even a kiss. I was nine years old. I wasn't sure where my father was taking me. All I remember was that I was excited to go on my very first bus ride. We travelled for hours with my father sitting beside me, silent and always looking away from me. We arrived in the village of Lefkara at night and my father introduced me to this very nice couple. I was fed oranges for the first time in my life. It wasn't until the next morning when I discovered that my father had left me behind to be adopted by this couple."

I asked Nina if she ever found out why her real parents gave her away. "Poverty, I imagine," she replies quietly. "They had five children. I was the middle child." She pauses and shakes her head. Then she begins to cry. "Could they not bring themselves to feed one more child? I never saw my real parents or siblings again. But you know Costa - I am content. I was raised by a loving and wonderful couple. They were very good to me."

Things certainly turned out much better for Nina. Despite the trauma she must have felt to lose her biological family she was thankfully raised by a good couple in a beautiful village. As soon as Michalakis had completed his army service in 1971 he married his Nina. He was twenty-one and she was eighteen. They had two sons and became grandparents in their early forties.

"Life was good for us," Michalakis exclaims. "After I was married I was earning around nine pounds a week as a silversmith. My father-in-law who had the *kafenion* (coffee house) was only earning about half of that amount."

Michalakis speaks fondly about his village. "Lefkara was prosperous. People lived a good life. There were over four thousand people living in the village back then. We had everything; the *Agora*, schools, a hospital, courthouse and a police station. We had a football team, even before Larnaca had one. We had everything. Praise God, we lived a good

Nina's father, Stelli Yialoniti. Pano Lefkara. Year unknown.

life. And Nina and I have always loved each other. We are happy."

Michalakis goes on to explain his views about life today in Lefkara compared with that of forty or fifty years ago. "The big difference, in my opinion - is debt. When I was growing up, most people owned their property and there was very little debt. Today, I would say maybe ninety percent of people (if not more) do not own what they have and constantly live in debt."

With the introduction of tourism to Cyprus in the 1960s, Nina and Michalakis eventually turned their family *kafenion* into a silversmith and lace shop where they still work today. Despite certain hardships they feel blessed to live in Lefkara and are content with their lot in life. Michalakis may in fact be the last of the original silversmiths in Pano Lefkara.

Nina's father in his kafenion. Pano Lefkara. Year unknown.

Although both his sons have also become silversmiths under his tutelage, he remains somewhat pessimistic about the future and believes that this ancient craft will not survive.

There are many age-old crafts that are now teetering on the edge of extinction. The emergence of machines, industry and technology over the last century has introduced faster and cheaper alternatives to the older time-consuming hand-made products. Lace embroidery, silverwork, dress making, boot making, kerchief making, violin making and basket making, to name a few, are traditional hand-made crafts that have been replaced by faster machine-made alternatives.

Only time will tell if these ancient traditional skills will disappear and become extinct. I certainly hope not.

ACKNOWLEDGEMENTS
I would like to thank Nina and Michalakis Christou for making time in their busy schedule to allow me to conduct this interview. I only wish I had more time to spend with them.

Nina's parents Stelli and Panayiota Yialoniti. Pano Lefkara. Year unknown.

Andreas
PAVLIDES

Andreas Michael Pavlides was born on the 6th of June 1934 in the village of Kornos, Larnaca. The village had a population of around eight hundred inhabitants in the 1930s and was famed for its beautiful pottery. "Everybody knew each other in the village," remarked Andreas. One of his earliest memories in Kornos was exploring the countryside with his friends.

Andreas attended primary school for four years from the age of seven until he was eleven. "I did not like school very much," he says. "I wanted to be outside all the time, exploring my village. There were two schools in my village, an upper and lower school. They were separated by about half a mile. In the morning, we would have lessons in the upper school then at lunch time we would all walk home to eat something and then return to the lower school for our afternoon lessons. My house was in between the two schools and I remember one time when I was around nine or ten I decided, while walking with the other children back to school in the afternoon, that I would sneak away and go and explore the countryside. I did this every afternoon for a week or so before the teacher asked my father where I was every afternoon. My father did not know where I was so he decided to follow me one afternoon and discovered my escape route. After that I once again became a regular student in the afternoon classes."

Andreas' father Mihalis Pavlides died suddenly in 1942, when Andreas was only eight years old. His premature death would place a heavy emotional and financial toll on his family. Although Andreas barely remembers his father, he does recall an extraordinary story about his father's life that is based on snippets

Andreas Pavlides' passport photo. c.1951

told to him by relatives over the years.

"I did not really know my father," begins Andreas. "I know he was born in Kornos in 1887, shortly after the British arrived. I believe he was a man ahead of his time. He was someone who sought a life beyond the hardship and poverty of the village. Even as a child, he wanted to improve his life."

According to Andreas, when his father was very young he left the village to travel to Egypt. "My grandparents had a herd of goats and I was told that at the turn of the century, my father sold a few of the goats and bought himself a ticket to go to Egypt. I do not think his parents knew about this." Andreas does not know why his father chose to leave Cyprus at such a young age and in such an extraordinary manner or why he decided to travel to Egypt. Was he sent by someone or did he run away? The circumstances that led to Mihalis' early exodus from Cyprus remains forever a family mystery.

Andreas recalls that his father had kept in touch with his family during his time in Egypt, never losing touch with his homeland. Later in life he remembers seeing photographs and letters that his father had written to his grandparents and brother when he was abroad.

Once in Egypt, Mihalis was adopted by a Pontian family living in Cairo. The circumstances that led to the adoption are unknown. Andreas does not know how his father met the family, only that their surname was Pavlides. "All I know is that this Pontian family helped to raise my father and even trained him to be a barber just like the other men in their family. They had a barbershop in Cairo. I also know that my father had an understanding and knowledge of Arabic, French and English, the main languages that were spoken in Egypt at the time."

LEFT:
Mihalis Pavlides (seated) with his brother Lefteris Georgiou. Buenos Aires, Argentina. Dated 1st January 1915.

BELOW:
Cabinet portrait photograph of Mihalis Pavlides (seated) and Lefteris Georgiou. Location unknown. c.1913.

Mihalis Pavlides. Location unknown. c.1915.

The Pavlides family took very good care of Mihalis. When he turned twenty, he became engaged to their daughter Eleftheria who was also the same age. "I remember seeing a photo of her when I was just a small boy," adds Andreas. "She was very beautiful with dark curly hair. I don't know what happened to that photo."

Shortly after their engagement, Eleftheria contracted meningitis and died. Mihalis was devastated. In memory of his dearly departed fiancé, he decided to change his surname to Pavlides. Heartbroken, he left Egypt for Argentina to reconnect with his younger brother Lefteris, who was living in Buenos Aires.

The two brothers stayed and worked together in Buenos Aires until the outbreak of the First World War in 1915. They then left Argentina and travelled to North America where they settled in Pennsylvania. Mihalis found work at a munitions factory producing weapons for the war effort. A year later a workplace accident occurred and Mihalis lost four fingers on his right hand. "I was told

that a grenade exploded in his hand and that is how he lost his fingers," says Andreas. "He received around one thousand pounds compensation from the government."

At the end of the war, Mihalis, aged thirty-one, decided to return to Cyprus and go back to Kornos. His brother Lefteris remained in Pennsylvania. Apparently, the journey by ship back to Cyprus took around six months - such was the distance and the many stops along the way.

Mihalis set up a barbershop in Kornos, utilising the skills he had learned in Cairo. With the money that he received in America for losing his fingers he bought quite a lot of property in Kornos, including all the land owned by a local priest. His cultured manner and his acquired Pontian accent were often at odds with many of the local peasant farmers in Kornos. He had left Cyprus as a poor goat herder and returned almost twenty years later as a cultured, worldly and highly qualified barber bringing a small fortune with him.

As a barber in Kornos, Mihalis was popular. He was earning up to four or five shillings a day when the average farm worker in Cyprus at that time was earning one shilling a week. Despite his disability, he still managed to use his injured hand to shave and cut the hair of his customers with remarkable dexterity. In the evenings, He enjoyed smoking cigarettes and playing cards at the local *kafenion* (coffee house) with the other villagers.

In 1923, Mihalis was introduced to Erifilli Yiangou, a master potter who was also the daughter of the *mukhtari* (headman) in Kornos named Yiangos.

They were married in 1924. Erifilli was around 15 years younger than Mihalis, who had just turned thirty-five. Together they had five children: Yiangos (born in 1925), Elefteria (1928), Varvara (1931), Andreas (1934) and Giorgia (1939).

On the 4th of December 1942, Mihalis died unexpectedly. Andreas was too young to recall the circumstances that led to his father's premature and sudden death. He remembers only that it was the holy feast day for Agia Varvara. "After my father passed away, I was sent to work as a *chouraki* (apprentice) with Giorgios

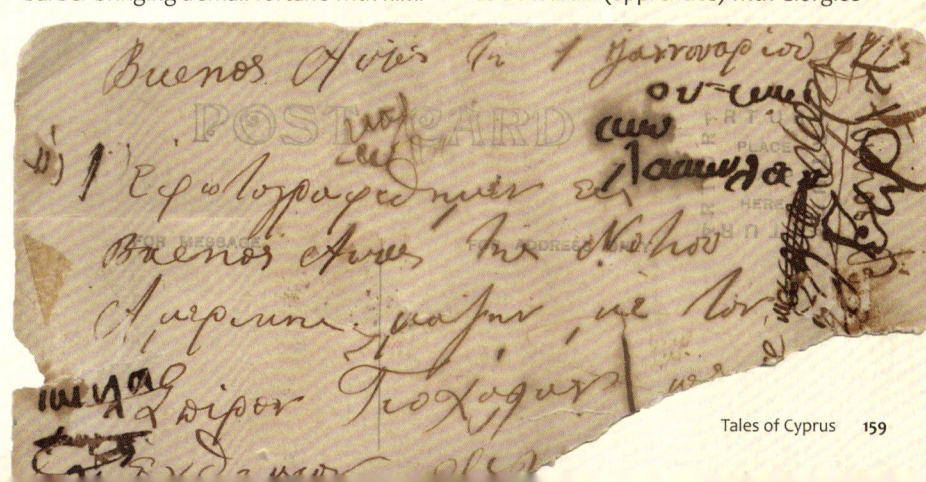

Reversed side of Buenos Aires studio photograph on facing page.

Stylianou who was a tailor in the village. My mother thought that if I could learn a trade I could help her with the demands of raising our family. My older brother Yiangos decided to immigrate to Australia for the same reasons. He would often send money home to our mother."

After the Second World War ended, Giorgios Stylianou left Cyprus to go to England so Andreas had to continue his apprenticeship with another tailor in Kornos whom he called Master Kostas. His apprenticeship lasted for five years and during this entire time, he was not paid. From Kornos, he started to work with other qualified tailors in places like Pera Chorio, Nisou, Varosi, Nicosia and Limassol. He was very deliberate in his travels around the island, as he was using this opportunity to hone his tailoring skills, by working under and observing other skilled tailors. In his early days as an apprentice, Andreas lived in the capital Nicosia, where he worked with a master tailor in a shop off Ledra Street. At sixteen, he began earning around four or five shillings a day. There were no set hours of employment. He worked as many hours a day and as many days a week as required. It all depended on the volume of work, which was based on the number of customers and orders the shop would receive. Sometimes he would work twelve or fourteen hours a day or seven days a week. "As an apprentice, I was hidden from the customers and required to stay in the workshop at the back of the shop," he explains. "In Nicosia, it was just me and another boy. The owner of the shop served customers from all over the neighbourhood including Turkish, Armenian and Maronite Cypriots. It was a popular tailor shop and for that reason, it was always very busy."

In Nicosia, Andreas rented a small room with a few other apprentices. The building did not have cooking facilities, so Andreas had to rely on various cafés, kiosks or markets in the neighbourhood for his food. "I did not like living and working in Nicosia," he tells me. "I much preferred my life in the village. I knew everyone there. I really missed my family and my relatives and of course my good friends in Kornos."

In April, 1956 at the age of twenty-one, Andreas decided to move to London. "I left Cyprus because there was no work or jobs," he explains. "There was a lot of unemployment. I wanted to go to London to learn more about my trade and see another part of the world. I left Scala (Larnaca) on the ship MS Messapia, stopping off at Venice and Bari in Italy. From Bari, I travelled by train to Paris and then on to Calais in northern France where we boarded a ferry and crossed the English Channel to Dover. I did not have any food with me on the train but I was lucky to be sharing a compartment with another Cypriot boy (also a tailor) whose mother had packed some eggs and bread in a bag and he kindly shared his food with me. There were a lot of other Cypriot migrants on the train. The whole trip from Cyprus cost thirty-two pounds. I had to borrow the money. Most of the Cypriots on that train had to borrow money to pay for their fare. No one, including me, had any savings. You worked and lived day to day back then. As a tailor at that time I was earning about five pounds a week and spending the whole amount on food and rent."

When Andreas arrived at Victoria Railway Station he was disorientated and confused with so many people rushing around. He had no idea how to find his cousin George who was meant to meet him there. "I didn't know where to go or what to do. I was completely stranded." Suddenly, he heard some men speaking Greek and approached them. They helped to direct him to the Cyprus Club in London and from there he was placed in a taxi to his cousin's house in Chalk Farm. The ordeal from Victoria Station to his cousin's house had lasted several hours. It was not a great introduction to London. "I wasn't

Katerina's parents Constantinos Mihaelis and Christina Stylianou and her aunt Mirianthi Stylianou. Kornos. c.1930

THIRD FROM LEFT: Katerina's step-grandmother Katerina Stylianou, her parents Christina and Constantinos Mihaelis, Mirianthi and Evangelos Stylianou. The young boy is Andreas Stylianou. Kornos, Larnaca. c.1930

the only one stranded in London," recalls Andreas with outstretched arms. "The whole city was full of migrants walking around lost and confused. You have to remember hardly anyone spoke English so communicating with the locals was impossible. I was lucky, I had my cousin's address written down on a piece of paper. That is how the driver knew where to take me. I was starving. I had not eaten anything all day and it was very cold."

London in the 1950s was a dark and dirty city. The dependence on coal for the heating needs of the population created a constant cloud of smog. The smog (and the fog) descended over all the buildings making visibility difficult on the streets and reducing the air quality dramatically.

Two days after he arrived in London, Andreas found a job at Harella International Fashions owned by a Jewish family in an area called Angel, in the Borough of Islington. Andreas worked mainly as a presser. It was very hard and tiring work. "In some ways, I liked London; in other ways I did not," he remarks. "My first priority was to get a job and pay off my debt. At the same time, I was anxious to send money back to my mother in the village." Andreas sighs and takes a sip of his coffee. "London was not my environment, it was not what I was used to. For one, I could not speak the language. Also, I didn't know many people. At the start, I lived quite a monastic way of life. In Cyprus

I could speak the language and I knew everyone. I used to roam by myself in the countryside, to wander over the hills and through the valleys. All these things I could not do in London. There was no empty space there."

Within five years of arriving in London, Andreas had opened his own tailoring workshop in the heart of London's West End. His business was well respected and specialised in making up hand-made suits for many of the menswear stores on Saville Row and other parts of London.

Despite his success, Andreas admits that London was never really a happy place for him, although at times he did experience some genuine moments of joy and excitement.

In 1957, a year after he arrived in London, Andreas was introduced to a young Cypriot girl named Katerina Constantinou. She was the niece of his old master, Giorgios Stylianou from Kornos, who he was again working with at his new workshop in Streatham. Katerina's brother Michael Constantinou and Andreas were also good friends at the time.

Four years later in 1961, Andreas and Katerina were married. They bought a house in Streatham before moving to Thornton Heath. Their three daughters were born in Streatham and Thornton Heath. Their youngest child Christina, was born in 1967.

Andreas had always fancied the idea of living in Australia. London was so crowded, with a cold, drab climate that he never really got used to. His brother and sister lived in Melbourne and they seemed happy living there so he thought that

Standing from left: Stavros Mayirou and Eleftherios Panayi and Andreas Pavlides (seated). Kornos. c.1952

maybe it would be a good place to raise his family there as well.

In December 1970, Andreas and Katerina made the decision to sell their house and relocate their family to Melbourne. "We left on the ship RHMS Ellinis, from Southhampton, and four weeks later we arrived in Port Melbourne. We paid ten pounds each. The children travelled for free. There must have been over one and half thousand people onboard that ship." The ship was very grand and there were plenty of activities and even a school for the children but

the sea was often rough with massive waves. His wife Katerina and youngest daughter Christina suffered terribly with sea sickness so the trip was quite difficult.

"The day we arrived it was so hot, I couldn't believe it," he says rather excitedly. "We went to my brother Yiangos' house and we just collapsed. We were all so tired and distressed from the heat and the trip."

Andreas and his family stayed at his brother's house for a month before he was able to purchase a brand-new brick-veneer house in Reservoir. "There were ten of us in my brother's small house in Glenroy – six children and four adults, and it was January in Melbourne."

Two days after he arrived, Andreas found work at the fashion house Travellers Apparel which was owned and established by Cypriot migrants Antonis (Tony) Toumbourou and Chris Christopher. Andreas joined their team of tailors and was quickly promoted to a senior tailoring position. He stayed at Travellers Apparel for five years. Travellers was known for their high-quality products and Andreas recalls having many high-profile customers including television personalities and politicians. Their factory employed many people and was often a landing place for new Cypriot migrants entering the local Melbourne community.

In 1976, Andreas opened his first retail shop in Box Hill, which he named Michael Andrew's Menswear. It was very successful and he had many devoted clients, but the business quickly outgrew its premises. In 1977, he moved his business to the Greek precinct on Lonsdale Street in the city before

Katerina Constantinou aged fifteen. Cyprus, May 1955

opening up his first manufacturing factory in Thornbury and then a second larger factory in Northcote in 1983. This company was called Ellesse Casual Wear and specialised in men's apparel, which Andreas manufactured for the high-end stores on Melbourne's Chapel Street. As always, his wife Katerina was by his side.

Andreas and Katerina worked together in the tailoring and fashion industry for thirty years and are fondly remembered in the business for their quality clothing and personal integrity.

Since his retirement in 2000, Andreas has enjoyed many overseas trips to Cyprus with his wife. He is an avid gardener and is renowned in his neighbourhood for his summer vegetables and beautiful garden.

He is now a devoted grandfather to his two grandchildren Andrew and Katerina who he spoils greatly.

ACKNOWLEDGEMENTS
I would like to thank my father-in-law Andreas Pavlides for taking the time to share his precious memories about the past with me. His ability to remember and recall names, places and dates is truly amazing. I would especially like to thank his daughter (and my wife) Christina Pavlides for her wonderful assistance in helping to document and edit her father's life story for this book.

Chrysanthi & Sotiris
CHARALAMBOUS

Chrysanthi Charalambous (nee Hajifrixou) was born on the 11th of August 1936 in the village of Yialousa, located about forty miles from Famagusta. Her parents Frixos and Andriana had seven children (Dimitris, Christina, Katina, Loukas, Haralambos, Chrysanthi and Cleo).

Chrysanthi's earliest memory of Cyprus was accompanying her parents into their fields and feeling the freshness of the air on her face and drinking the cool water from the spring. Although Chrysanthi's memory of her youth is now fading she does remember the photo of Queen Victoria hanging on the wall of her school room and that her village had three automobiles. The main road through the village was made of asphalt and all the other roads were dirt and gravel. "I can sometimes still smell the fresh *basturma* (cured spicy meat) that the Armenians in my village would cook."

Chrysanthi's father Frixos struggled to feed his family solely with the tiny profit that he made from his harvest. He would therefore often leave the village to help build new roads for the British administration in order to earn a little extra money. During the Second World War, he enlisted with the Cypriot Volunteer Regiment (CVR) to earn more money to help his family survive.

Chrysanthi was four years old when her father left for the war in 1940. Her younger sister Cleo was only forty days old. The two sisters did not recognise

their father at all when he returned to the village, five years later.

In 1945, Frixos accepted the position of sentry at the Akrotiri military base in Limassol where he stayed for another two years living away from his family. He eventually moved his family from Yialousa to Varosi (Varosi) so that his older children could attend the Gymnasium (high school) there and so they could be closer to his workplace in Akrotiri. At first, Chrysanthi did not like living in Varosi. She found the town intimidating, with its cosmopolitan society and large buildings. "We didn't have the freedom to move around the way we did in the village," she would say. "As I grew older, I eventually grew to love the place."

When she turned twelve, Chrysanthi was sent to learn dressmaking with a Turkish Cypriot seamstress who lived near her house. "She was very good. She taught me quite a lot about how to measure and make patterns and eventually how to sew. I can't remember if we had to pay her. I think her name was Mouroutha, or something like that. It was a long time ago."

When Chrysanthi turned twenty, she was introduced to a young tailor named Sotiris Charalambous.

Sotiris was born on the 30th of December 1933. He lived with his parents Humbi and Christina and his three sisters Maria, Christalla and Giorgoula in the village of Agios Sergios. His father, who was orphaned from a young age, could

Engagement photograph of Chrysanthi Hajifrixou and Sotiris Charalambous. August 1956

not read or write - nor had he learnt a trade. He worked as a field hand digging trenches and ploughing fields for some of the wealthier land owners in the village. Inevitably, Humbi was paid a pittance for his labour.

Sotiris believes that because Cyprus was a British colony the island was able to progress quicker and further than other countries in the region. "I believe we had television before Greece," he boasts. As for his relationship with the Turkish Cypriots, Sotiris is quite vocal. "We

were just fine," he shouts. "There was no difference and certainly no animosity between us. They could all speak Greek and some of them even came to our Church on Sundays. Our priest had no idea. And I'll tell you another thing you may not know. There were villages in Cyprus; Turkish villages, where all the inhabitants spoke only Greek. They didn't know any Turkish."

Sotiris is unwaveringly animated and passionate when recalling the Cyprus of his youth. It seems that our conversation about the past had somehow unleashed some raw emotion. "No matter how much poverty existed at the time, I believe

Cleo Hajifrixou aged sixteen. Varosi, 1956

that people back then were somewhat more grateful, more respectful and more pleasant. That's what I believe. That's what I know to be true. We respected our customs and traditions with a strict obedience that you don't see today. For instance, in those days if a man liked a woman or if a woman liked a man they would need to get engaged in order to spend time together. It was a serious affair. You were required to sign an agreement, like a contract in front of your parents and a priest. If you broke your word you could be sent off to court and made to pay a fine."

Unlike his father, Sotiris went off to Varosi to learn the tailoring trade. Aged only thirteen, he was taken under the tutelage of his Godfather, Iacovos Stavrou, who owned a tailoring workshop in a tin shed next door to a garden shop. Sotiris recalls that it was mostly English customers from the garden shop who would walk into their shed on impulse and have their suits made. "Because of that garden shop, my Godfather was able to make a good business."

In 1954, Sotiris and a friend named

Artemis Laoudaris went into partnership and opened up their own tailor shop. Later, when Artemis moved to England, Sotiris bought his friend's share of the business and became a sole trader.

Sotiris recalls visiting many places in Cyprus as a young adult. His best friend Christakis hired a motorcycle and together they rode to Bellapais and Troodos reaching as far as Polis in Paphos. "We visited places we had never heard about. It was a fantastic time. When we had travelled too far and could not return home on the same day, we would sleep overnight at a monastery." Sotiris noticed a big difference with the Cypriots he met in the various districts. "It was mainly their accent and the words they used, sometimes even their food and customs were different."

In 1956, Sotiris' friend Andreas mentioned that his fiancé knew a lovely young girl named Chrysanthi who might make a suitable wife for him. By sheer coincidence, Chrysanthi's sister Cleo had already met Sotiris. He would often visit the Armenian photo studio where she worked to have his films developed. "I remember asking Cleo to take me to his tailoring shop so I could sneak a look at him," Chrysanthi tells me with a broad smile. "When we got there, I saw this unshaven man about to mount a bicycle with a large watermelon strapped onto the rear rack. I must admit, my first impression of him wasn't good. I didn't like what I saw. I was a bit fussy, you see. I wanted someone special."

At hearing this, Sotiris laughs out loud. "But what did you think after I turned up at your house with my mother and I was all dressed up and looking pretty smart?" Chrysanthi waves her hand dismissively in the air, "Well yes, then I thought you looked good." They both laugh.

Once Chrysanthi and Sotiris were engaged, they were allowed to spend

time together as a couple. "In those days, once you got engaged, you had to proceed to get married, Chrysanthi tells me. "You cannot back out. No matter what! It was just the way it was back then. You got married purely on physical attraction and what you heard about each other. That was it. Reputation was everything."

At this point of the conversation Sotiris remembers a custom that he believed only occurred in the village of Deryneia (just outside Famagusta).

"Every Easter, the youth of the village would gather in the main square with the boys seated on one side of the street and the girls seated on the other side. If a boy liked a particular girl, he would send the waiter from the *kafenion* (coffee house) to her table with a plate of *loukoumia* (Turkish Delights) If she accepted the gift, it meant that she liked him. If she didn't accept the gift, the boy might try his luck with another girl. Either way, he still had to pay for the sweets." Once again, this courting ritual was based purely on physical attraction, as the boys and girls were not allowed to converse directly with one another.

While Chrysanthi and Sotiris were planning their wedding day, a tragedy

Chrysanthi Hajifrixou aged sixteen. 1952

Chrysanthi Hajifrixou (left) with her sister Cleo (seated) and their mother Andriana. Varosi, early 1950s

occurred that shocked the whole family. Chrysanthi's younger sister Cleo was struck and killed by a speeding British military jeep as she was riding to work. According to Sotiris, the jeep was probably speeding to avoid an ambush. It was common for members of the liberation movement (known as EOKA) to hide in the fields and throw grenades at passing British military vehicles.

Chrysanthi remembers the day all too well. "It was the holy day of Apostolos Andreas; the 30th of November. My sister went to church in the morning to light a candle before riding her bicycle to work. She had just approached a bend on the main road when out of nowhere the jeep appeared. We were told that the jeep struck the back wheel of her bicycle at such a speed that she was catapulted over the handlebars smashing her head against the trunk of a tree," Chrysanthi speaks slowly and softly. It's clear that the emotional trauma she experienced that day still haunts her. "Although Cleo was rushed to hospital, she died a few hours later. The jeep didn't stop. There was no investigation conducted, no compensation given and not even an apology from the British. Nothing!"

Sotiris believes that the British authorities would never have admitted that they had killed a Cypriot girl, especially during the ethnic conflict. Cleo had become yet another innocent victim of this unfortunate era.

"You know, there was a young boy named Kostaki who was in love with my sister," Chrysanthi added. "When the accident happened he rushed to be by her side at the hospital. He was heartbroken to lose her. He would have married her for sure. I remember seeing him in the church lighting candles and praying for a miracle the night of the accident. It was a horrible time for all of us."

Understandably, Chrysanthi and Sotiris' wedding was delayed during their time of mourning. They eventually got married on the 8th of February 1959. Nine months later, they welcomed the birth of their son Haralambos (Harry).

In 1965 their daughter Andri was born and then another son, Frixos, in 1975. "I had three children across three decades," Chrysanthi says with a smile. "It was just the way things worked out for us."

In August 1974, Sotiris and Chrysanthi (and close to forty thousand other residents) were forced to evacuate Varosi following the second phase of a Turkish invasion. "We ended up in Scala and then Limassol with nothing more than the clothes we were wearing," laments Chrysanthi. "Initially, we all believed that we would return to our homes because the world would not allow Turkey to stay. I even cleaned my house from top to bottom and locked all the windows and doors. We thought we were leaving for a short time and then returning back home after a few weeks. All my photos, my clothes and a house full of furniture; everything was gone."

Sotiris also laments the loss of his tailoring business. "I went from making suits for upper class clients to sewing patches and repairing the clothes of refugees." At the time of the *coup d'état* and subsequent Turkish invasion, Chrysanthi's oldest son Haralambos was studying at the prestigious English School in Nicosia. Thankfully, he emerged unharmed and was immediately sent to London by his parents to continue his studies and avoid the trauma of remaining in a divided Cyprus.

In 1976, Sotiris and Chrysanthi made the decision to leave Cyprus with their children for Australia, which is where Chrysanthi's older brother Dimitri lived. After a short period of adjusting and settling into their new home in Melbourne, Sotiris found work as a tailor in a small Italian fashion company called Dressbon. Disappointed with his lowly wages, he left after two years and went to work for a larger and more established menswear company named Stafford Ellison, located on Swanston Street in the heart of the city. Eventually, his wife would join him at the Preston outlet of the Stafford Group.

Sotiris and Chrysanthi are a prime example of a Cypriot couple that have stuck together and supported one another through thick and thin.

They have endured great upheaval, personal loss and tragedy. In many ways, they represent the unwavering Cypriot spirit that I have come to expect from their generation. Their resilience and ability to 'pick up the pieces' and simply carry on with life is a true testament to their survival.

ACKNOWLEDGEMENTS
I would like to thank Chrysanthi and Sotiris for always making me feel so welcome in their home and for sharing their memories about the past with me. Sadly, Sotiris passed away in 2018 following a short illness. Thanks also to their daughter Andri for helping to clarify the facts, especially when her parents' memories would at times start to wane.

Chrysanthi and Cleo Hajifrixou with a friend at the beach in Famagusta. c.1952

Stella
KOMODROMOU

Stella Komodromou was born in the town of Rizokarpaso on the 3rd of June 1938. She was the second youngest child of Nikolas and Eleni Komodromou. Her sister Andriana was born in 1933, followed by her brother Zacharias in 1935, her sister Maroulla in 1940 and her youngest brother Christos in 1945.

Rizokarpaso had around five thousand inhabitants during the 1930s, all of them Greek Cypriot. At one point Rizokarpaso was the largest town in Cyprus. Despite the size of the town, people had enough food to eat all year round. It was said that even a homeless man could survive in Rizokarpaso. The surrounding fields were fertile and full of wild vegetables and edible grasses and the nearby ocean had plenty of fish and crabs. Most of the town's farmers grew cotton, wheat, corn, tomatoes and tobacco with beneficial harvests due to the fertile soil and the ideal climate.

Two thirds of the tobacco grown in Cyprus came from farms surrounding Rizokarpaso. This was harvested during the summer months. Stella remembers the locals were paid around ten *grosha* (around one shilling) per *oka* (about 1.3 kilos). "Before independence, we sold the tobacco only to the British buyers," she recalls. "They would select only the best tobacco leaves and ask us to burn the rest. There was a lot of wastage. A lot of our hard work went up in flames because the British were very fussy."

The region around Rizokarpaso was also blessed with thousands of olive and carob trees. The poorest of the townspeople were often employed by the wealthier landowners to work in their fields and therefore everybody managed to earn a living – although some earned more than others.

Rizokarpaso was divided into three suburbs: Lefko, Anavrisi and Agia Triatha. There was a *mukhtari* (headman) governing each suburb. The town boasted several *kafenia* (coffee houses) two schools, a town hall, two or three doctors and even a cinema that showed American movies. "The Louisiana Cinema was a two-story building with an outdoor rooftop cinema that operated during the summer months," says Stella. Nearly every house in Rizokarpaso had an outdoor wood fire oven, a well and a cesspit.

Stella's father Nikolas Komodromou was born in 1892 and was a blacksmith by trade (like his father). The name Komodromou literally means 'blacksmith' in Greek. Nikolas used traditional tools and coals burnt from the roots of local trees to create a furnace. He would make shoes for horses and mules and long metal skewers used to thread tobacco leaves. When the combine harvesters and tractors were introduced to the region in the late 1930s, his work dried up and his family experienced a period of great poverty. His love for taverns and *kafenia*

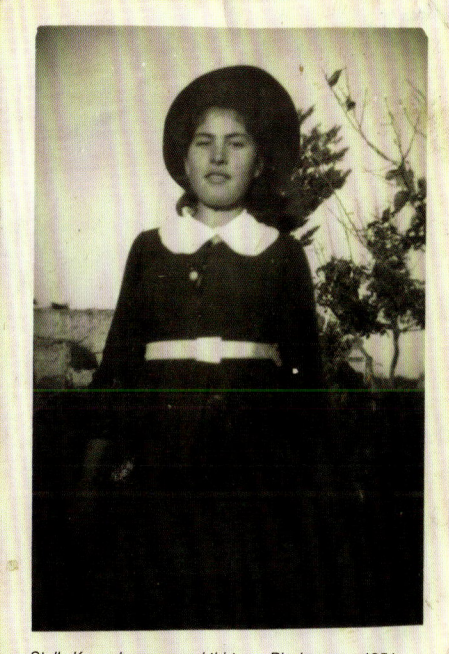

Stella Komodromou aged thirteen. Rizokarpaso, 1951

meant that Nikolas spent most of his earnings dining out with his friends.

Despite his spendthrift ways, Nikolas was a kind and caring man who adored his children. By comparison, his wife Eleni was very strict and thrifty, if not a little too tight with money. "My mother was fifteen when she was married," explains Stella. "People said that she was so little she had to stand on a stool in the church just to reach my father. I know she did not want to get married so young but family pressure and old-fashioned customs overruled her wishes. She was eighteen years younger than my father. Perhaps that's why she was so strict with us."

Stella's brother Zacharias was the first member of her family to leave the village. At fifteen he went to work as a junior pastry chef at his cousin's shop in the seaside town of Varosi. Many teenagers in Cyprus left home to alleviate the financial strain that was placed on their families. At nineteen, Zacharias left Cyprus to go to England and was lucky to find work as a waiter at the prestigious Hotel Café Royal located in London's Piccadilly area. In 1958, he met and married Vasiliki Papasavva and together with their ten month old son Nick, they immigrated to Melbourne, Australia.

Andriana was the eldest of the five siblings and was therefore required to stay at home to help their mother Eleni with the chores of the house and to look after her younger siblings. "My big sister's regret in life was that she wasn't allowed to go to school like the rest of us," Stella says sadly. "She did not learn how to read or write."

Andriana Constantinou. She is wearing the first dress she had ever bought. Rizokarpaso c.1948

In 1956, Andriana was sent by ship (Gumhuryat Misr) to meet her fiancé Dimitrios Constantinou in Melbourne. He had agreed to marry her after his cousin showed him a photograph. She was twenty-three and he was thirty-seven. His parents travelled from Pyrgos to Rizokarpaso to negotiate the dowry agreement with her parents.

"My sister couldn't wait to leave Cyprus," exclaims Stella. "She hated her life in Cyprus, especially working on the tobacco farms." Because Andriana could not read or write she would ask her younger sister Stella to write her letters to Dimitri in Australia while she dictated. "Whatever she told me, I would write." Stella recalls.

From a young age, Stella worked on tobacco farms that were owned by wealthy land owners; planting the seedlings and then in the summer picking the leaves in the dark before the dawn. "We had to wake before the sun rose to go and pick the tobacco leaves. This way the leaves did not stick to your skin so much and were easier to handle. It was a very dirty job. I hated it." Once the leaves were gathered, Stella and the other children would sit in the shade and thread each leaf onto a string using a long metal skewer. It was tiresome work. When all the tobacco was sold to the mostly English buyers, the tobacco farmer would pay the child labourers their share.

To escape the hardships of her town, when Stella was around fifteen or sixteen she would sometimes go and visit her

Rizokarpaso girls school. Stella Komodromou (middle row, sixth from left) aged about eleven. c.1948

two aunts in Varosi. With them she was allowed a lot more freedom.

In 1958, Stella left Cyprus to go and live with her sister Andriana in Melbourne. It was during this time that she was introduced to a taxi driver named Dimitri Kounas who had migrated to Australia from Kalavasos in Larnaca. They eventually married and had four children (Panayiotis, Helen, Alex and Nikki) but divorced after fourteen years. During her married life Stella moved house over six times to various suburbs around Melbourne. At one point, she found work at Brockhoff Biscuits in East Burwood.

Stella's younger brother Christos was the only family member to complete both primary and secondary school. The church bell in Rizokarpaso would ring before 8am to signal that the school day was about

to commence. At midday, the students would go home to have their lunch and have a short rest before returning for more lessons in the afternoon. Rizokarpaso was such a large town that some of the houses were over a mile away from the town centre where the schools were located. Many of the school children lost a lot of valuable time walking home and back to school again. "It's a pity no one thought of allowing the students to bring their lunch to school in those days," says Stella. "It would have saved a lot of time and the students would not have been so tired."

Once Christos finished high school he went to serve in the Cypriot army for eighteen months. He left Cyprus on Boxing Day, 1967 with the intention to study Civil Engineering in Australia. Thankfully, because he could speak English he was able to enrol at the Royal Melbourne Institute of Technology where he attended night school whilst working in a factory during the day.

In 1971, Christos rushed back to Cyprus after learning that his father Nikolas was seriously ill. After his father's death, Christos decided to stay in Cyprus and was encouraged to enrol in a hospitality course to become a waiter. Some of his lessons were conducted at the popular and exclusive Ledra Palace in Nicosia. The course fee was 100 pounds, which included all meals and accommodation.

Upon graduating a year later, Christos found a job as a waiter at the Constantia five-star hotel in Varosi.

He worked eight hours a day, six days a week and was paid around 120 pounds a month, earning more with tips and bonuses.

The Constantia had around 200 rooms and was always full, according to Christos. "Most of the guests came from England but there were also German and Swedish

Christos Komodromou aged fifteen. Varosi, 1960

tourists," he recalls. "A room with all meals provided was around seven and a half pounds a day. I remember a two week stay including airfare plus two meals a day would cost around 110 pounds."

Christos left the Constantia and went to work at the prestigious Grecian and Trojan Hotels where at the latter, he was promoted to Head Waiter. "I loved my time working in Famagusta at these fancy hotels," he remarks. "The staff were mixed and we all got along wonderfully well. There were Armenians and Greek and Turkish Cypriots. I used to socialise a lot with the Turkish Cypriots. You had to speak English to work in a hotel. If the *coup d'état* and invasion did

ABOVE: Nikolas Komodromou Rizokarpaso. c.1956
RIGHT: Christos (aged fifteen) with his parents Eleni and Nikolas Komodromou. Rizokarpaso, 1960

not occur in July 1974, I would have liked to have stayed working as a Head Waiter in Varosi. I liked my job a lot and the money was good."

Stella's sister Maroulla was the only sibling who stayed in Cyprus. Even after the Turkish invasion in 1974 (which occupied the north of the island - including Rizokarpaso), Maroulla stayed in the town to look after her elderly widowed mother. She later married Yianni Sporikou and had a son.

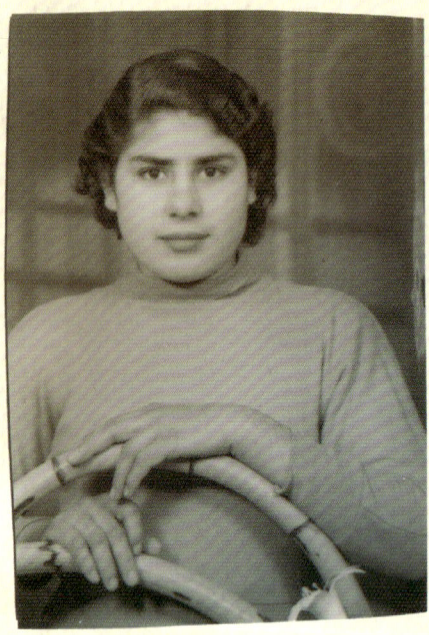

Maroulla Komodromou. Famagusta. c.1951

After her divorce, Stella eventually moved into a house in Reservoir with her children in 1984. Three years later, she could finally afford to return to Cyprus to see her widowed mother and sister Maroulla. It had been twenty-six years since Stella last saw them. Her father Nikolas had died in 1971. Rizokarpaso was now part of the occupied territory in the north of the island.

After a long and stressful application process, Stella was finally allowed to travel (under escort) from the U.N. checkpoint in Nicosia to her home town. As expected, it was a very emotional reunion with her mother and sister. She was only allowed to stay for six hours and she spent most of the time crying and embracing her distraught family members. "I made time to visit my father's grave," she says softly, choking back tears. "The last time I saw him was the port of Limassol when I was leaving

Cyprus. As the boat was moving away, he was standing on the pier waving goodbye to me."

Stella's mother Eleni died in 2010 at ninety-nine years of age.

Stella still lives in her Reservoir home and feels blessed to be surrounded by her children and grandchildren. "I have endured many, many hardships in my life," she tells me with open arms. "But I have survived because of my family. My children are the reason I am still here."

ACKNOWLEDGEMENTS

I would like to thank the Komodromou siblings Stella, Andriana and Christos for their kind assistance in helping me to document their family story and for allowing me to scan and preserve their old family photographs. Special thanks to Stella's daughter Helen for her support and for checking the details in her mother's story and also to George Komodromou for his input.

CLOCKWISE FROM TOP LEFT:

Kyriakou Varnava,, Stella Komodromou, Kikoura Varnava, Stavroulla Giorgalli, Andriana Varnava and Christos Komodromou. Rizokarpaso. c.1953

Maroulla Panagiotou, George Katsouris and Elli Anemouri. Rizokarpaso, c.1953

Eleni Komodromou and Nikolas Komodromou. Rizokarpaso. c.1953

Sisters, Stella and Maroulla Komodromou. c.1951

Zacharias Komodromou aged around eighteen on his horse. Location unknown. c.1953

Christos Komodromou, Nikolas Komodromou, Athoula Katsouri, Stella Komodromou and Kikoura Varnava. Rizokarpaso. c.1953

Eleni Komodromou, mother of Christos. Aged 50 in this photo. Studio photo taken in 1960 at Stylianos Photo Studio in Varosi.

Porosina Taousiani, Maroulla Saxli and Eleni Solomou. c.1953

CENTRE PHOTO:
Androulla Varnava, Kyriakou Varnava, Maroulla Levendi and Kikoura Varnava. Rizokarpaso. c.1953

Ν Σ Κωνσταντζόπου
εξένα Σ Κωνστζόπου

Harry
SHIAMARIS

Harry Shiamaris aged nineteen. 1948

Harry Shiamaris was born in Lefkoniko, Famagusta on the 21st January 1929. Lefkoniko, at the time, was a mixed village boasting around 3000 inhabitants. Harry's parents were poor and like so many other rural inhabitants, they worked ceaselessly on the land to make ends meet.

As a young child, Harry remembers spending his school holidays cultivating tobacco on his father's small plot of land, in the heat of the summer. In those days, nobody knew or cared much about the hazardous conditions of tobacco farming, especially for children.

Harry recalls an average day spent on the tobacco farm. "I would be woken up at 4am by my father (Anastasis), two hours before the sun would rise, to go to work until three or four in the afternoon. We would begin by cutting the tobacco leaves and then later in the day sit on the ground threading the leaves together with a needle. That was our summer. After we finished we could go and play games with other children until it was time for us to go to bed. The next day, we would wake up at 4am and do the same job all over again."

Sometimes, Harry and his younger brother Kiki would receive one *grosi* from his father as payment for the work they performed on the tobacco farm. Harry recalls his great joy receiving that one coin. It meant he could go and buy some sweets for himself - a rare treat. "Imagine that one *grosi* could make me so happy," exclaims Harry with a broad smile. "No one knew what it was like to be rich in those days. We didn't know any rich people. When I was young, it was my dream to one day own a watch or a bicycle."

Harry recalls playing football (soccer) as a youngster. He would use a homemade ball fashioned out of a pig's bladder stuffed with cloth. "Every family bought a piglet at the start of the year that they would fatten for the feast of Christmas. No part of the animal was wasted." Certain villagers were well trained with the proper method for slaughtering a pig and would arrive at each house at Christmas to assist in the annual ritual. In the days before refrigeration, many households used ancient methods of preservation by storing the meat in earthenware jars filled

Harry Shiamaris on his motocycle aged thirty. Unknown location. 1959

Cypriot customers, the three brothers became fluent speakers of the Turkish Cypriot language.

Harry was fortunate enough to be able to complete both primary and secondary school in Lefkoniko. In 1945, at the age of sixteen, he became a teacher's assistant in the village of Diorios, near Kyrenia. He was paid six pounds a month. His room and board (including all meals) was two pounds a month, which left him with four pounds in his wallet for his own amusement - a small fortune back then.

In 1946, Harry attended the Teacher's College in Morfou, where he graduated two years later with his diploma. At the same time, his father found work as a night watchman for a company in Nicosia, which proved to be more profitable than farm work. Even though Nicosia was only twenty-four miles from Lefkoniko, Harry's father would often stay in Nicosia for a week (or sometimes even a month) before returning to the village. Eventually, Harry's mother, who was tired of being left on her own, moved to Nicosia to be with her husband. In May 1949, Harry's father died of a sudden heart attack and his mother returned to her village. That same year, Harry's younger brother Kiki became a fireman and went on to marry a young girl from Limassol.

Harry's father Anastasis Shiamaris aged sixteen with his mother Marikou (Harry's grandmother) and baby Kyriakou (Harry's aunt). Location unknown. 1925

with pig fat. Curing using salt, smoking and drying were other popular methods of preserving food in the village.

I asked Harry if he visited his friends at their homes. "No, what for?" he replied. "There was nothing to do in our homes apart from eat and sleep, so I would always meet my friends outdoors and we would either go and play somewhere nearby or sit under a tree and just talk."

Harry played with both Turkish and Greek children. It didn't matter.

Lefkoniko had a barbershop that was owned and managed by three Greek Cypriot brothers. In the nearby Turkish Cypriot village of Platani there was no barbershop, so the male inhabitants would come to Lefkoniko to have their hair cut or to be shaved. Through frequent encounters with their Turkish

Popi Gregoriades aged nineteen in Limassol. 1949

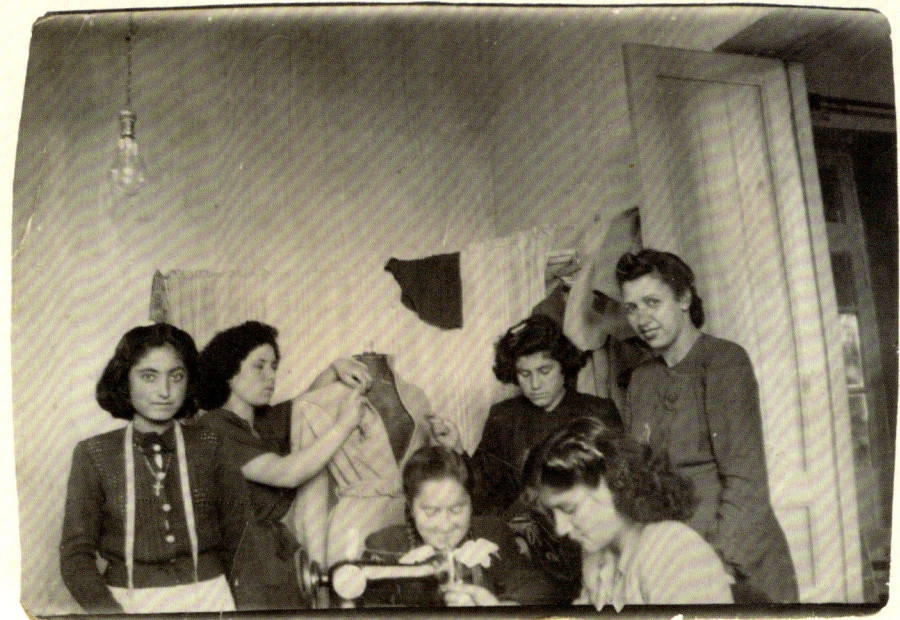
Popi at her machine with fellow students in a sewing class in Limassol. 1947

When Harry started teaching and earning a steady wage (around eight pounds a month) he bought himself a motorcycle, which he kept for three years. As a single young man, he rode all over Cyprus; sometimes with a friend, but more often on his own.

Harry met his wife Popi (Pathenopi) at the Arakapas village *panayiri* (festival), which was held on Saturday, the 7th of September 1950. Harry was twenty years old and about to commence his second year as a qualified school teacher at the school in Arakapas. The festival was held every year at the end of the school holidays. Harry had decided to go to the festival with some of his friends.

A few teenage girls recognised the young teacher and started to follow him around. Harry was modest but always charming. He knew that being a teacher in Cyprus was a distinguished and respected profession. The girls asked Harry to show them around the school building. He agreed and struck up a conversation with one of the girls, named Archisti. Later that night, during the festivities in the village square, Harry noticed that Archisti was sitting with another girl who seemed to be giving him the eye. The girl's name was Pathenopi (Popi) and she was from Limassol, but living with her parents in Arakapas. He found himself staring back at her for a long time, until he mustered up the courage to walk over and introduce himself. Harry and Popi then spent the rest of that evening getting to know one another. Their courtship had begun.

The following week on a Saturday afternoon, Harry set off with his friend Lakis to collect his motorcycle which was having minor repairs at a mechanic's workshop in Nicosia.

The two friends were riding together on Lakis' motorcycle through the village of Skarinou when a bus from the company KEM struck their bike. Harry was thrown off the bike and hit the ground with a hard thud. The bus driver stopped - but only to curse the two young men for getting in his way before driving off in a huff. Harry had suffered a deep gash to his right leg, but there was minimal blood loss and no other major injuries. It was common in Cyprus for bike riders not to wear any protective clothing or helmets.

Luckily, a passing taxi driver agreed to take the injured Harry to a hospital in Limassol about twenty-four miles away. Lying in a hospital bed, Harry

Popi aged sixteen. Limassol, 1946

asked a friend to find the girl named Popi Gregoriades that he met at the *panayiri* and to tell her what had happened. The following day, Popi arrived at the hospital with her mother Stella. Harry summed up the courage to announce to Popi's mother that he liked her daughter very much and wanted to marry her. There was no sneaking around or flirting in those days. Harry spent a week in hospital and upon his discharge, was invited to Popi's house for dinner.

On the 10th of October 1950, (a month after they met), Harry and Popi were

Popi Gregoriades (far left) with friends. 1947

Harry Shiamaris aged eighteen. 1947

my third application in 1965. I had had enough. In 1966, we packed our bags and left Cyprus for Australia."

Upon their arrival in 1966, Harry and his family moved in with Popi's brother who was already living in Melbourne with his family. Harry found work almost immediately at the Huntingdale High School before being transferred to Saint Albans High School. He eventually settled at Westall High School where he stayed for twenty years teaching mathematics.

In February 1979, Harry's brother Kiki died of a heart attack, like their father, twenty years earlier. Kiki was only forty-eight. Six months later his mother also died. Harry Shiamaris had now lost every member of his family.

engaged. When I asked Harry why he rushed to get engaged, he simply replied. "So I wouldn't lose her to another man." He then went on to tell me about a letter he had sent to his mother before he got engaged. "My message was very direct. I told my mother to come and meet the girl that I had selected to marry. I warned my mother that whether she likes her or not, she must say that she likes her. You see, I was going to marry Popi whether my mother wanted me to or not."

Harry and Popi were married on the 31st of December 1950 on New Year's Eve.

Harry confessed to me that after he left the *panayiri* that fateful evening in September he went straight home and started to write a diary, which he called 'The Diary of Love.' He wrote his thoughts and desires in this diary every day until the day he married Popi.

Harry worked for seventeen years in Cyprus as a primary school teacher before he decided to emigrate to Australia with his wife and three children. His decision to leave Cyprus was prompted by a series of setbacks regarding his teaching position. "In 1961 I was required to teach at a school in Pelendri village which was some twenty-two miles from my house in Limassol," he begins to explain. "The distance meant that Popi had to raise our three young children alone. I would only see them briefly on the weekends. At that time teachers were entitled to a transfer after completing a three-year term. Once I had completed my three-year term in Pelendri, I applied to the Ministry of Education for a transfer to Limassol to be close to my family. My application was rejected. I sent them a second application in 1964. That was also rejected, as was

BACK ROW: Popi (aged ten) and her brothers Neophytos (left) and Yianakis. Seated in front are Popi's parents Koumis and Stella Gregoriades. Her other brother Christos was in America at the time. Limassol, 1940

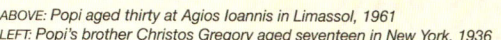

Harry remembers a time when teachers were revered and were highly respected in their community. When they spoke, people listened and they were entrusted with shaping the future of each generation of students in their guardianship.

I am sure that there are hundreds of former students who fondly remember Harry Shiamaris and have been guided and influenced by his teaching. So on behalf of all the students who have benefited from having Mr Shiamaris as a teacher, I would like to say '*σε ευχαριστώ δάσκαλε*' (thank you teacher) - for everything.

ACKNOWLEDGEMENTS

I would like to thank Harry Shiamaris for allowing me to visit him to capture and record aspects of his life story. Popi Shiamaris passed away in 2017 aged eighty seven. I would also like to acknowledge the generous support of Harry's daughters Stella and Mary.

LEFT: Harry and Popi's engagement photograph. October, 1950

BELOW: Popi and her friend Kallistheni in Limassol. 1947

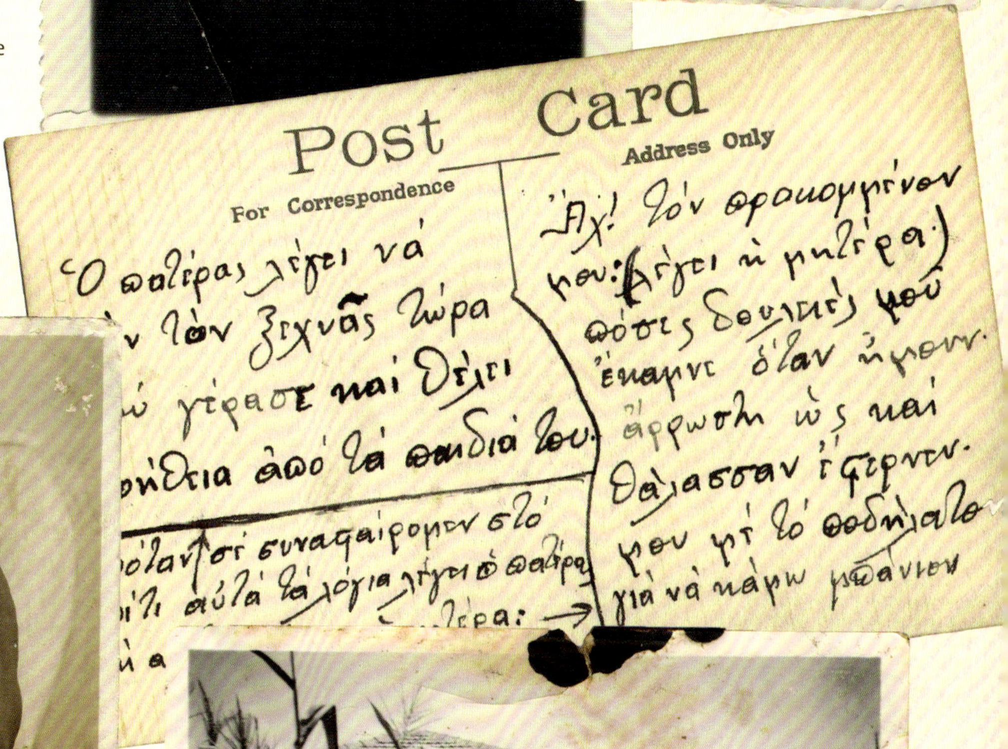

ABOVE: Popi aged thirty at Agios Ioannis in Limassol, 1961
LEFT: Popi's brother Christos Gregory aged seventeen in New York, 1936

Erol
ERALP

Erol Eralp was born in the village of Sygkrasi (Singrassi) in the Famagusta district on the 13th of November 1935. Sygkrasi was a small, mixed village not far from Trikomo with an estimated population of around 343 inhabitants, most of them Muslim just like Erol's family.

Erol's father, Galip Mullaosman was born in 1896 and his mother Refiye was born in 1904. They had six children, three sons Osman (born 1927), Erol (born 1935) and Ali (born 1939) and three daughters Fatma (born 1926), Akile (born 1931) and Naciye (born 1933).

Erol had a brother named Ahmed, who died as a child from dysentery, most likely caused by contaminated food or water. "My parents were too poor to take him to see a doctor," he says softly. "My poor brother died at home from diarrhoea."

Erol's father Galip was a shoemaker by trade who struggled at times to make a living. When Erol was still a toddler, his family moved to Nicosia, where they lived together with his uncle Mustafa's large family. "We loaded all our belongings onto a cart that was pulled by a horse," says Erol. He remembers that his father opened up a makeshift workshop on the ground floor of the house, but business was slow. He also remembers hiding under his big sister's skirt to escape the taunts from his female cousins who kept pestering him.

In 1940, with the onset of World War II, Erol's family were forced to leave Nicosia and move back to Sygkrasi after German planes started to bomb the capital and Famagusta port. "Many Cypriots fled the towns to move to the safety of the mountains or the rural villages," Erol explains. "I remember the curfews and the total blackout and how all the villagers in my village were asked by the authorities to dig trenches."

Back in Sygkrasi, Erol's family continued to struggle to survive. Their living conditions became bleaker and more desperate during the war. "One time we did not have any food to eat for three days," he recalls. "We did not know how poor we were. For us it was normal life. Today we are in paradise. We have no idea what poverty is."

During the summer months, things improved for Erol's family. Their fruit trees were in season and would bear fruit, such as *babutsa* (prickly pears), plums, figs and dates. "We had pomegranates too," he adds. "We used to eat the fresh leaves from the grape vine. But in the winter we ate bread. Only bread most days. That is why even today, I do not like the winter. I do not feel secure."

Erol's mother Refiye was fortunate to own a small loom. She was taught how to weave when she was just a small child. During the harshest years, she would exchange eggs for thread in order to weave cloth that she could sell to passing traders. The cloth was more valuable than the eggs. Erol's father would also barter and trade goods. Once, at a village festival, he exchanged a pair

Erol and his younger brother Ali, most likely at the Glaszner Studio in Larnaca. c.1952

of boots for a pig. He then sold the pig to a Greek man at a *kafenion* (coffee house) for a few coins. Bartering was a common practice amongst the peasantry in Cyprus, especially in the absence of a monetary economy.

When Refiye contracted malaria one year, the family watched and prayed as she became very sick; her body trembling with the fever. She eventually recovered

Erol's sister Fatma's official wedding photo. Back row, left to right: Najiye, Ali, Erol, Akile. Front row, left to right: father Galip, Fatma, Osman and mother Refiye. The groom was in London at the time so Fatma's brother Osman sat in his place. Larnaca, c.1952

and was able to return to her loom and to caring for her children.

In 1942, Erol's family was on the move again; this time to Scala (Larnaca). His father bought a derelict old baker's shop near the Turkish Quarter for three hundred pounds. Galip converted the upper story into living quarters for his family and the lower lever into a makeshift cobbler's workshop. "The place was very dirty," says Erol, shaking his head. "My brother and I would fill tins with sand from Scala beach to pour over the oil that covered the ground. The oil came from the cars that belonged to the previous owner."

Business during the war years was slow across Cyprus. Shoemakers like Erol's father found it especially difficult as stocks of leather and even shoe tacks were massively depleted. This made it virtually impossible to repair shoes.

In order to help alleviate his parent's financial strain, Erol's older brother Osman decided to enlist with the Cypriot Volunteer Regiment (as did thousands of other young men). Osman lied about his age, being only sixteen when he joined. He served for three years, travelling as far as Port Said with the British Forces. During this time, he was earning his family back in Cyprus an astonishing one shilling a day.

In 1947, when Erol was attending his final year of primary school in Scala, his mathematics teacher Mr Kemal announced to the class that the Turkish Boy's Lycee in Nicosia was offering free education to young boys interested in learning a trade. Erol told his parents, and they jumped at the chance to enrol him.

But fate intervened on the very day that Erol and his mother set off to enrol. As the story goes, they were waiting by the side of the main road for a bus to take them to Nicosia. They waited for hours but no bus arrived. Erol's mother noticed that the building near the bus stop housed the American Academy. She had a thought. "You know, Erol, I heard there is an entrance test at this school today. Let's go there instead."

Erol passed the test at the American Academy and began his studies in the autumn of 1948. The American Academy was operated by the Reformed Presbyterian Church of North America. That same year, Erol's father decided to abandon the dismal shoemaking trade and opened a small *bakaliko* (grocery store) on the ground floor of the family home. This decision made it possible to comfortably afford the monthly school fee required for Erol's enrolment at the American Academy. The *bakaliko* also meant that for the first time, Erol's family were able to eat reasonably well. Apart from selling grains (barley seeds), beans, fresh fruit and vegetables they also sold fresh *haloumi* cheese and yoghurt.

Erol had a wonderful time at the American Academy. He recalls that all the students would commence the day with a chorus of 'God save the King.' Erol mixed freely with all the other students at the school. "We all played together. Christians, Muslims, Greeks, Turks, Armenians. It did not matter. We loved baseball," he adds. "Especially when the female students would watch us. I remember the girls. The Armenian girls were the prettiest. But we could not really interact with them. You know, in those days it was difficult. It was not allowed."

Erol's best friend was a fellow student named Hasan Cemal. They used to ride around Scala town every day after school on their bicycles. Erol and his friends visited many exciting places across the island thanks to a busy schedule of school excursions. They went to places he had never seen or heard of before.

Erol remembers visiting a monastery in Paphos and seeing monks for the first time. "It was like stepping back in time," he said. "The monks there were really quite dirty and did not wash except for their hands. I believe it had something to do with the sacrilege of washing or bathing after being baptised. I noticed how their hands were a different colour to the rest of their body. They were quite smelly too."

American Academy. Erol is in the back row (second from right) and his best friend Hassan Cemal is leaning on the railing next to column. The teacher is sitting in the chair facing the students. 1952

At the American Academy, Erol excelled in typing and mathematics, often finishing at the top of his class. He remembers the school principal Mr William W. Weir and his teachers Mr Silvestre and Mr Kingston, Mr and Mrs Mavrides, Mr Christides and Mr Edgards.

Mr. Weir began teaching at the American Academy in 1916. He was named director of the 300-student school in 1921 and remained so until he returned to the United States in 1961.

The main emphasis at the American Academy was placed on teaching English and Bible Studies. Unfortunately, Erol failed to pass the final exam for Religion (by only three marks) and therefore was not awarded a graduation Diploma.

After six years of study at the American Academy, Erol decided to emigrate to the historical town of Izmir in Turkey. His decision to go to Izmir was largely inspired by the promise of employment after a few college

friends had returned from holidaying there and had boasted about the career opportunities for English-speaking Turkish Cypriots.

On the 28th of October 1954, aged only nineteen, Erol said goodbye to his family and travelled to Turkey. He stayed at a cousin's house in Izmir where he slept in a tiny attic. After a few months he was able to secure work with an American engineering company named Tippetts, Abbett, McCarthy, Stratton (TAMS). The engineering company was assisting the local government with the construction of a dam in the region. Erol worked for the consultants for almost two years as their chief translator and secretary.

In 1956, Erol joined the Turkish army. He was stationed in the ancient city of Konya, located around 162 miles south of Ankara. According to Erol, his family had been registered as Turkish citizens back in 1926, following the international call made by President Atatürk as part of his Turkification initiative. "When I was in the army, I was the only person who could speak English apart from the Full General, so I ended up working as his personal secretary and translator."

While Erol was in the army, his parents decided to move to Turkey along with his brother Ali. They sold nearly everything they owned in Cyprus. Much to their surprise, they were not allowed to bring money into Turkey. In an extraordinary leap of faith and trust, Erol's mother took

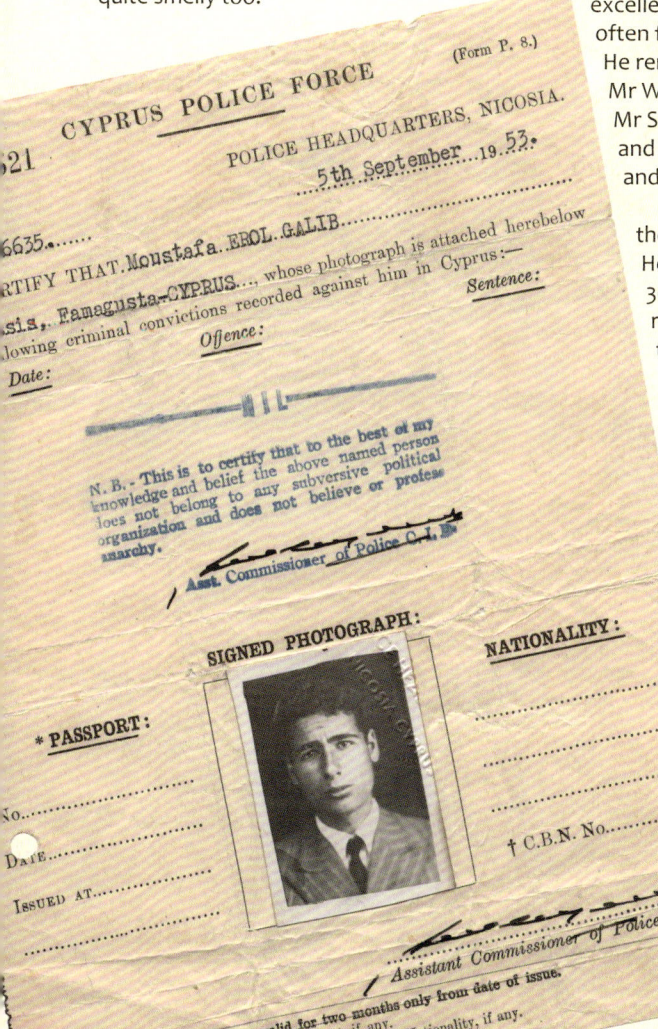

Erol's British passport application. 1953

Erol's younger brother Ali (aged seventeen) standing in front of a statue of Mustafa Kemal Ataturk in Izmir. 1956

nationalities including Greeks, Italians, Americans, Canadians, British and Turkish personnel. He was paid around 740 Turkish Lira a month (about 21 pounds Sterling) and did not have to pay tax thanks to the North Atlantic Treaty that was signed in 1949.

Erol was an exceptional typist. He could type more than eighty words per minute. He was also one of only a handful of people at NATO who could speak fluent English – except for a few high-ranking Colonels and Generals.

Erol remembers a moment of great innovation that transpired on his first day at NATO. "I noticed that the layout of the keyboard on the Turkish typewriter was not the same as the English typewriter. I suggested to my officer-in-charge, Colonel Eino R. Aho to get the typewriter mechanic to rearrange the keys on the Turkish typewriter to match the position of those on an English typewriter. He agreed and it was a huge breakthrough. My idea would allow 'touch typing' to occur in Turkey for the first time, saving countless hours of work and effort." Erol is proud to state that the new keyboard layout was named the 'LandSouthEast Turkish-English keyboard' and added to the official NATO Regulations Document.

Erol had always wanted to return to Cyprus to find a Cypriot wife but the escalating tensions on the island had kept him away. In 1960, when he was twenty-five, his cousin's wife introduced him to a young seventeen year old girl named Sukran. Erol was immediately smitten by the beautiful Sukran. They were married and had two children; a son named Suat in 1961 and a daughter named Janan in 1964.

Erol and Sukran divorced in 1965 after only five years together. In 1967, however, Erol was married again, this time to a woman who was also divorced, named Gülcihan. They had two sons together (Engin and Ertan). After a while, Gülcihan became despondent with married life and indeed, life in Turkey. She began insisting that they should all move to Australia. Erol's two children from his first marriage, were also living with them by now.

Erol finally gave in to his wife's constant demands to move to Australia. In 1973, he left his job at NATO, sold his house and moved his whole family to Melbourne. He was lucky to find work almost immediately at the Department of Immigration (thanks to his references

a thousand pounds to a money-lender in Nicosia and was given a simple card stating that when they arrived in Turkey they would receive 35,000 Turkish Lira - in accordance with the exchange rate at that time. "Can you imagine that?" remarks Erol, wide-eyed. "When my parents arrived in Izmir, I took this card to a Jewish moneylender in Istanbul and he gave me 35,000 Turkish Lira. What a gamble we took. It could have been a terrible tragedy."

In time, all of Erol's family members were to leave Cyprus. His two sisters Fatma and Naciye moved to London and his older brother Osman and other sister Akile moved to Australia.

After he completed his military service, Erol found a job at the North Atlantic Treaty Organisation (NATO). He began work on the 1st of July 1958 as a secretary in the translation department in the 'LandSouthEast' headquarters in Izmir. At NATO he worked alongside many

Erol (bottom-right) on a school excursion to Paphos. The bus driver is second from the left. The Greek school teacher is standing in the middle. Erol's best friend Hassan Cemel is back row far-right. 25 May 1953

village. Three stray (but well fed) cats are his constant companions.

"I've had a very interesting life, Costas," Erol remarks as I conclude the interview. "My personal life was not as stable as my working life but still; I have four wonderful children and six grandchildren."

It is quite extraordinary that a poor boy such as Erol Eralp from a small village in Cyprus could have achieved such academic success in his life to secure work at an institution such as NATO. It clearly demonstrates that ambition, determination and resilience really are the key prompts to success.

from NATO). He was employed as an interpreter for the office of Ethnic Affairs. He used the severance pay he received from NATO to buy a small but comfortable house.

After five years, Erol and his family moved back to Turkey. "My wife Gülcihan was very unhappy in Australia and she kept begging me to take her back to Izmir," he says In a whisper. "Once again, I had to sell everything and in 1978 we went back. What could I do? Thankfully, I was able to get my job back at NATO. This time, however, I worked in their Logistics Department."

Six years later, in 1984, Erol and his family returned to Australia. Once again Gülcihan prompted the move. Erol was reinstated at the Department of Immigration where he stayed until he retired in 1989. His marriage with Gülcihan did not last. They divorced in 1992.

Erol did remarry for a third time. His wife sadly passed away after battling cancer in 2016.

When I met and interviewed Erol he was living on his own and happily investing a good deal of time caring for his vast and impressive fruit and vegetable garden. It appeared that he had succeeded in recreating a little bit of Cyprus in his own back yard. There were plum, fig and pomegranate trees similar to those that he would ambush as a small boy in Sygkrasi. He even had a cane crop growing just like the one he knew in the

ACKNOWLEDGEMENTS
I would like to thank Erol Eralp for sharing his life story with me with the poise and grace that befits his high level of communication skills. I would also like to thank Mr Ahmet Polat and Hakki Abdurazak for introducing me to Erol Eralp in the first place.

Erol's sister Fatma with her husband and two friends in London. c.1950s

Eleni
THEODOTOU

Eleni Theodotou (nee Nicolaou Anastasi) was born on the 13th of October 1926 in the small village of Livadia in the Pitsilia region near Troodos. She was the eldest of five children. Her parents Melanie Michail and Nicolas Anastasi Shabanis lived a humble but fortunate lifestyle in the mountainous village and were able to earn some money through farming, hunting, building, carpentry and dressmaking.

Eleni only attended primary school for two years. At the age of eight she was required to help her parents with various home duties. Being the eldest female child in her family, she was also expected to help with the rearing of her younger siblings.

When Eleni was thirteen, her mother gave birth to twins – who, heartbreakingly, died soon after they were born. Her mother had lost twins previously, so her grief and sorrow were unimaginable. A few days after the twins were buried, Eleni's mother fell ill.

Eleni remembers the day she rushed to tell her father that her mother was very ill and could not walk. "My grandmother advised me to go and fetch my father," she recalls. "He was at the bottom of the mountain building a house in a neighbouring village several miles away. I struggled climbing down the steep pathways and down the steep slopes of our village to reach him. By the time I finally arrived at his building site I was breathless. My father knew just to look at me that something was wrong. 'What

Eleni Nicolaou in Nicosia. 1948

is it?' he asked me. 'Why did you come here?' At first I couldn't speak and then I told him. 'My mother is unwell. You have to come quickly and take her to the doctor'."

Eleni's father abandoned his work immediately and rushed home. He carried his wife to the side of the road and waited for an automobile to drive past from the neighbouring village to transport them both to the nearest hospital in Nicosia. In those days, children were not allowed

to visit a loved one in hospital. Eleni and her siblings had to wait at home with their grandmother. Despite some (albeit clumsy) efforts by the doctors at the hospital, Eleni's mother died twenty-nine days later. It was suspected that she had died from an infection following the delivery of her twins. She was only thirty-five years old.

Just over a year later, Eleni's father Nicolas decided to remarry so that he would have someone to help him raise his family. Eleni was almost fifteen when she met her stepmother. She took it upon herself to make her father's new wife feel welcome and enjoyed helping her to cook and clean and look after the family.

Life was extremely hard in Cyprus during the 1930s, especially in a mountainous village such as Livadia where Eleni had to navigate the steep, slippery slopes and cliffs every day. She remembers waking up before sunrise, putting on her studded boots and criss-crossing the rugged, rocky terrain to work all day in the fields and vineyards, which were located a fair distance from the village. At dusk she would return home and work a few more hours helping to prepare the evening meals.

The cool climate up in the mountains did make working in the outdoors bearable. There was always plenty of fresh cool running water. "Everywhere you would dig a little hole, cold water from underground would appear. The slope, however, made it difficult to farm the land. My father would have to dig a

α. Ζη ●5-1-926

γένη 13-10-926

φραφία 2- 4-928.

ευ υοἰ 25-9-930

ἐς γ.Χρίσου 2-11- 934

αγιόλης 21-11-935

φία γ Χρι 23- 2-940

ἡ 5-5-941

γιαννοὐ ἡ 12-5-942

---

hear the hooves of the large draft horses plodding along the dirt roads pulling their milk carts before the sun would rise.

When the Maltese and Italian migrants arrived and settled in Sunshine, many Greek housewives (including Eleni) slowly began to learn English. At every opportunity Eleni would attempt to learn to read, write and speak English to communicate with her neighbours.

Eleni not only taught herself to speak English, but is credited as being the first Greek woman from the western suburbs to gain her driver's licence. By her own admission, it may have taken four instructors to help her learn to drive a car, but she eventually succeeded. When

Eleni and her family at the Massey Ferguson Christmas party in 1957. Little Kleoniki is holding a Christmas present from Santa who came to the factory.

others had heard about the rigorous ordeal she had to endure to get her licence, they simply said, "Why didn't you just bribe the first instructor with a hundred dollars and just be done with it?"

In the 1980s, Eleni became the proud owner of a new Ford Falcon XF and became the talk of the town. She was able for the first time to drive around the streets of Melbourne with her young family and visit faraway places with relative ease.

Andreas and Eleni also worked tirelessly to help establish the Greek Orthodox Church of Apostolos Andreas in West Sunshine. Apparently, Andreas had raffled a block of land that he owned to help raise the necessary funds to build the church. The estimated cost was around £6000. Many of the workers (carpenters, plumbers, etc.) offered their services for free.

Andreas was always eager to continue to build strong links amongst the local Greek Cypriot community. In 1965, he helped to set up the Western Suburbs Soccer Club where many youth from Greece and Cyprus could join and create lifelong bonds with other players and club members.

In October 2009 Andreas passed away after succumbing to failing health.

"I don't regret coming to Australia," Eleni says proudly. "This is my home now. All the Cypriots here in Sunshine are like a large family to me. I am happy here. Of course I miss the mountains of Cyprus and I miss the way things used to be. But Cyprus has changed and all our family are here now. So this is now my home."

ACKNOWLEDGEMENTS
I would like to thank Eleni Theodotou for sharing her life story with me. Thanks also to Eleni's daughter Rita Efthymiou and granddaughter Eleni Efthymiou for their wonderful assistance, especially with the scanning of their old family photographs.

Eleni's children Nicholas, Kleoniki and Margarita in the backyard of their house in Sunshine. 1956

Stellios
PANAGIOTOU

Stellios Panagiotou aged eighteen. 1946

Stellios Panagiotou was born on the 2nd of October 1928 in the village of Lagoudera, Nicosia. His parents were quite poor and could not afford to keep him in school beyond the age of ten. This was something he regretted. Being someone who loved learning; he was always regarded as a keen and hard working student.

Stellios is the youngest of four children (two boys and two girls). His older brother died tragically in 1942 after contracting a fever. Stellios believes that the lack of proper medical services in Cyprus at the time were to blame for his brother's sad and preventable death.

In 1940, when Stellios was twelve years old, he went to work with his uncle at the Palace Hotel in Nicosia. His uncle was the head cook in the restaurant at the hotel and young Stellios was hired as a kitchen boy to wash plates and glasses. Other duties included peeling potatoes, running errands and general cleaning. He remembers working from 6am until 9pm, seven days a week. Though his employer provided food and accommodation, Stellios earned just one pound a month.

In 1942, Stellios left the Palace Hotel and found employment at the Gosselin Hotel in Kyrenia. It was the middle of the Second World War and many soldiers stationed at Kyrenia were frequent visitors to the hotel's restaurant. Stellios remembers one night when a senior officer invited him and a few of the soldiers to sail by boat to Turkey just for fun. They rowed for many hours during a moonless night until they were close enough to see the sleepy Turkish houses dotted along the Turkish mainland. They

Stellios at his mother-in-law's house in Nicosia. 1949

then quietly and slowly rowed back to the safety of Kyrenia harbour. In hindsight, this was a risky and careless thing to

LEFT: Stellios aged eighteen at the Elyssia Hotel in the mountainous village of Pedoulas. 1946
RIGHT: Stellios' identity photograph (1944) and a work reference letter. Nicosia, 1950

HOTEL "ACROPOLE"

9A TENNYSON STREET
NICOSIA - CYPRUS
TEL. NICOSIA 26

PROPRIETOR: C.H. SOFRONI

HEAD OFFICE :
GOURMETS RESTAURANT
47/48 LISLE STREET LONDON W.C. 2

MANAGER : ROLAND A. MEO

Nicosia the 21st May 1950

TO WHOM IT MAY CONCERN.

THIS IS TO CERTIFY that Mr Stellios Panayiote has been in our employ as a First Cook for the last two years.

Mr Panayiotou has proved to be an excellent cook, honest and trustworthy and willing at all times.

I strongly recommend him for any such employment he may apply for.

Manager

do. It was probably alcohol that fueled the commanding officer's desire to take young Stellios on this midnight adventure.

Feeling isolated in Kyrenia and missing his friends and relatives, Stellios decided to return to Nicosia six months later. He soon found work in the kitchen at the Cleopatra hotel where he stayed for three years.

The history of the Cleopatra hotel begins in 1916, when a young boy by the name of Charalambos Ioannides, was forced to leave his family in Paphos to move to Nicosia. He walked barefoot for three days to reach the capital. On his arrival, he was offered a job as kitchen boy and waiter at the newly built Cleopatra Hotel; the first hotel in Nicosia. He was only eight years old.

After fifteen years of working at different establishments in the capital, Charalambos opened his first restaurant. By saving every single penny from his earnings, he was able to buy the Cleopatra Hotel. Charalambos is better known as 'Loucoullos', a nickname that refers to the rich and tasty food he offered his guests.

At the Cleopatra Hotel, Stellios again worked as a kitchen boy, but was later invited to cook and assist the main chefs who worked there. Stellios mentioned that it was common for 'Loucoullos' to find two or three young boys loitering in a nearby street and offer them a shilling each to help peel potatoes or run errands during a particularly busy period at the restaurant.

After the war, in 1946, Stellios decided to leave the Cleopatra Hotel to seek his fortune elsewhere on the island. He was eager to work as a junior chef and earn more money. He found employment at the Elyssia Hotel in the mountainous village of Pedoulas where he was paid fifteen pounds a month; an impressive wage for an eighteen year old. Eager to further his career, Stellios moved back to Nicosia in the late 1940s where he was employed as First Chef at the Acropole Hotel.

In 1949, aged 21, he met his wife Anna, a seamstress who was working for his landlady. Anna (who was a year and half older than Stellios) insisted that he would need to get her parent's consent before she could agree to marry him. It was improper at that time for a man to pursue a young lady without parental consent. Stellios did as he was instructed and met with Anna's parents. He recalls how her mother spoke to him sternly and said, "Listen young man, we are a poor family so therefore, we cannot provide a dowry for our daughter." Stellios told the mother he was not interested in money or gifts. He simply wanted to marry Anna – as she was. With Anna's parents now in agreement, Stellios turned his attention to his own family, eager to receive his own parents' approval and blessing. He was well aware that his two older sisters were still unmarried and village custom dictated that they should marry first. Stellios joked that in Cyprus a man who had sisters might have to wait until he was fifty before it was his turn to marry. Stellios pleaded with his mother that he was living all alone in Nicosia, with no one to look after him or to wash and iron his clothes. Upon hearing his pitiful plight and seeing how determined and anxious her son had become, his mother finally agreed that he could marry Anna. Her only condition was that he did not leave Cyprus to travel abroad.

Stellios and Anna, now engaged, bought a property in Nicosia with the intention of building their family home on

LEFT: Stellios and Anna at Agios Dometios church on their wedding day in Nicosia. April 1950

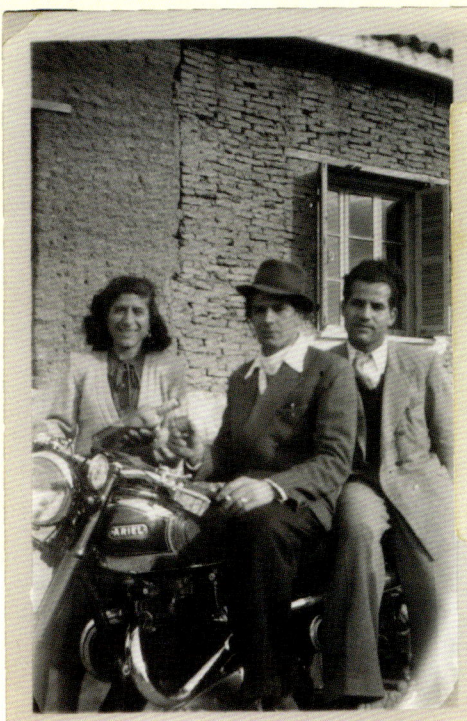

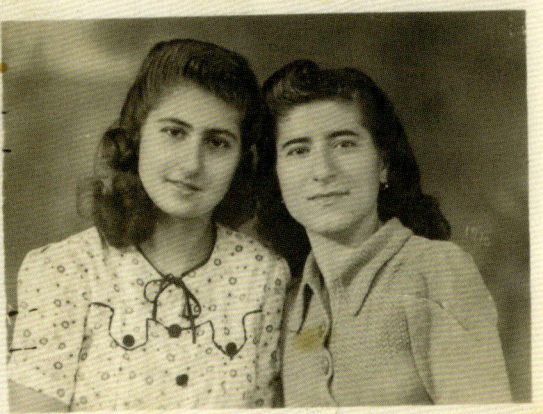

LEFT: Anna with Christaki (a friend) and her brother-in-law Andreas seated at the back of his motorcycle. Nicosia, 1949
BELOW: Anna Panagiotou (right) with a friend. c.1950

it. The property located on the road that leads out to Kykkos monastery cost 200 pounds. Stellios contributed 75 pounds and Anna paid the remaining 125 pounds. They were married on the 16 April 1950. Not long after, Stellios became tempted to travel to Australia. In doing so, he would break the promise he had made to his mother.

Many Cypriot men and women left Cyprus on their own to seek work and stability during the late 1940s and early 1950s. Cyprus at that time was suffering economically and unemployment was rife.

And so it was that on the 28th of April 1950, twelve days after Stellios was married to Anna, he left Cyprus bound for Australia onboard the ship SS Cyrenia. Exactly one month later, on the 26th of May, the 22-year-old Stellios arrived at Port Melbourne in Australia.

Upon his arrival, Stellios chose to live with his brother-in-law Evripides (Anna's brother) in a small flat in Carlton. Evripides had arrived in Australia a few months earlier. Before long, the two men became increasingly frustrated with their greedy and mean-spirited landlord who was charging them around 25 pounds a month in rent. This was an astronomical amount to pay in 1950. Evripides convinced the young Stellios to buy some land for 125 pounds in the western suburb of Sunshine and together they built their first home; a tiny, weatherboard bungalow. The bungalow was small but accommodated the two men comfortably until their wives arrived in 1951.

Stellios was soon able to earn and save enough money to build his own house in the same suburb.

Over time, Stellios purchased a few more blocks of land in Sunshine for twenty-six pounds each, which he then sold a few years later for twenty times their original value. Land was plentiful and cheap in the 1950s. Many migrants with

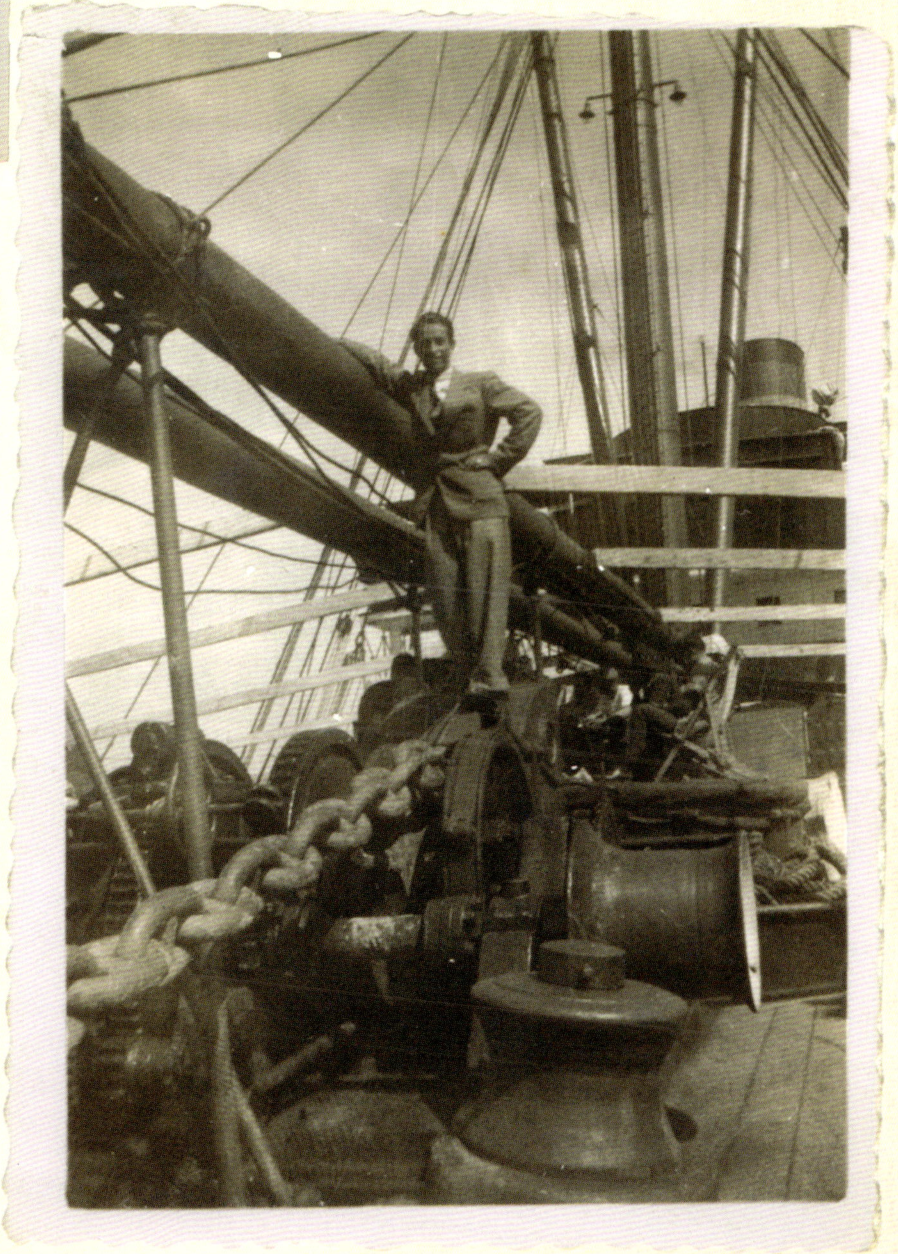

Stellios Panagiotou on board the ship SS Cyrenia. May 1950

a keen sense for investment were able to purchase land outright by saving a few pounds a month for about a year; an impossible scenario in today's world.

The industrial suburb of Sunshine was a rather flat and barren wasteland, surrounded by factories, farms and bush. Wild rabbits would often roam the unmade streets that ran alongside sheep and cattle farms. There was no plumbing and many Cypriot immigrants had to fetch buckets of water by hand, exactly as they had done back in their villages in Cyprus.

The suburb became a popular place for migrants to live, as there were many large employers in the area (such as the Massey Ferguson Factory).

Soon after Stellios settled in Sunshine with his wife Anna, he became a member of the newly established Greek Cypriot Community of Apostolos Andreas. The mission of the committee was to build a

Stellios Panagiotou on board the ship SS Cyrenia. May 1950

The church was established to help provide a nearby and convenient place of worship for the many Greeks and Cypriots who lived in the outer Western suburbs of Melbourne. At the time, the nearest Greek Orthodox Church was located in East Melbourne. With virtually no regular or adequate public transport system in the western suburbs it was an almost impossible journey for a Greek Orthodox family to undertake on a Sunday morning.

Stellios found work as a cook at the Wentworth restaurant located above an emporium on Collins Street in the heart of Melbourne. The restaurant was owned by Mr Pappas and was open 24 hours a day. Stellios was introduced to Mr Pappas by his brother-in-law, Evripides. Many migrants found work largely by word of mouth or by knowing someone who knew someone who knew someone. Stellios introduced a delightful repertoire of Cypriot dishes to the menu during his time at the restaurant. His training in Cyprus had served him well. He was paid around seven pounds for working six days a week. The distance he had to travel from Sunshine to work each day meant his days were even longer. His wife Anna endured a lonely existence at home while he was away, with few friends for company. With limited English skills, she did not dare to interact with any of the locals.

Stellios left the Wentworth restaurant in 1952, largely due to the difficult daily commute from his suburban home. He soon found work as a welder and sheet metal worker at the Austin Motor Company in West Melbourne. Like other migrants, Stellios enjoyed the privilege of finding steady work that provided training on the job. The cost of living was low enough to allow these workers to save enough money to buy land and houses in a relatively short amount of time. Australia soon became known as 'the lucky country'. In the early

Anna Panagiotou. c.1948

church for the growing outer Melbourne Greek Orthodox community. In fact, Stellios became the first president of the Greek Cypriot Community of Apostolos Andreas between 1956 and 1965 and was instrumental in helping to gather the funds to build the church. Stellios himself donated ten pounds while others contributed a pound or a few shillings until they were able to afford the £650 needed to purchase the block of land.

1950s, the price of a loaf of bread was 5 pence. The average yearly wage for a male factory worker was around 305 pounds. Female workers had to put up with earning about half that amount.

In 1958, Stellios decided to leave the Austin Motor Company and went to work at the Massey Ferguson Factory which was conveniently located in his home suburb of Sunshine. His travel time was reduced significantly. He was employed once again as a sheet metal worker. Stellios sadly came to the realisation that he would never work in restaurants or cafés again. Only at home could he continue to put his culinary finesse to use.

In the late 1960s, Stellios left Massey Ferguson to buy a Milk Bar (in Deer Park), which he owned and operated with Anna and his family for 32 years.

In 1975, Anna was diagnosed with breast cancer and had to undergo extensive treatment followed by surgery. Though her health improved after surgery, a few years later the cancer returned and had spread to other parts of her body. In 1989, aged only sixty-three, Anna passed away in her home. She died peacefully lying on her matrimonial bed next to her husband who stayed faithfully by her side until the end.

Stellios and Anna lived a peaceful and happy life in Melbourne. They were blessed with three children (Georgina, Andrew and Jimmy) and were fortunate to have made many life-long friends in Australia. They travelled frequently and extensively around the world including two trips back to Cyprus in 1969 and 1980.

Although he misses his wife deeply, Stellios is grateful to have the constant and reassuring company of his family and friends.

ABOVE: Bus trip to Phillip Island. The driver is holding up a penguin to the amusement of the other passengers. c.1952

ACKNOWLEDGEMENTS
I would like to thank Stellios Panagiotou for his hospitality and for sharing his life story with me. Special thanks to his daughter Georgina Morabito for her kind assistance and to Mary Demetriou for introducing me to her uncle Stellios.

Stellios with his first car. A 1928 Chevrolet bought for £58. Melbourne, 1954

Taki
LEPTOS

MORPHOU-NICOSIA

Taki (Christos) Leptos aged seventeen. 1946

T aki (Christos) Leptos was born in July 1929 in the town of Morphou, Nicosia district. His parents Maria and Nicholas Leptos had six children; Andreas, Taki, Tasoulla, Nitsa, Giorgios and Harita.

Taki's father Nicholas owned a large general store in the heart of Morphou, selling a vast array of goods including food products, farming equipment, home wares, building supplies and leather goods. Nicholas was raised in Egypt where he taught himself to speak six languages. Taki is unsure as to how his father ended up in Egypt but believes his grandparents gave him away to a wealthy family. Perhaps they were too poor to look after him. His father returned to Cyprus as a young man where he eventually married Maria Bogiatzis (Taki's mother) and settled in Morphou.

Taki remembers that Morphou had a population of around six thousand residents comprising of Greek, Turkish and Maronite Cypriots. Morphou has always been famous for its vast orange and citrus fruit plantations as well as the monastery of Saint Mamas. The saint is believed to have lived as a hermit in a cave near the town in the 3rd century AD.

When Taki was eight years old, he contracted malaria and was bedridden for over a month. His mother gave him a small pill he believes was called *Quinine*. He recovered and completed his education, which included studying English at the Sylvestre School. "I was a rather cheeky young boy growing up," admits Taki with a grin. "I was always getting into mischief and being reprimanded by my father or my school teachers."

During the Second World War, Nicholas Leptos was forced to close his general store in Morphou because many people were unable to pay him what they owed for goods provided. "The British wouldn't let my father take anyone to court," he laments. "He had all these people owing him money and he couldn't do anything about it. His business was suffering and he was losing money. So my father decided to move to the mountainous village of Prodromos where he found work at the Berengaria hotel."

After the war, Nicholas returned

Taki (Christos) Leptos aged eighteen. Melbourne, 1948.

to Morphou where he opened a large *kafenion* (coffee house) in the middle of the *Agora* (market). "My father's *kafenion* had three large billiard tables and was frequented by both Christians and Muslims. I have fond memories of mixing openly and conversing freely with members of both communities. We didn't distinguish any difference between Greeks and Turks," Taki adds. "We were all Cypriot. We were all the same."

From the age of ten, Taki was allowed to work with his father at the *kafenion* and became accustomed to mixing with adults as they drank, sang, argued and laughed. They sometimes harassed the youngster but always in good spirits. "We even had a Communist Club in Morphou," Taki remarks. "The leaders of this club would spend many hours at night promoting the benefits of Communism to whoever would listen in an attempt to recruit new members." Apparently, there were many men in Cyprus who adopted Stalin's communist ideology without understanding anything about it.

When he turned eleven or twelve, Taki discovered girls. He took particular notice of a young girl named Kostandinya who would accompany her father when

Taki's younger brother Giorgios aged around ten.

he went to prune trees. Kostandinya had long dark hair that was tied into two long plaits that extended down the length of her back. Although Taki went to some trouble to try and sneak a peek at this girl, he was frustrated by the fact that she barely noticed him. "You have to remember," he tells me. "In those days boys and girls were kept apart. You were not allowed to mix or try to have any

relationships. Yes, there were some boys who had secret affairs; but that was rare and very risky in those days."

Taki would go on to tell me that many young men from Morphou would seek to release their sexual frustration by visiting the prostitutes in Nicosia. Apparently, the average visit to a brothel would cost around two shillings. Some young men would go to the brothels once a week until they were old enough to consider marriage. Then they would prefer to marry a 'demure and pure' girl from their village. Taki explained how some girls were forced into prostitution after a secret affair or sexual encounter was discovered. Regarded as sullied, these girls were abandoned by their parents. Even girls who were victims of rape or incest were sometimes banished from their village and forced into prostitution.

During the 1940s, it was a common sight to see truckloads of English troops driving through Morphou. Taki and his friends were always keen to chase after these vehicles shouting 'cigarettes, cigarettes, cigarettes' until the amused soldiers in the trucks would throw packets of cigarettes at them. "I remember one day smoking an entire packet and then

Friends and neighbours sitting together at the front of the Morphou football club. Taki thinks he took this photo in 1946

going to my father's *kafenion* worse for wear. My legs were like jelly. Boy, did I get a beating from my father that day. I remember he used a long branch from our Jasmine tree."

When Taki turned fourteen he decided to get a motorcycle licence. He figured this would allow him the freedom to escape from Morphou and the strict work regime set up by his father. With his motorcycle he was free to explore the world beyond Morphou, to visit the beach or ride to other towns such as Limassol, Kyrenia and Nicosia. He soon developed an interest in the black market. With the little pocket money he received from his father, he would buy various products and trinkets in Nicosia and then sell them at slightly inflated prices to the inhabitants of Morphou.

It was around this time, when Taki met a Turkish watchmaker named Mustafa in Morphou who agreed to show him how to mend watches. "Everyone called him 'Koutso Mustafa' because he was lame and walked with a limp." Seeing another opportunity to make money, Taki became an attentive and competent apprentice. He would accompany his grandmother Hajinou to the outdoor markets in the village of Kambos around thirty-seven miles from Morphou. There he would set up a makeshift workshop and advertise his services as a watchmaker. "People started calling me *kyrios* (master) and I quickly developed a reputation as a gifted young watchmaker."

In early 1947, Taki saw an advertisement in his local newspaper from the Australian Government asking for qualified tradesmen to emigrate and work in various States such as Victoria, New South Wales and Queensland. The young seventeen-year-old managed to convince seventeen of his friends from Morphou (including two Turkish Cypriots) to travel with him to Melbourne. Taki was also inspired to leave Cyprus by his older brother Andreas who managed to successfully settle in South Africa.

In October 1947, Taki and his fellow companions left Cyprus in a small boat and travelled to Port Said in Egypt. They then boarded a Yugoslavian ship named Partizanka bound for Australia. He recalls that his friends objected to the food on the Partizanka and decided to stage a hunger strike. "I'm not sure whose idea it was," says Taki. "But it was

Taki's younger sister Tasoulla, Year unknown.

unsuccessful. All we wanted was for the chefs in the ship's kitchen to cook Cypriot food – proper food. We didn't like their Yugoslavian food."

When the Partizanka reached Australia it docked in Perth initially for a few days. Taki and his friends were astounded by the warm reception they received from all the young Australian girls who had flocked to the wharf to greet them. For the first time in their lives, the Cypriot men were approached by members of the opposite sex who seemed keen to hug and kiss them. "We were definitely not in Cyprus anymore," laughs Taki.

"We didn't stay in Perth long," he added. "But I can tell you that the place made a great first impression on us. I mean the Australian girls. That's all we talked about on the ship as we set course for Melbourne." The Partizanka with its six hundred plus passengers on board did not dock in Melbourne, however. An alleged workers' strike at the port forced the ship on to Sydney.

As they disembarked, Taki and his friends were surprised to find a fellow compatriot from Morphou waiting

Taki standing inbetween his God brother Andreas (left) and a friend in Morphou. c.1946

Toula on a school field trip. Year and place unknown.

for them on the wharf. His name was Diomedes and he had travelled to Sydney from Melbourne to greet the new arrivals from Cyprus. Diomedes paid for their train fares back to Melbourne and was able to find all of them suitable lodgings.

"He helped us a lot," remarks Taki. "In fact, I remember it was a Friday or Saturday when we arrived in Melbourne and by Monday he had found most of us jobs at a paper mill factory in Carlton." Taki discovered that Diomedes had migrated to Australia directly after the Second World War and had even married a local Australian woman. He owned a Cypriot café in the heart of the city and was keen to meet and direct any new arrivals to visit his establishment.

Soon after Taki arrived in Melbourne he started to question his decision to leave Cyprus. "I had a moment when I felt uncertain and a feeling of dread came over me," he says. "I told myself, 'what are you doing here Taki? What are you looking for'?"

Things improved for Taki however, when he began to explore the exciting

cosmopolitan life that Melbourne had to offer. He would frequent the Greek bars and cafés on Russell Street including the Athenean, Dimocratos, Zenon and

A young Toula on her bicycle. Location and year unknown.

even the inappropriately named Café Poutzos. Taki was surprised again by the forwardness of some of the local women. "You could board a bus at one end of Swanston Street and by the time you got off the bus at the other end you would have two or even three women hanging off your arm," he boasts. "It was not uncommon for many Cypriot migrant men to bring an Australian 'sheila' (as the local women were sometimes called) back to their flat or rented room, sometimes two or three times a week. I knew a Cypriot man who was overdoing it by flirting with two or three woman in a single day. All you needed to say was 'hello' and the women would flock to you. They loved us. It was incredible. I think there must have been a shortage of Australian men after the war."

The seventeen young friends from Morphou did not stay together for long. Many of them decided to explore other parts of Victoria. In time, they would all marry and settle in towns and suburbs across Australia. Taki was fortunate to have two of his closest friends remain

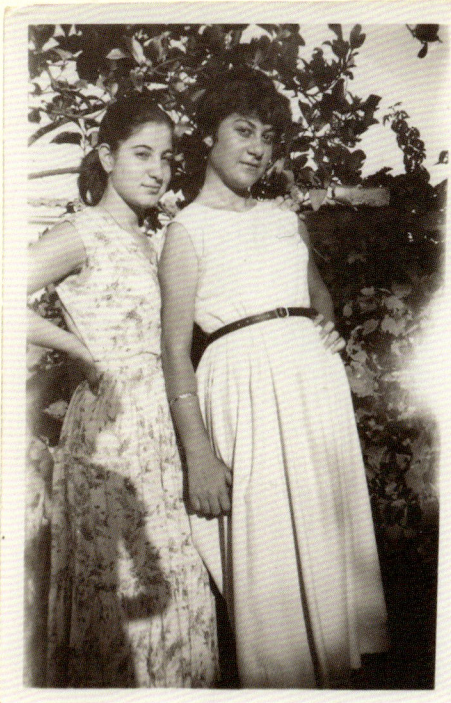

with him in Melbourne; namely, Dimitris Petrou and Andreas Katsineris.

Taki left the paper mill factory and found steady and well-paid work in a number of popular cafés and restaurants in the city. The first establishment was a popular restaurant called Mario's owned by Italian immigrants Maria and Mario Viganò. He worked as a waiter and was instantly surprised by how much money he could make, especially in tips.

Melbourne in the late forties was enjoying a post-war euphoria and the theatres and cinemas were again full of patrons. Once a show was over, many patrons would go to places like Mario's for a late night drink or supper. Young men out with their wives or sweethearts were only too happy to push an extra shilling into Taki's hand or waistcoat pocket as he served their drinks. Mario's also attracted plenty of ex-servicemen who would get drunk after spending their government allowance on alcohol. When Taki returned the following morning to sweep and clean the restaurant he would find plenty of loose coins and even pound notes scattered all over the floor. "Finders keepers," the head chef would say and instructed Taki to take what he could.

In 1949, Taki was earning enough money at Mario's to rent a weatherboard house in Thornbury for four pounds a week. At last he could put an end to sharing rooms with boisterous bachelors.

One night he returned home from work to discover that a thief had broken into his house and had stolen all of his suits. Fortunately, the thief did not open the wardrobe drawer that contained all of his cash savings.

After a while, Taki left Mario's to go

Toula (on the right) with a friend. Unknown location. c.1955

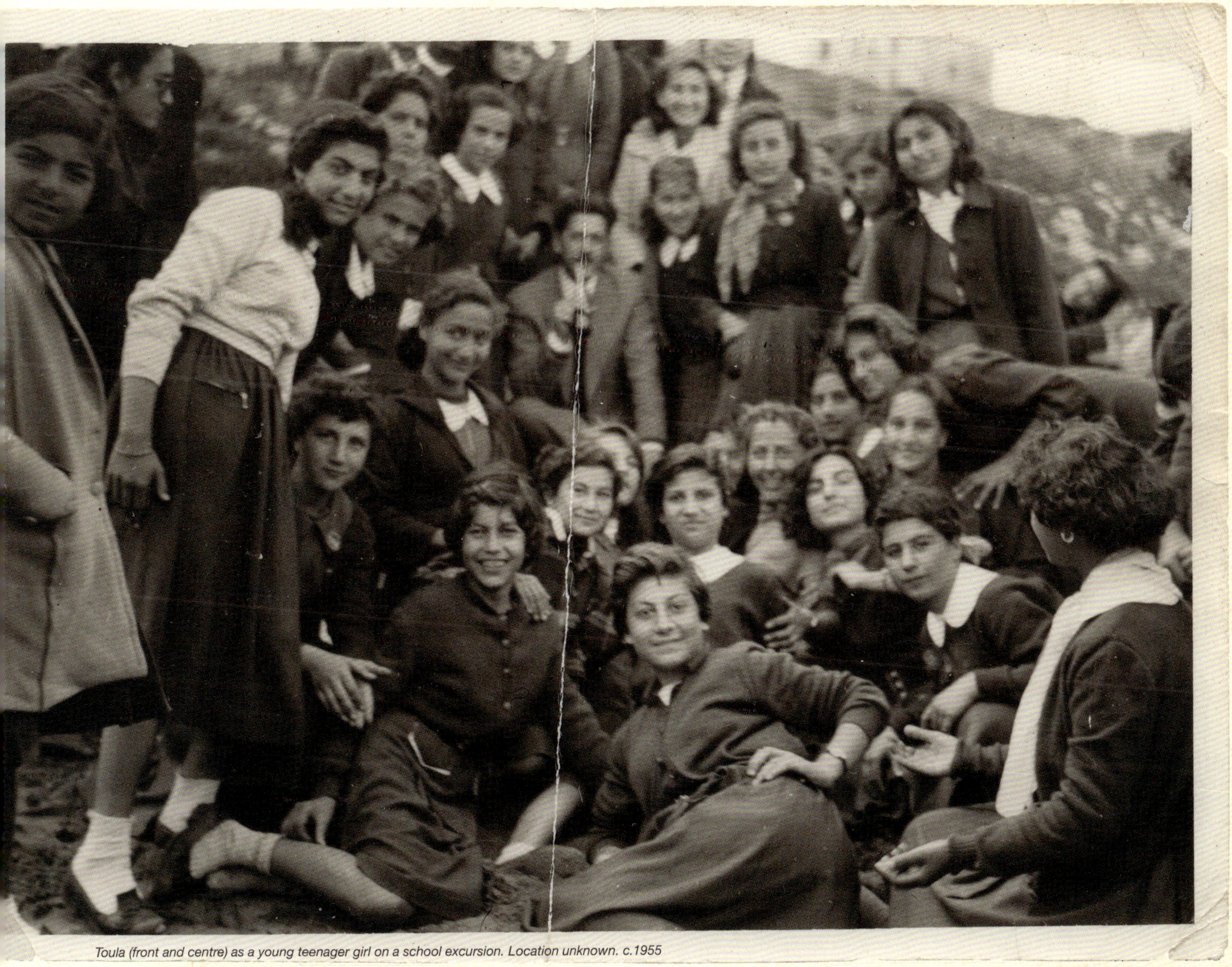

Toula (front and centre) as a young teenager girl on a school excursion. Location unknown. c.1955

and work at the Astoria Restaurant. He also worked the evening shift at a dance club opposite the Astoria. Six days a week, he would serve lunch and dinner at the Astoria and then drinks at the dance club until his shift ended after midnight. "I remember that a glass of beer would cost one shilling," Taki says. "The customers would usually tip me one shilling. By the time I finished my shift, my pockets would be bulging with coins. I made a lot of money in those days."

By 1950, Taki took his savings and bought a combined milk bar and fruit shop in the leafy suburb of Hampton. At first it was a very demanding venture. Not only was he required to get up at 2am to go to the Victoria Market and buy fresh produce but he was also required to work long hours six days a week. As a business owner, his contact with friends had waned considerably and so did his social life. He did, however, continue to attend the dance halls of Melbourne most weekends. Twenty-one year old Taki had no previous experience in selling fruit and vegetables or running a milk bar. This was very different from helping his father in his general store and *kafenion* in Morphou or fixing watches at the Kambos market with his grandmother.

In 1953, he purchased a fruit-shop on Lygon Street in Carlton. "My fruit shop was very successful and very popular," he says proudly. "It was even more popular than the Italian-owned fruit shops in the area." Taki claims that his success as a green grocer was largely due to his ability to provide the best local produce and his commitment to establishing long-lasting relationships with his customers.

In 1959, after almost twelve years living abroad in Australia, Taki decided to go back to Cyprus to visit his parents and family. He had left Cyprus as a wide-eyed teenager seeking adventure and was he now returning as a very successful business owner.

While Taki was visiting relatives in Nicosia he met his cousin's friend who insisted that he should marry a girl he knew named Toula (Demetra). At first Taki was unsure about entering an arranged marriage, especially when he discovered that Toula was twelve years younger than him. But Taki was swayed by Toula's innocence and good looks and agreed to marry her. Toula did not have much say in the matter. Once her parents gave their consent she had no choice but to go along with their wishes. Two weeks after they met, Taki and Toula were engaged.

Almost a year later in February 1960, they were married.

Taki brought his young wife back to Melbourne where they worked together in the Carlton fruit shop. In 1961, they welcomed the arrival of their son Nicholas and in 1965, their daughter Mary was born.

In 1970, Taki bought a beef cattle farm on the outskirts of Geelong with a hundred head of cattle. His main intention was to use the little stone cottage on the farm as a holiday house for his young family. "I bought the farm for pleasure," he said. "But I couldn't look after it, so I had to sell it - which was a shame."

In 1975, Taki slipped and fell in his shop and shattered his kneecap. As he spent time recovering, he decided to sell his business. The injury depressed Taki and he laments that he sold the shop for only twenty thousand dollars, which was a quarter of its true value.

At nearly fifty years of age, Taki was now unemployed for the first time in his life. Unwilling to just give up, he took a friend's advice and enrolled in a Real Estate course at Prahran College.

In 1992, he bought a Real Estate business in Ivanhoe, which he kept for a few years. In 1996, after suffering a mystery illness he sold his business and retired from Real Estate altogether.

Today Taki still lives in his original house in the eastern suburbs of

Taki and Toula visiting Salamis in 1960.

Taki Leptos in front of his fruit shop located opposite the Williamstown railway station. 1951

Melbourne. Unfortunately, his wife Toula has developed dementia and now resides in a nearby nursing home.

It is a real testament to the human spirit and sheer determination that a young boy from Morphou who became a master watchmaker at fourteen years of age could then go on to became a successful businessman, green grocer and real estate auctioneer in a metropolis such as Melbourne.

ACKNOWLEDGEMENTS
I would like to thank Taki Leptos for sharing his living memories with me. Thanks also to Mary Leptos for her assistance and for proof-reading her father's life story.

Taki in his fruit shop on Lygon Street. On the right are his sister Harita and brother Giorgios. Melbourne, 1962

Hakki
ABDURAZAK

Hakki Abdurazak was born on the 24th of March 1925 in the *mahalla* (neighbourhood) of Yeni Jami in Nicosia. He was the third of four children born to Abdu Razak and Fatma Suleyman. His older brother Dervish was born in 1918, his older sister Hatice in 1921 and his younger brother Muzaffer in 1928.

Hakki's father Abdu Razak worked for the municipal council sweeping and cleaning the streets of the capital. The council, which was run by British officials, employed both Greek and Turkish Cypriot workers. When Hakki was eight years old, his father developed an aggressive eye

Hakki Abdurazak aged seventeen. Nicosia, 1944

cancer that spread to his brain. He died in 1933, aged thirty-three, leaving his wife Fatma a widow at twenty-five with four children to raise.

After the death of her husband, the municipality provided Fatma and her children with a house on the outskirts of Nicosia. Despite a number of marriage proposals, she decided to remain a single mother working long hours as a servant and washer-woman to provide the bare essentials for her children. Her oldest son, Dervish found work at the Magic Palace cinema in the centre of town and was therefore able to contribute his lowly income to help his family.

Hakki attended primary school for only three years before he was sent to work for a barber named Ismail Salih. Ismail's shop was located opposite Hagia Sophia in the heart of the capital. Hakki worked six days a week for two years without earning a wage. In the beginning, he was only required to sit and watch his master at work or to do odd jobs such as cleaning the mirrors or sweeping the hair on the floor. Ismail was able to teach the young apprentice how to cut hair and provided Hakki with all his clothes and daily meals.

Ismail Salih was a talented and popular barber who had many regular customers, both Christian and Muslim, rich and poor. "In those days, everything was peaceful," says Hakki. "No one would ask you if you were Greek or Turkish or anything like that. People were mixed. There was no trouble at all."

An average haircut in 1936 would cost around one and a half *pakires* (about one ninth of a shilling). Hakki remembers that Master Ismail would often shave or cut the hair of a poor person for free. Sometimes the poor person would repay the barber's kindness with a small basket of fruit or perhaps a few loaves of home-baked bread.

Hakki was often invited to eat lunch with Ismail's family in their home. He was unaware at the time that the master's young daughter Sevil would one day become his wife. She was only two years old in 1936 and eleven-year-old Hakki would have to wait another fourteen years before she would be eligible for marriage; but more about that later.

Hakki's mother Fatma was happy that her two sons were now employed. Dervish had steady work at the Magic Palace cinema and Hakki was now a junior apprentice working for a well-respected local barber. At least where Hakki was concerned, it was one less mouth to feed on account that all his meals were provided by his kind Master Ismail.

On his day off, Hakki and the other local boys would play *mappa* (football) or *lingri* (a game similar to baseball) in the churchyard of Agios Loukas, which was next to the Jami cemetery. Hakki played together with Greek, Turkish and Armenian boys without any prejudice or concern. Like most of the other boys, he often played barefoot. One day, he accidentally kicked a rock instead of the ball and injured his foot. With his large toe

Hakki's brothers Muzaffer and Dervish (seated) and Konchi the dog. Yeni Jami, Nicosia. October 1946

now bleeding, the quick-thinking Hakki hid behind the minaret, quickly pulled down his short pants and urinated on the wound to disinfect it. It worked.

When Hakki was around twelve years old, he became unwell and began to spit blood. His distressed mother took him to see a doctor at the Central Hospital in Nicosia. Hakki was immediately admitted for treatment. He was suffering from tuberculosis. Unfortunately, Hakki's mother was very poor and after two weeks she could no longer afford to keep her son in hospital. In those days, hospital patients were required to pay two *pakires* a day to stay in a hospital bed. When she arrived to take her son home, a Greek Cypriot doctor named Doctor Kourea intervened and kindly insisted that he would pay the hospital fees on her behalf. He did not want Hakki to be discharged until he had fully recovered.

Hakki stayed in hospital for two months, receiving excellent treatment from Doctor Kourea and the mostly Greek nurses. He even managed to learn Greek during his time there.

When Hakki had recovered from his illness, the generous Doctor Kourea drove

him to Ismail's barbershop and placed two shillings in his hand. "Take this money Hakki," he said. "and please spend it only on food to fatten your bones." Hakki made a full recovery from his bout of tuberculosis and continued to work at Ismail's barbershop throughout his teenage years and into adulthood.

After the Second World War, in late 1945, Hakki bought himself an Ensign photographic camera and travelled all over Cyprus with his friends, taking many photographs of major events, famous landmarks and the natural environment. He had a keen interest in photography and managed to take a great deal of photographs in the late 1940s, trusting his film development and printing to Mustafa Diana, who owned a popular and successful photography studio in Nicosia named Foto Diana.

In 1947, twenty-two year old Hakki decided to open his own barbershop, not far from Master Ismail's shop. His brother Dervish helped him to set up his business by purchasing all the shop fittings and chattels such as the mirrors and the chairs. Dervish had left the Magic Palace and was now a qualified policeman.

After six months, Hakki was attracting enough customers to employ another barber. He also took on a young Greek

apprentice named Kypro from the village of Dikomo. "I had many Greek customers just like my boss," Hakki boasts. "Kypro was the son of one of my loyal customers. I could speak Greek quite well, so communicating with my Greek customers and my apprentice was not a problem."

Hakki maintained his friendship with his former boss Ismail, sharing business knowledge (and even customers) from

Hakki (on the right) together with his future father-in-law Ismail Salih. Nicosia, 1947

time to time. He was still invited to Ismail's house every Sunday for dinner.

By 1950, Hakki started to express an interest in finding a wife. He was now twenty-five and his barbershop business was a proven success. He mentioned his intention to marry to a few people including Ismail's wife Suzan. "What about my Sevil?" she asked him referring to her daughter who was now almost sixteen. Hakki immediately gave his consent. He had watched Sevil blossom into a beautiful young woman over the last fourteen years.

Sevil was born on the 26th of July 1934 and was one of five children. She went to the American Academy in Nicosia where she studied English for three years before being sent to learn dressmaking with a local Greek seamstress. "We weren't that free to go out or anywhere by ourselves," she explains. "We always had to have a chaperone with us. Even when I used to

Hakki together with his younger brother Muzaffer and Konchi the dog. Yeni Jami, Nicosia. October 1946

Hakki Abdurazak (left) his brother Dervish, sister Hatice and younger brother Muzaffer. Nicosia, 1931

the wedding celebration was held in the large courtyard of her parent's house. Her mother used three large dressmaking benches to place all the food for the guests. Many family members and friends were invited, including many Greek and Armenian neighbours.

Once married, Hakki and Sevil appealed to their local Justice of the Peace to sell them a new house in Neopoli in North Nicosia. Unfortunately, the house was sold to another buyer who was able to pay in cash. Dejected, Hakki decided to travel to Australia where he was told he could make a lot of money in a short amount of time. Coming from a very poor background, he did not want to start a family that would endure the same hardships and impoverished life that he had endured.

Australia was beckoning and promising to be the solution to his financial problems. His plan was to work abroad for five years, and return to Cyprus with enough money to buy a new house in Nicosia. He sold his barbershop business to a popular football player named Defterali for one hundred and fifty pounds and he used this money to pay for his ship fare.

On the 30 January 1951, Hakki left Limassol on the ship SS Jenny bound for Australia. He remembers that the front section of the ship was reserved for passengers and that the crew could all speak Greek. The trip took thirty-seven days. He arrived in Melbourne on the 27th February 1951. He had fifty pounds in his pocket, which compared to other migrants was a small fortune.

go to school, my mother used to walk me there. It was so embarrassing for me. She would walk behind me and call out 'be careful Sevil. Don't look at anyone Sevil. Don't speak to anyone.' I was so embarrassed."

Sevil's mother Suzan was an orphan from the age of two and it seemed that the experience of moving from house to house with relatives had made her very nervous and overly-protective. "She was

not a very caring or affectionate person," Sevil remarks. "Perhaps her mood was affected by her difficult upbringing."

Once Sevil's father and Hakki's mother had given their consent, the young couple were able to officially announce their intentions to marry. Ismail the barber, (Hakki's old master), would soon become his father-in-law.

Hakki and Sevil were married on the 26th of March 1950. Sevil remembers that

Hakki was fortunate to have a few friends in Melbourne who helped him to settle into the city. He shared a room in a house in Richmond with a Turkish Cypriot acquaintance. They each paid two pounds and ten pence a week in rent. If they wanted to have a shower they had to walk to the nearby City Baths on Swanston Street.

Hakki found work almost immediately after he arrived at the General Motors Holden plant in Port Melbourne. With almost no knowledge of English, he worked on the production line earning an amazing eight pounds a week.

In his spare time, he would join other Turkish Cypriot migrants at the various Greek-owned clubs and cafés in the city of Melbourne. They mingled freely with Greek Cypriot migrants, conversing and exploring Melbourne together.

Hakki's wife Sevil arrived in Melbourne on a ship named Corsica on the 4th of February 1952. Reunited after almost a year apart, the couple rented a place in Richmond together with another migrant couple, Mehmet and Cemaliye. The tenants had to burn wooden logs to boil pots of water for cooking and bathing due to the lack of gas and hot water plumbing.

Sevil struggled to settle into her new Australian home. "I did not want to come to Australia," she says softly. "To tell you the truth, I really didn't want to come. I was so miserable in that little rented room in Richmond. Hakki would go off to work

Sevil in Nicosia. 1951

at six-thirty in the morning and he would come home late in the evening. I was left at home all by myself. I did not know anyone. It was hard for me in those days."

In December 1952, Hakki and Sevil welcomed the arrival of their first child; a daughter whom they named Suzan (Sue). The following year, Hakki had saved enough money to purchase a house in Port Melbourne. The house cost £2,500 and came complete with gas and hot water. Despite working at General Motors Holden, Hakki's first car was a

second hand Triumph Mayflower that he purchased in 1957. That same year, the Abdurazak family sold their house in Port Melbourne and moved into a brand new house in the suburb of Keon Park.

Just before the birth of their son (Serhat) in March 1960, Hakki left General Motors and bought himself a tip-truck. The housing and construction industry in Melbourne was booming and Hakki was keen to work as a sub-contractor delivering soil to various building sites around Melbourne. Before too long, other immigrants bought themselves tip trucks and soon the contracts began to dwindle. Hakki went from earning thirty pounds an hour in 1959 to only one pound an hour just two years later.

In 1961, Hakki made the decision to sell his truck. He went to work as a forklift driver at a local foundry. Once again, he had proven that he was able to learn new skills far beyond the comfort of cutting hair. His ability to accept new challenges was truly astonishing and admirable. Towards the end of 1963, Sevil received a letter from her father Ismail in Cyprus announcing that he had built her family a brand new house in Neopoli. Spurred on by the invitation and reminiscing their old life, Hakki and Sevil decided to sell their house and car in Melbourne and move back to Cyprus for good.

Just before they departed, a family friend from Cyprus contacted Hakki warning him to stay away because the political situation on the island had become unstable and quite dangerous. Having sold everything, Hakki and Sevil decided to travel to London instead since Sevil had two sisters already living there.

In December 1963, the Abdurazak family moved into the suburb of Newington Green in North London and Hakki bought himself a barbershop on Green Lanes road. The family lived in the space above the shop. "I had not cut hair for over twelve years and I was glad to see that my skills as a barber were still there," he tells me. "In fact, in London I

Hakki and Sevil in 1950. Photographed by Mustafa at his Foto Deanna studio in Nicosia.

Hakki (front) at Machairas Monastery. 20th July 1950

In 1971 Hakki opened a barbershop on High Street in the suburb of Thornbury. Over the coming years, he entered and won many hairdressing competitions. His trophies and awards were proudly displayed in his shop window, which helped to attract many new customers. The skills that he brought back from London also increased Hakki's reputation as a professional hair-stylist.

Unfortunately, in 1980, Hakki contracted glaucoma, an eye disease, and was forced to sell his business. Even though his eye surgery was successful, he decided to retire at the age of fifty-five.

Hakki has enjoyed his retirement now for over thirty-six years. He has taken his wife on many

Sevil's Aunt Shifa and Hakki's sister Hatice relaxing in the Troodos mountains. 1947

ACKNOWLEDGEMENTS
I would like to thank Hakki and Sevil Abdurazak for inviting me into their home and allowing me to record their life story. I am also grateful to their two children, Susan Osman and Serhat Abdurazak for all their support. Special thanks to Ahmet Polat and Sermen Erdogan for introducing me to Hakki Abdurazak and for their ongoing encouragement and assistance.

Hakki and Sevil with friends Mehmet and Cemaliye. Melbourne, 1952

Hakki's mother, Fatma Suleyman.1957

was able to learn how to become a hair stylist and not just a barber."

Life in Newington Green was anything but peaceful for Hakki and Sevil's young children. His twelve-year-old daughter Suzan was constantly getting teased and even punched by the other schoolgirls who would sometimes steal her lunch money. Hakki and his family lived in North London for three years before deciding to move back to Melbourne.

overseas holidays and has watched his children grow up, get married and have their own children. Hakki and Sevil have four grandchildren and four great-grandchildren.

These days Hakki spends most of his time at home with Sevil and working in his garden and garage. He visits his local Turkish Cypriot clubhouse twice a week where he sits and enjoys the company of others as they sip coffee and play *tavli*.

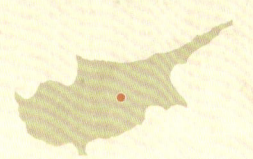

George
PAPOUIS

George Papouis was born in the village of Nisou on the 2nd of June 1928. He was one of seven children (two sisters and four brothers) born to Alexandros and Anna Papouis.

Nisou was a mixed village of Greek and Turkish Cypriots. George's best friend was a Muslim boy named Kuzey. The two boys were inseparable. They went everywhere together, roaming the village from daybreak to sunset. Gradually, they taught themselves to speak each other's language. No one in the village considered it strange that a Christian boy and a Muslim boy spent all their spare time playing together. "I didn't think Kuzey was any different to me," said George. "As far as I was concerned he was Cypriot just like me."

All the children in Nisou played in the main square of the village. The children relied on traditional games such as hide and seek, *lingri*, *mappa* and *pirilia* (baseball, football, marbles).

George attended junior school for two years. At the age of eight, his father took him out of school to work on the family farm. Alexandros Papouis was an elderly man and unable to tend to his own fields so he ordered his sons to do most of the work outdoors such as ploughing and threshing. Other chores included planting cotton, sesame, grains and potatoes.

"My father was extremely lazy," George tells me. "He would spend all his days at the *kafenion* (coffee house) while we were out in the burning sun doing all the farm work. It was the way it was. You didn't dare disobey your father in those days."

When I asked George to describe his life as a youngster he suddenly stiffens, leans forward and looks me straight in the eyes. "Listen!" He says sharply. "Life was very hard in those days. If anyone tells you otherwise, don't believe them. We worked from dawn to dusk and most days went to bed hungry." His wife Maria who is sitting beside him nods in agreement. "Poverty," she utters. "There was severe poverty. It was awful."

George becomes animated when asked to explain the life of a Cypriot farmer in the 1930s. "It would take fifty days to plough the fields with only a pair of mules, compared to only seven days with a tractor. My brothers and I begged our father to buy a tractor but he just wouldn't listen."

Because George's father owned many large parcels of land in Nisou he would sometimes hire workers from outside the village to help on the farm. "I remember my father would hire twenty workers from Paphos to help us tend to the crops and the fields. My mother would feed them breakfast, lunch and dinner and they

George's brother Stavrinos who died in 1933 in the United Kingdom aged eighteen.

would sleep under the trees in the open air at night. There were men, women and children of all ages. I believe that the workers from Paphos were the hardest workers in Cyprus."

George explains that many people in Nisou lost a lot of money because of the unscrupulous and cunning behaviour of the representatives from the export companies who were sent to the village to buy their farm produce. "They would promise to come to the village on the day the fruit was picked but instead turn up a few days later. By then the fruit had started to spoil and the buyers would only agree to pay half of the price. What could we do? Do we throw the fruit away and lose everything? No! We had no choice but to sell everything at a loss. These were the tricks the export companies would play on the poor."

Maria Constantinou. Larnaca, 1950

At age fourteen, George undertook extra work at a marble and mosaic workshop in Nicosia. He worked alongside twenty young boys polishing the stones and earned around ten shillings a week. George would often share his earnings with his family and give money to any relative or friend who was experiencing financial difficulty.

Many young Cypriot children were forced to live and work away from home during the first half of the twentieth century in order to help support their families during bleak economic times. The unlucky ones were treated like slaves. Despite working extremely long hours, many child workers earned a pittance and were often mistreated and even beaten by their masters. George was one of the lucky ones. The owner of the marble workshop was a kind-hearted man

named Michalis who was generous and supportive of young George and the other boys. George liked his boss and he made a fair amount of money. "I spent a lot of my money on helping to stock my sisters'

dowries. One week I would buy spoons. The next week I would buy forks."

As George approached his late teens he decided to become a barber. He set-up a makeshift salon at the local village *kafenion*. "I loved my job," he remarks.

"I was able to meet people from all classes; rich and poor, Muslim and Christian – it didn't matter. The only part I didn't like was dealing with the hot-headed, quick-tempered customers who

George's brother-in-law Panayi who married his sister Lisou, The little girl is their daughter Maroulla. Nicosia. c.1944

might slap you across the face if you made a mistake."

When George was twenty-eight years old, he left Cyprus and migrated to England like his brothers had done a few years earlier. It was 1956 and he was single and full of ambition.

He arrived at Victoria Station in London having travelled for six days by train through France and then by ship to Dover. Unfortunately, there was no one to meet him at the station upon his arrival. He would discover later that the letter he had sent his brother had not arrived. George was stranded. Unable to speak English and without a clue where to go, he wandered around the streets of London looking for a Greek face so he could ask for directions. Eventually, he showed a policeman the scrappy piece of paper that had his brother's address

Maria (left), her sister Varvara, step grandmother Katerina Stylianiou, mother Christina and her younger sisters Eleni and Katerina. Kornos. c.1946

written on it and he was promptly placed in a taxi and driven to the house. It wasn't unusual to see immigrants and new arrivals wandering lost around the streets of London in those days.

George's first impressions of London were not good. He remembers a dark and bleak city choking with fog and smog. "In those days, people used coal to heat their homes so wherever you went - you inhaled coal dust" he remarks. "It was everywhere. Up your nose; on your tongue and on the soles of your shoes. The whole place was covered in black soot and coal dust."

George settled with his brother Alekos and soon found work as a barber. Two weeks after he had arrived in London he found a bag in a stairwell that was full of bank notes. He had estimated that there must have been around two thousand pounds in that bag. "Enough money to buy a house," he says. Remarkably, George was not tempted to keep the money for himself. Instead, he took the bag to the nearest police station and through the help of an interpreter explained how he had come across the loot. The policeman on duty thanked him, saying: "You're a good boy Mr Papouis. Tell you what. If no-one claims this money after a week, we'll give it back to you." George never saw or heard from that

policeman again. Maybe the policeman had tracked down the owner of the bag of money. Maybe not.

Once settled in London, George decided to undertake a proper education for the first time in his life. He studied and completed a Diploma of Hairdressing. A year or so later he also decided to get

Maria's sister Varvara Frangou holding her daughter Christina in Kornos. 1959

married. A family friend introduced him to Maria Constantinou and the two were married six months later in 1958.

When I asked George why he waited until his late twenties to settle down he told me that he had to wait his turn in the family. It was a tradition in Cyprus to wait until older siblings were married before you could try your luck at the altar: especially if you had sisters.

"But what if your older siblings didn't get married?" I ask politely.

"I would have stayed single," he laughs. Then his expression turns serious. "It was a big mistake to have this rule in Cyprus. A big mistake."

Maria (Maroulla) Costantinou was born in the village of Delikipos on the 18th of December 1932. She is the eldest of six siblings and her parents were Constantinos and Christina Mihaelis.

She remembers that her village was very poor and life was a constant battle for survival. She would often walk barefoot to her school in Kornos (about two miles) and some days she would not have even a crust of bread to eat.

After school there were always chores to do. Maria's mother was riddled with arthritis and was often bedridden, unable to move. Being the eldest child, Maria was lumbered with the responsibility of looking after her parents and younger

George and Maria Papouis in Trafalgar Square, London. c.1958

siblings. Cooking, cleaning and fetching water from the well were daily chores for the young teenager.

George spoke fondly about his first few years as a barber in London. "I couldn't speak much English, but somehow I was able to communicate and understand my customers," he states. "They were always very good to me and I have nothing but praise for the English people."

In 1958, he opened a barbershop in Richmond, London. He called the shop Gino's Continental Hairdressing. He deliberately chose an Italian name for his business to attract the local migrant residents who had recently arrived from Italy. It was a smart move because George was soon inundated with customers. He became so popular in fact that he had to employ more barbers. The business was booming and at its peak George had eight barbers working for him.

George tells me that the Cypriots in Cyprus were often the toughest customers to please. "When I was cutting hair in my village *kafenion*, people would

often try to haggle the price with me or arrange to pay me in goods a month or even a year later. I would cut the hair of a shepherd for instance and a year later he would give me a lamb as payment."

Setting up shop in London, George found the English customers kind and very well mannered. "They appreciated my skills as a barber and often gave me tips and compliments." He was amazed to see how in England he would often receive a one or two shilling tip after each haircut. "My pockets were full of coins by the end of the day," he laughs.

George left the Richmond shop in 1961 and went to Camberwell where he worked until 1966. At this time he moved his family, (he now had a daughter named Anita born in 1965) to Southend. Here he opened a new salon called Maison Francis which he ran for over twenty years. In 1988 he opened a barber shop in the suburb of Rayleigh called Hair by George and Savvas. By this time Anita had married Savvas Savva from Kornos and together with Anita they forged a new business. Although, George retired in 2000, Anita

George and Maria Papouis. London. 1958

LEFT: George Papouis in his barber shop in Richmond, South London. 1958

and Savvas continue to run the business and have a strong local and loyal clientele.

Maria and George have been married now for almost sixty years. Although they are older and frailer they still have such a lively spirit.

At times during my interview, Maria would break into song. She has a lovely voice and it was nice to hear some old Cypriot tunes sung with great joy. Every now and again George would join his wife in song and together their melody was very sweet and touching.

ACKNOWLEDGEMENTS

I would like to thank George and Maria Papouis for making me feel so welcome when I went to visit them at Southend by Sea with my family in October 2016. Special thanks to their daughter Anita Savva for her support and assistance with documenting her parent's story.

ABOVE: Maria Papouis with her aunt Betty and sister Katerina (right). London. c.1956

LEFT: Maria Papouis at work in a ladies wear factory in the West End of London. c.1950s

Nicos
FALEKKOS

Nicos Falekkos was born of the 5th of June 1927 in the village of Kaimakli near Nicosia. He is the only son of Iphigenia and Kyriakos Falekkos and brother to Maroulla who was born a year earlier. His father Kyriakos had emigrated to America as a single young man to seek his fortune, as there was little work in Cyprus after the First World War. When Kyriakos returned in 1924, he met and married Iphigenia Papageorgiou.

In the early 1930s there was an estimated four and a half thousand Greek Cypriots living in Kaimakli and only thirty-one Turkish Cypriot residents. Apparently the Muslim population of the village had always remained at thirty-one. According to Nicos, the patron saint of the village Agia Varvara had prevented the Muslim population from increasing beyond thirty-one as punishment for trying to burn down her church years earlier.

In 1929, when Nicos was only eighteen months old, his father left for America a second time, leaving him and his three-year-old sister Maroulla in the care of their mother. At the time, the family were living with Nicos' grandparents, Nikolas and Ioulia. Nicos was later told that his father had gone to America to find steady work. His plan was to send money back to the village so they could have a better life.

In 1933, when Nicos was six years old, the family moved into a larger house that was built by his maternal grandfather.

His grandfather was an outstanding carpenter who had modern and sophisticated tools that were custom made from stainless steel. He had purchased these tools during his travels to Egypt, Morocco and Spain, where he went as a young man to master his trade. The skills and techniques he was taught overseas made him the envy of all the other carpenters in Kaimakli.

When Nicos attended primary school he earned a reputation as a rather mischievous student. He would often crawl and hide under the teacher's desk

Nicos Falekkos aged thirty-six. 1963

and wait for her to be seated so that he could pinch her legs. The teacher would become furious and insist that he remain at home with his mother. Nicos managed to curb his enthusiasm for school pranks and completed primary school in 1939.

Life in Kaimakli was rather pleasant during the 1930s and Nicos was never bored. There was always activity in the village with plenty to see and do. On weekends he would go and watch the village football team 'Achilleas FC' where his good friend Giorgios Zodiates played in the left wing. Sometimes Nicos would volunteer as a linesman during the home games. Whenever an English team played against Achilleas the stadium would fill with English supporters, mainly soldiers and their commanding officers. Watching the football on a Sunday afternoon was a simple pleasure enjoyed by the youth of Kaimakli. Besides church and the village fair, it was also one of the few times when young boys and girls could share the same space together.

Another place that was frequented by children of all ages was the movie theatre - often chaperoned by a parent, relative or older sibling. Like most children, Nicos loved the movies. One of his most enduring memories was visiting the Magic Palace cinema in Nicosia with his mother and sister for the Sunday matinee or evening screening. The Magic Palace cinema was located about fifty yards from Metaxas Square (now Eleftherias Square)

Nicos' mother Iphigenia seated on the left. Next to her are her parents Nikolas and Ioulia Papagiorgiou. In the back row are Nicos' aunts Thekla, Athena and Androniki. Nicos is standing next to his grandmother and his sister Maroulla is standing next to her grandfather. c.1936

opposite Kafenion Hadjisavva (a popular snack bar and cafeteria).

Nicos remembers that the Magic Palace had an indoor cinema and an outdoor summer cinema. The price of a movie ticket was one *grosi*. A popular snack enjoyed by many moviegoers was lightly roasted pumpkin seeds, known as *passatembo*. The trick was to crack the seed between your teeth, suck the kernel into your mouth and spit the shell onto the floor. It was common after a movie for the marble floor of the cinema to be covered in pumpkin seed shells.

Most of the movies shown at the Magic Palace were British or American with Greek subtitles. Westerns and action films were particularly popular. Nicos recalls how a movie would be shown in two parts (forty-minutes each) over two weeks. This was a clever way for the cinema to sell more tickets. Sadly, the Magic Palace was demolished in the 1970s

to make way for a supermarket.

Nicos also enjoyed going to the theatre and often participated in local plays in his village with his good friend Pepe. He would spend up to six months rehearsing with the other actors at the back of the *kafenion* before putting on a show for the locals and visitors. One particular play was called 'The Shepherdess and her Beloved'. A decade after his youth theatre days, Pepe went on to become a much-loved professional actor in Cyprus.

During the Second World War, Nicos and his sister were sent to live with their aunt Androniki, who was a teacher in the village of Pelendri at the foothills of the Troodos mountains. Many young children were sent away during the war to protect them from the possible German bombardment. One day, Nicos had a disagreement with his aunt Androniki. He stormed out of her house and decided

to walk to his aunt Athena's house in the village of Agros. He walked a distance of six miles, jumping over farm fences and hedges along the way. When he was thirsty he would drink water from puddles in the road. Unfortunately, the water was contaminated (most likely by dog urine) and he became very ill. He was rushed to hospital where it was discovered that he had contracted a parasite disease known as Echinococos (Echinococcosis). Thankfully, after undergoing surgery, he made a slow but full recovery. "My poor mother had to change the large bandage around my stomach each day for months," he recalls. Nicos still bears the scar today as a constant reminder of his near-death experience.

Venturing beyond the outskirts of their village was a rare activity for Nicos. He does remember one occasion when he went on an overnight family pilgrimage to the monastery of Apostolos Andreas.

He can also remember travelling by train to Kythrea to visit a family friend. The old railway station was located near his house on the outskirts of Kaimakli. Nicos and his friends would often run down to the railway tracks to watch the trains go past as they knew the exact times they would be arriving each day.

Nicos recalls that some people in his village were not very nice. "My mother was often cheated by the owner of the *bakaliko* (general store) in Kaimakli. When she did not have enough money to pay, he would simply write down what she owed on a tab so she could purchase her goods on credit. When her debt grew, the store owner would convince my mother to sign over family property in lieu of the money she owed. The property was worth a lot more than the debt owed." Nicos suspected that the store owner was also stealing money that his father was sending from America. "In those days all letters were delivered to the *bakaliko* which was like our village post office. The store owner would have known that a

padded letter coming from America most likely contained bank notes."

Nicos attended a high school for boys in Nicosia. He remembers walking to school with his male companions on one side of the road, while the female students who were attending the girl's school walked on the opposite side of the road. The youngsters could only admire each other from afar in those days. To

engage in conversation or flirtatious behaviour was out of the question as it was deemed disrespectful and forbidden by the elders. Overall, the moral code that kept Cypriot society in check at that time, whether for religious or cultural reasons, was well respected and observed by all.

Nicos remembers a neighbour in Kaimakli named Panjaros who had five daughters. Panjaros was very protective

ABOVE: *Iphigenia and Kyriakos Falekkos together with baby Nicos and his sister Maroulla. Nicosia. 1928*
LEFT: *Kyriakos Falekkos in America. Unknown location and date.*

of his daughters. Whenever Nicos went to play in front of their house Panjaros would shout at him. "What are you doing here? Go and play in your own yard and keep away from here."

When Nicos completed his schooling, he found work as a clerk at an import and export business in Nicosia. His job involved typing customer orders (in English) for goods that were to be imported into Cyprus from abroad. He would also arrange for goods to be exported. Although he had a good job that paid seven pounds a month, Nicos wanted to travel abroad. He was inspired by the stories a family friend named Evripides would tell him about South Africa. Evripides lived in Johannesburg and would often return to Cyprus and Kaimakli with great stories about life in South Africa. When Nicos heard that people were paid up to fifty pounds a month he was determined to go and work there. Being a British colony, South Africa became a popular and obvious destination for many Cypriots.

In 1947, aged nineteen, Nicos (and around a dozen other men from his village) left Cyprus to try their luck in Johannesburg. His mother did not want him to go, but his grandfather supported his idea of going abroad to seek a better life. In fact, it was his grandfather who took out a loan of 180 pounds to pay for his grandson's airfare and living expenses.

Nicos had only intended to work a few years in South Africa and then return to Cyprus with enough money to start a new life. Since Nicos was taught English at his high school in Nicosia, he was able to communicate easily with the local residents in Johannesburg. He lived with Evripides for the first three weeks and soon found work in a corner store after which he could afford to rent his own place to live. He remembers sharing a room with five other young Cypriot men who also worked in the city. His starting salary was around twenty pounds a month, ten pounds of which he would send back to his mother in Cyprus. In time, Nicos was able to buy his own corner store and run his own business.

Nicos lived in South Africa for twelve years before returning to Cyprus in 1958. He was thirty-two years old, unmarried and earning enough to live a good life. What prompted his return to Cyprus was a significant event. His father had

returned from America and was now back in Kaimakli living with his mother. Nicos' first cousin Ermioni insisted that he should return to Cyprus to see his father.

Nicos had remained in touch with his

Nicos with his sister Maroulla. c.1933

father in America through letters. Once a fortnight, if not once a month, he would write and receive a letter from his father. Communication between the two men had improved once Nicos had moved to South Africa.

Nicos sold his supermarket business in Johannesburg and boarded a plane back to Nicosia where he was finally reunited with the man he had not seen for thirty years. His father, mother and a few relatives were all there at the airport to greet him. Needless to say, it was quite an emotional moment.

Nicos recalls the surreal feeling of being introduced to a stranger at the airport and told, 'this is your father.'

The two men spent many hours in conversation (often through tears). "All I knew about my father was that he worked as a chef and waiter in various bars and restaurants in Virginia and South Carolina during the Great Depression. What I really wanted to know was why he left Cyprus in 1929. Why did he leave us for such a long time? This was my chance to find out some answers and the truth."

Nicos was respectful with his father and tried not to become angry or emotional. He remembers staying up late most nights, sometimes until two or three in the morning, conversing and exchanging stories with him about their life apart. Unfortunately, after countless hours of questioning Nicos never received a substantial answer that would reveal the truth, the absolute truth as to why his father had stayed away for all those years. The sense of loss and abandonment he felt as a young boy would remain with him for the rest of his life.

Now that he was back in Cyprus and reunited with his family, Nicos tried to find work and resettle in Kaimakli. Although his reunion with his father was somewhat bittersweet, he would eventually find other forms of distraction to fill the void in his life – marriage being one of them.

In 1959 Nicos was introduced to a young girl named Tsikkina Michaeli Savva, from the nearby village of Sia.

Tsikkina was born in 1941 and was the daughter of Myrianthi and Michaeli Savva. Her mother Myrianthi was from a poor family from Kornos and when she married Michaeli Savva she thought she would be marrying into wealth. This was not the case. Michaeli was a simple farmer and worked in his *perivoli* (field),

BACK ROW: Nicos' aunt Androniki, his mother Iphigenia, sister Maroulla and Nicos.
FRONT ROW: His grandparents, Nikolas and Ioulia Papageorgiou. c.1943

fourteen pounds a month.

"I was a very good student at school," states Tsikkina. "In fact, I was the only one of my four sisters to be sent to Nicosia to complete a formal education. In those days, a high school diploma would often lead to a good and respectable career."

In May 1959, a family acquaintance arranged a meeting between Tsikkina and Nicos as they were deemed to be of marriageable age and a good match. Tsikkina had just finished school and was employed as a clerk at a reputable law firm in Nicosia. In order to conceal the fourteen-year age difference between them, Nicos was told that Tsikkina was twenty-two years old (not eighteen) and Tsikkina was told that Nicos was twenty-eight years old (not thirty-two). Their actual ages were only revealed after the wedding.

Nicos and Tsikkina were married on the 28th of June 1959. Nicos decided to return to Johannesburg with his new bride. Their plan was to work solidly for five years and then return to Cyprus to settle permanently close to their families. Although Tsikkina was daunted by the prospect of leaving her friends and family behind in Cyprus she agreed with the move, providing it was only for five years. As it turned out, Tsikkina and Nicos stayed and raised four children in Johannesburg: Kyriakos, Anthia, Michael and Iphigenia.

Life in South Africa was difficult for many Cypriots. Due to a lack of language skills, most immigrants chose to work long hours in convenience stores. Nicos would wake before sunrise and be ready to open his store at 6am and work until 10.30pm. His store was open seven days a week all year round. He would only close for half days on Greek Easter Sunday, Christmas day and New Year's Day. Tsikkina would join Nicos at the store after taking the children to school. Nicos often went home for a nap in the afternoons. Tsikkina would go home at 7pm to cook and bathe her children before returning to work in the store until closing time. There was a strong Greek Orthodox community in South Africa that helped many Cypriots to keep a close connection with their religion and cultural background.

It was impossible for Nicos and his family to take any holidays together, as someone had to always look after the store. He did manage to return to Cyprus a few times while his parents were alive.

growing vegetables, pulses and wheat to take to the market in Nicosia and also to sell in the neighbouring villages. Myrianthi worked in the fields and quite often worked on the roads around Sia repairing and replacing the stones before and after the winter rains. She also worked in the local copper mine near the village to earn extra money to raise her four daughters and one son.

Although Tsikkina was born in Sia she attended the PanCypriot Girls Academy on Ledra Street. This was a private boarding school owned by Athena Ioannidou. Tsikkina recalls that the school fees were four pounds a year and her parents had to pay an additional two pounds a month for board. The students had to provide their own food. By the time she graduated in 1958, the boarding fees had risen to

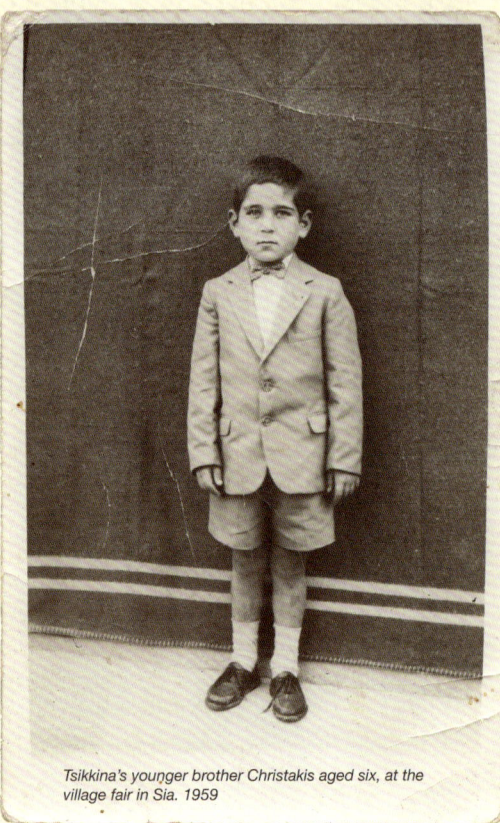

Tsikkina's younger brother Christakis aged six, at the village fair in Sia. 1959

Tsikkina (back row in the middle) at the village school in Sia. 1953

He saw his father two more times, once in 1966 and again in 1971. As it was, he could only calculate nine months of his entire life that he spent together with his father.

Like most Cypriots, Nicos and Tsikkina worked hard and concentrated on raising and educating their children and providing a comfortable family life together

They always strived to ensure that they remained connected to their Cypriot heritage. Nicos was also proud to be able to help his sister Maroulla in Cyprus by sending her money to support her children's university education in Greece.

In 2005, after forty-five years in South Africa and after their four children had become independant adults, Nicos and Tsikkina Falekkos finally retired and moved back to Cyprus.

What they discovered was a vastly different homeland to the one they left behind. Gone were the sleepy towns and villages with their mostly farm-based inhabitants. Gone too were many of the traditional and cultural crafts so readily available and practiced during their upbringing. Instead they found a modern, built-up environment designed for tourism, consumerism and commercial enterprise.

It was my great pleasure to meet Nicos and Tsikkina Falekkos in 2016. Even at ninety years of age, I could sense the pain and sorrow Nicos still felt by the mystery of his father's absence. As his voice quivered and his eyes welled up, I was aware that the hurt he must have felt as a young boy had always remained with him. Despite not having a father figure in his own life, Nicos overcame the loss by becoming an ever-present and loving father and grandfather himself.

Sadly Nicos Falekkos passed away in May 2017 just shy of his ninety-first birthday. He will be sadly missed.

ACKNOWLEDGEMENTS
I am grateful to have met Nicos and Tsikkina in Cyprus in 2016. I feel privileged to have been trusted to record their living memories for *Tales of Cyprus*. Special thanks to their son Kyriakos (Kyri) Falekkos for all his support and assistance both in London and Cyprus. I am sure this interview will become a treasured keepsake for the entire Falekkos family.

LEFT: Tsikkina and her friend Katina walking through the streets of Sia. 1957

FAR LEFT: Nicos Falekkos (aged twenty) in Johannesburg in 1947.

BELOW: Nicos and Tsikinna walking down the streets of Kaimakli on their wedding day, 28th June 1959.

Elias
PEPPIS

Elias' brother Yiannis (left) with his cousin at the Dimosios public park in Nicosia. c.1942

E lias Peppis was born in the Maronite village of Agia Marina in 1931. At the time, the village boasted a mixed community of both Turkish and Maronite Cypriots. Although Maronite Cypriots lived in several villages and towns across Cyprus, they were mostly settled in the villages of Agia Marina, Kormakitis, Asomatos and Karpasia.

Elias' mother Christalla Iosifidiou was only fifteen when she married twenty-eight-year-old Peppis Bartella from Asomatos in 1928. Shortly after Elias was born however, his parents separated due to a financial dispute between their two families. Separation between couples was frowned upon in Cyprus at that time. "Anybody who separated from their wife or husband was shunned and discriminated by all other Catholics in the village," Elias tells me.

Elias and his older brother Yiannis were forced to live with their father in his village of Asomatos. Their mother went to live with her parents in Varosi. The two boys felt like outcasts; their parent's separation had a profound and devastating effect on them. For Elias, the feeling of not having a mother to visit was sad, and depressing.

In 1937, twenty-four year old Christalla converted to the Orthodox faith in order to be granted a divorce.

As a Maronite, the Catholic religion did not allow divorce. In 1939, two years after her divorce was granted, Christalla decided it was best to leave Cyprus (and the scandal) to travel to England.

Life for Peppis Bartella was also difficult following the divorce. Elias remembers that whenever his father would go to sit at his local *kafenion* (coffee house) the other villagers would immediately get up and leave to avoid being seen with a sinner. After a few years, Peppis became so depressed that he decided to leave his village and go and live and work in Nicosia. He sent his two sons to Varosi to live with their maternal grandparents Ioannis and Eleni Iosifidou. By this stage, their mother Christalla had already left Cyprus.

Peppis eventually remarried. This time to an Orthodox Cypriot who herself had an interesting past. As the story goes, she was engaged to a man who was wanted for murder. Her fiancé stabbed and killed a man after a heated argument and then fled into the mountains to avoid being captured, leaving her behind to the wrath of the locals. Like Peppis, she was shunned and outcast by the other villagers. That was until she met Peppis. They decided to escape to England together, away from the persecution of the Catholic Church and the scorn of their fellow Cypriots.

In 1942, Elias went to study at the secondary school in Varosi. For two years he did not tell anyone he was a Maronite for fear he would be teased. Instead he pretended to be an Orthodox Christian just like the other students at the

Ioannis and Eleni Iosifidou with their daughter Christalla (mother of Elias Peppis). Christalla was around five years old when this photo was taken. c.1917

Gymnasium. One day however, during a religion lesson the Orthodox priest asked him to recite the Nicene Creed. When he left out the word 'apostolic' his secret was out and he was teased and bullied by many of the students.

Elias also remembers that on New Year's Day, he would wander around the village collecting money from his relatives. "On the first day of the year," he explains. "The children of the village would wear little hessian bags around their necks and go and visit their Godparents, Grandparents and other relatives to wish them *Hronia Polla* (a long life). The relatives would then place some money in the bags." Elias collected around eight *dekares* that day which was around one-quarter of a shilling.

Every Easter, grandmother Eleni would make *flaounes* (cheese pies) just like the Greek Orthodox mothers. Many Maronite Christians share the same customs and traditions as their Greek Cypriot neighbours.

A few years after Elias' mother Christalla had settled in England she met and married a young Greek Cypriot soldier named Victoras who was serving in the British Army during the Second World War. Elias suspects that as a British solider, marrying a single mother such as Christalla, Victoras could double his salary to around fourteen shillings a week.

In 1944, Christalla sent a telegram to her parents in Varosi requesting that her sons be sent to her. The following year Elias and his brother Yiannis were reunited with their mother. At first, they all lived together in a rented three-story flat in Central London, near the British Museum. "Twenty people were cramped together in that house," recalls Elias. "My brother and I slept in the kitchen while our mother and stepfather slept in one of the four bedrooms. There was one toilet for twenty people and it was located outside the house. It was terrible. There was no bathroom and our gas was supplied by the use of a coin-operated meter. In winter, my mother would buy paraffin oil from the 'paraffin man' every morning to light the heater. It was very basic accommodation."

Christalla had relatives who owned a restaurant on Charing Cross Road near Trafalgar Square called The Anglo-America. Elias would spend time after school washing dishes at this restaurant

Elias' parents, Peppis Bartella and Christalla Iosifidiou on their wedding day in Nicosia on the 5th August 1928.

earning around one pound a week. This was quite a lot of money for a fifteen year old boy. "I remember the steak and chips deal at the Anglo-American was about two and half shillings," says Elias. "The sausages and chips deal was one shilling and three pence. You couldn't eat more than five shillings' worth. There were days when the queues extended out of the restaurant and down the street. I was allowed to eat as much as I wanted since I worked there."

During and after the Second World War, the British government were concerned about food shortages in Britain and therefore introduced a food rationing system. Each person was given a coupon book and had to register and buy their food from chosen shops. There were no supermarkets, so people had to visit speciality shops on the High Street to buy meat, vegetables, bread and other goods.

Christalla and Victoras eventually moved out of their rental property and bought their own house in London. They had earned enough money to also buy a fish and chip restaurant on the popular seaside resort of Barry Island in Wales. The shop was appropriately named 'Barry Fish and Chips' and was only opened during the summer months. Victoras used to travel back and forth from Barry Island

George Bartella (aged around thirty-seven) with his mother Varvarou. Standing behind are first cousins Marie Bartella (aged seventeen) and Michael Bartella (aged four). 1924

used the money that he earned working as a waiter in a very exclusive night club called The Cyros Club. The Royal family were amongst many famous patrons that would dine at the club.

Elias retells a funny story that happened at the Cyros Club one night in 1947. He was ascending the marble staircase holding hot plates of food to serve to the newly engaged Princess Elizabeth and Prince Phillip. When he got to the top of the stairs to approach Phillip, who was sitting at the head of the table, the Prince made a particularly large and expressive hand gesture which knocked the hot plates out of Elias' hands, causing them to fall and crash onto the marble staircase. Everyone jumped out of their seats thinking they had heard gunshots.

The furious manager immediately fired Elias on the spot, but thankfully Prince Phillip intervened to say that it was his fault and Elias was able to keep his job.

Elias jokes that perhaps it was Phillip's Greek genes that were to blame for the elaborate hand gestures that he made whilst he was talking.

When Elias turned twenty in 1951, he began his compulsory military service for the British army. On the completion of his service two years later, he decided to enter the fashion trade and became an experienced pattern-cutter.

Although Elias had dated several English girls in London he decided in his late twenties that he should return to Cyprus to find a wife. He discovered that there were few eligible Cypriot girls in London at that time.

In 1958, he returned to his father's village of Asomatos. "The first time I entered the *kafenion* in Asomatos, the owners arranged for me to meet and marry their daughter," says Elias. "Her name was Eleni Ioannou. She was eighteen and I was twenty-seven. Within three months we were married."

When Elias enquired about asking Eleni out on a date he was promptly warned by the locals that dating was not allowed. It seemed that living in London had caused Elias to forget the cultural and traditional norms of his village. He was advised to watch Eleni from afar as she walked through the village. He waited patiently for the moment to arrive where he could get a good look at her. Unfortunately, just as Eleni walked past, some cattle appeared and blocked

to his home in London. Yiannis did not get along with his stepfather Victoras and so in 1946 he left to go and live with a Greek friend. Elias left soon after and went to live with the owners of the Anglo-American restaurant.

In 1962, Victoras was driving back home one night from his Barry Island restaurant when he collided with a car that was stationary in the middle of the road. He died as a result of the accident. He was fifty-four years old. Christalla was devastated, but continued to run the restaurant on her own until 1971. After that she retired and was able to live out the rest of her life on a State pension.

When Elias arrived in London in 1945, he went to study at a Catholic School for two years. He then funded his own private education to improve his English. He

Elias aged fifteen. London, 1946

his view. He had to therefore base his decision to marry her on a fleeting glimpse of her that day.

Elias and Eleni were married in Asomatos on the 28th of June 1959. They left Cyprus by ship two months later and arrived in London after a five-day voyage. A year later, their daughter Katrina was born, followed by their son Michael (Mike) in 1963.

ABOVE: *Elias during his compulsory military service in Bicester, Oxford, 1951. He was twenty years old.*

Elias and his family lived for six years in a rental property on Gower Street in the heart of London. In 1966, they bought a house approximately ten miles away in Dollis Hill, North West London.

Elias eventually used his pattern cutting skills to open a dressmaking factory, together with his wife Eleni, in Camden Central. They worked hard together and were able to establish a very profitable business. Eleni became a competent machinist and began to teach other women at the factory how to sew.

In 1993, after thirty years in the rag trade and with the fashion industry in a steady decline, Elias and Eleni decided to close their factory in Camden Central. Elias continued to work for a further three years at several other fashion houses until at sixty-five years of age, he finally retired with a pension.

ACKNOWLEDGEMENTS

I would like to thank Elias Peppis for meeting me in Palmer's Green in London in 2016 to share his wonderful family photographs and memories with me. Thank you also to his daughter Katrina Makrides for her kind assistance in helping to proof and check this translated version of her father's life story. Special thanks to Kyri Falekkos for introducing me to Elias.

Elias (aged twelve) and his brother Yiannis (aged fourteen) with their grandparents, Ioannis and Eleni Iosifidou. Famagusta, 1943

Costas
KARATZAS

Costas Karatzas' passport photo. 1975

Costas Karatzas was born in the town of Lapithos on the 25th of July 1930. Lapithos at that time had a population of around five thousand inhabitants with over a third being Turkish Cypriot.

Costas was the middle child in his Greek Cypriot family. His parents Petros Karatzas and Anastasia Panayiotou had four other sons (Yiorkos, Chrysostomos, Panayis and Apostolos) and two daughters (Eleni and Maria). The family owned around three hundred olive trees as well as carob and fig trees. The children would often accompany their mother Anastasia into their fields in late August and early September to gather the ripe olives and carobs.

Costas and his family lived in a large house above the *kafenion* (coffee house) that was owned by his Godfather. This building was next to a house that was full of rabbits. In those days, it was common to own part of a house, or a field or even a tree. One person may own a parcel of land while someone else might own the trees that grew on that land.

From his house Costas could hear the dogs barking at night on the Turkish mainland, sixty miles away.

From the age of six, Costas spent a lot of time at his Godfather's *kafenion*. On occasion; he would even be taxed with the task of making coffee for the patrons. He enjoyed watching his grandfather playing *tavli* (backgammon) and cards with the other men at the *kafenion* and

was able to learn the rules of the game purely by observation.

As a young boy, Costas played football barefoot with the other neighbourhood children on a dirt road near his house, using oranges as balls. One time, a Jeep with English soldiers drove by and stopped to watch the youngsters at their game. "Can you spare a few oranges for us?" one of the soldiers asked. Costas obliged and watched in astonishment as the soldiers ate the fruit, skin and all. Before they departed the soldiers gave the boys a carton of cigarettes in gratitude. That was the day ten-year-old Costas and his friends began to smoke.

As well as playing football, Costas was also a keen swimmer. On very hot days, he would walk two miles down the mountain path with his friends to a nearby beach and swim out to a great distance. "I would swim so far out that I could no longer see the Pentadaktylos Mountain," he boasts. "We used to all run into the water naked without any bathing suit and swim until we were tired. Then we would flop onto our backs and bask in the sun. If we were hungry we would eat shellfish and crabs that we plucked out of the sand. If we were thirsty, we would drink fresh water from natural fountains that squirted up out of the sea."

During the Second World War, Costas and his friends would swim out to greet the refugee boats that were arriving from Greece. They would scamper onto the boats (much to the surprise of the

refugees) and direct them towards the shore. Lapithos was soon full of refugees from Greece, placing further strain on the financial viability of the town. After the war, many refugees chose to make Cyprus their new home.

Chrysoula Karatzas (nee Charalambitdou). Nicosia, 1952

Costas and his friends had many adventures in and around the village and they enjoyed a rather idyllic childhood. The boys were also quite resourceful. On their many treks beyond the village they would find and eat wild mushrooms. They would eat cucumbers, tomatoes, lemons, oranges or whatever other edible delights God had placed in their path (or perhaps, over a stone wall in someone's field).

In the evenings Costas and his friends would spend their time with the adult men at the *kafenion* listening to British and Greek broadcasts from a tiny radio connected to a car battery.

Costas' father Petros Karatzas was a talented blacksmith and welder, continuing on with a family trade that spanned a few generations. He was a master craftsman and was able to fashion nearly anything out of metal, including farming tools (such as sickles and ploughs), axes, knives and even shotguns.

Apart from working with metal, Petros would cut bottles in half with a hot wire to make drinking glasses. He could also fashion combs out of animal bone.

Before the outbreak of the Second World War, Petros had steady work receiving many orders for his metal objects. At times he was making around twenty-four knives a day to meet the demand coming from Nicosia and had to employ other metalworkers and a few apprentices.

During the war however, a lot of people in Cyprus became unemployed and the demand for handmade goods and handicrafts declined rapidly. Due to a lack of business, Petros joined the Cypriot Volunteer Regiment (CVR) mainly because the British Army paid the volunteers two shillings a day while their families received an additional half shilling. Petros had volunteered once before during the Great War back in 1916. He was twenty-four years of age then and was part of the Cypriot Mule Corps travelling as far as the city of Varna in Bulgaria. Petros, who was born in 1892, was forty-eight years old when he enlisted with the CVR. He had to ask the *mukhtari* (headman) of Lapithos to forge his application so that he would appear young enough to qualify for the Regiment. In any case, he was not sent overseas but remained in a training camp for a year before returning to Lapithos.

Costas attended both primary and secondary school in Lapithos. "I remember that in my first year at the Gymnasium I was taught, English, French and Latin. Many of our teachers came from Greece. The school fees were five shillings a term. Unfortunately, my education came to an abrupt end when I was kicked out of the ninth grade because my father did not pay the first term fees on time." The year was 1945 and Costas had just turned fifteen.

In 1946, a family friend from Lapithos found Costas a job at the Magic Palace cinema in Nicosia. His main task was to clean the aisles and collect the rubbish. The Magic Palace provided sleeping quarters for its employees in a ramshackle old building. Costas remembers that he taught himself to ride a bicycle by practicing on the cinema bike that was used to collect and deliver movie reels.

In the late 1940s, Costas found work at the Hotel Atlanta in Nicosia as a kitchen boy and pageboy. One day he met King

Farouk of Egypt who had a most unusual request. "He asked me to go and find him a Cypriot telephone book that he could keep as a souvenir. I jumped on my bicycle and rode to the offices of Cable and Wireless Limited (the British-run telecommunications company) to seek one out. At first the girls at the exchange were suspicious and ignored my request. It was only after my boss from the Atlanta intervened that the operators relented and gave me a telephone book." The king was very grateful and rewarded Costas with five shillings. Even the king's sister, Princess Fawzia, who was also staying at the hotel gave Costas a gift; an embroidered napkin.

Costas' next job was at the Forest Park Hotel in Platres (in the Troodos mountains). He worked as a waiter in the junior dining room, helping to serve the children of the guests their morning, noon and evening meals. At times there would be up to seventy-five children gathered together in the junior dining room. Parents ate separately at the hotel, enjoying a more relaxing and quieter dining experience in the main hall.

Costas was paid around three pounds a month as a junior waiter but often earned a few extra shillings in tips from some of the grateful parents. He was soon able to afford his own bicycle (a brand new, green Rayleigh), which he bought for eighteen pounds.

One day, Costas became very ill after eating a sesame pita. "I cannot remember why I got so sick after eating that pita," he says. "But I was advised by a local doctor to have my appendix taken out and I was sent by car from Platres to the Central Hospital in Nicosia. From there I was sent by bus to a hospital in Kyrenia. I remember that Doctor Thornton operated on me and stapled my wound shut using eighteen metal clips. This doctor even loaned me his bicycle to ride back to Nicosia after my operation. Would you believe I rode about eighteen miles on this bicycle straight after my operation?"

Costas enjoyed working at the Forest Park Hotel. He laughs as he remembers sleeping in the cellar or on top of a bench. "The junior staff at this hotel were not provided with any sleeping quarters," he exclaims. "We had to make do with sleeping anywhere that was dry and warm." He also enjoyed interacting with people from all over the world. In time,

Costas Karatzas on his bicycle in the Public Gardens opposite the Paphos Gate in Nicosia. c.1949

special barracks located behind the hotel and they even had their clothes washed and ironed for free.

Costas met Chrysoula Charalambidou at the Ledra Palace in 1951. Chrysoula would often ride her bicycle to the hotel to visit her mother Maria who worked in the hotel laundry. Chrysoula's father Giorgalis Hajicharalambos had died when she was only eleven years old. Her widowed mother was left to raise five children on her own. Chrysoula was born in the neighbourhood of Agios Loukas in Nicosia on the 2nd of February 1937. Her parents originated from the village of Karmi, four miles west of Kyrenia.

"When I asked her how old she was, she told me she was eighteen," Costas laughs. "She lied to me. To tell you the truth, she looked a lot older so I believed her. It was only after her mother gave her consent for us to get married when I discovered that she was only fourteen and a half years old. The church would not allow us to get married. The legal age in Cyprus at that time was sixteen." Chrysoula's mother approached a priest (Papa Giorgkis) from Trahona and convinced him to change her daughter's date and place of birth on an official document to show that she was older.

Costas' parents were understandably concerned that their son was besotted with a girl so young. Like most parents in Cyprus, they preferred their son to marry somebody older and preferably, someone from a family that they knew. Costas was adamant. "Don't come to meet her if your answer is no," he told his parents. "Don't even ask for *prika* (dowry)." Costas had strong personal views about the custom of bride-dowry. His views were influenced by the unreasonable behaviour of a man betrothed to his sister Eleni. The man was promised a parcel of land and six traditional reed chairs. When the chairs arrived he threatened to call off the wedding because they did not have a coloured pattern in the weave. The villagers forced him to reconsider and he was unceremoniously frog-marched to the church to marry Eleni. The fuss over his sister's dowry left a lasting impression on Costas who decided he just wanted his young bride and nothing else, much to his parents' surprise. Costas boasted how he built and furnished his matrimonial home with his own money, ignoring another age-old family tradition whereby the

Costas became fluent in Italian and French by conversing with the guests. He also managed to learn quite a few words and phrases in Arabic and both Turkish Cypriot and mainland Turkish. Many of the guests who visited the hotel came from Egypt, Palestine, Syria, England, Sweden, Hungary and Yugoslavia.

Between 1949 and 1955, Costas worked as a room service attendant and

waiter at the Ledra Palace where he met a fair number of famous and wealthy people including British actors Dirk Borgarde and Sam Kydd and a number of American aristocrats. His job was to deliver lunch-boxes and evening meals as summoned. At times he was asked to take various guests on private tours to visit some of island's famous landmarks.

At the Ledra Palace, the staff slept in

bride's family built the matrimonial home.

In 1951, Costas met a popular post-war Greek singer named Sophia Vembo at the Ledra Palace when he was asked to deliver breakfast to her room. Sophia was visiting Nicosia with her mother and performing a few shows at the Pallas Cinema Theatre. Sophia took a liking to Costas and invited him (and his fiancé) to come to her evening show. "Thank you Miss Vembo," he said politely. "But I work day and night and it would be difficult for me to find the time." Sophia was furious. "What did you say?" she shouted, "People fight one another to get tickets to my show and you don't want to come." She then slapped Costas hard across the face

papers stating otherwise. The newlyweds lived together in Trahona.

Two months after they were married Chrysoula gave birth to her first child Giorgia. Her second child Anastasia was born 17 months later and her son Marios three years later. By the time Chrysoula had turned twenty, she had three children under the age of five. Three years later, her fourth child Eleni (Elli) was born.

Costas was working at the Ledra Palace in November 1955 when a fellow worker (and EOKA member) Yiannakis Pafitis attempted to assassinate Field Marshall Sir John Harding. At the time the Governor was expected to arrive, Pafitis (the hotel electrician) plunged

the grenades exploded he flung himself onto the floor and remained there face down until the lights came back on. Pafitis was also questioned but remarkably was let off, as he successfully fooled the authorities about his whereabouts.

At the beginning of 1956, Costas was approached by the Italian head waiter at the Ledra Palace who, for unknown reasons demanded that he should shave off his moustache. "And if I don't?" Costas insisted. The head waiter became furious. He told Costas that if he didn't shave off his moustache he could kiss his job good-bye. "In that case, ciao!" replied Costas. He packed his belongings and left the Ledra Palace.

With his hospitality career now over, Costas made the decision to join his brother in the fire brigade. In those days, the ambulance, fire brigade and police force belonged to the same department. Even though Costas was applying for a job with the fire brigade he was actually applying for a Police Constable position. Because he was only five feet and five inches tall he was deemed too short to serve as a fire fighter, so instead he was given a post at the central command centre (switchboard) in Nicosia.

His ability to speak perfect Greek, Turkish and English helped to secure his position there.

Costas was required to work in alternating shifts of eight hours and twenty-four hours. His gruelling work schedule caused him at times to suffer from insomnia. He remembers that on one particular Sunday he received seventy-five emergency calls from across the island. His job involved answering the phones, recording each emergency into a special logbook and alerting the fire fighters in each district. In those days, wireless radio was used for audio or spoken messages and a Teletypewriter was used to send written messages. In the 1950s, Costas discovered that members of the opposing guerrilla groups EOKA and TNT deliberately lit many of the fires.

Before Cyprus gained its independence in 1960, Costas was required to answer the phone in Greek, Turkish and English. "I would answer each call with '*fire brigade, πυροσβεστική, itfaiye*' and depending on the caller, I would continue to speak in their preferred language. After independence, I only answered and spoke in Greek."

Chrysoula (aged eighteen) with her bicycle and two friends. Trahona, Nicosia. c.1955.

and he promptly accepted her invitation. The next night Costas and his fiancé Chrysoula found themselves seated in the front row of the theatre. "It was funny," he said amusingly. "When we turned up to the Pallas Theatre, the door attendant refused to let us in. He didn't believe that I knew Sophia Vembo. I guess we didn't look like the typical theatregoers. Once I showed him her personal invitation, he stepped aside and with an angry frown let us enter."

Costas and Chrysoula were married on the 5th of October 1952. Chrysoula was still only fifteen, despite the forged church

the ballroom into darkness. He then rolled two grenades across the floor towards the Governor's table where they exploded. Unbeknown to Pafitis, the Governor was not there. He had been delayed at a previous appointment and therefore managed to escape the assassination attempt.

Fortunately, nobody was killed by the explosion. All forty-two employees of the Ledra Hotel were rounded up and questioned by the British authorities. Whoever did not have an airtight alibi was immediately dismissed from their job. Costas was able to prove that after

4

These pages must

DL/49858

not be removed or defaced

Form P. 167.]

CYPRUS POLICE — DRIVER'S PERMIT

No. 302

Name COSTAS P. KARATZAS

Rank PC

Date of issue 25/5/1965 No. 2874

Valid for vehicles : Class A, B, C, D, E, F, G, H, I, J.

Date 25/5/1965

Issuing Officer

for C.F.O

Keep this Permit in your Driving Licence.

Costas' Driver's Permit and Identity Card. Date of issue: 25th May 1965

The Karatzas family lived happily in Trahona, Nicosia until their world was turned upside down in 1974. Just after daybreak on the 20th of July, Costas was finishing his night shift in the control room when he received a terrifying phone call from his wife, Chrysoula. "She told me she could see Turkish paratroopers landing in the distance not far from our house. I couldn't leave my post so I just ordered my wife to run to safety. 'Take the car and the children and get out of there at once', I shouted down the phone."

Chrysoula gathered her children, Giorgia, Marios and Elli (as well as a live chicken) and sped off to her sister's house in Pallouriotissa in Nicosia. Giorgia was especially fragile and distraught. She had just celebrated her wedding a month earlier and her husband had been captured and imprisoned during a military *coup* at the Presidential Palace.

Chrysoula's other daughter Anastasia had immigrated to Australia to study a few years earlier and was living with her aunt Maria. She would play a pivotal role in organising the official papers and visas to help her family immigrate to Australia.

Costas' father Petros (now a widower) refused to leave his home in Lapithos. He was captured by the invading Turkish army and remained a prisoner in his own home for six months until the Red Cross managed to secure his release.

Costas and his traumatised family arrived in Melbourne on the 2nd of May 1975. They stayed with Costas' sister Maria and her family until they moved into a nearby house that was owned by Anastasia. Without a bicycle or a car, Costas walked everywhere, sometimes covering thirty miles a day. The long walks gave him time to reflect on his past life and to contemplate the future. Returning to Cyprus was not an option anymore for his family. They were now refugees.

By the end of 1975, Costas managed to get his Australian driver's licence and almost immediately bought himself a car; a Mazda 1500 sedan. He decided to take his family on a road trip to Adelaide for Christmas where his wife's brother and family lived. When the family stopped to have fish and chips in the town of Dimboola, the owner of the shop recognized Costas. He was Cypriot too and remembered Costas from the Ledra Palace when he came for a visit in 1952. He especially remembered Costas delivering his egg and bacon breakfast in the mornings. The two men embraced and spent time reminiscing about the past.

Costas was unemployed for a little while but eventually found work at Sidchrome Tools in West Heidelberg. A few months later he left Sidchrome and joined the staff at Commonwealth Industrial Gases (CIG) in Preston where he worked until he retired in 1995.

When I first met Costas to interview him for *Tales of Cyprus* in 2014, he was comfortably seated in his 'man-cave' (which was actually his garage) surrounded by many gadgets and tools. He kept himself busy by tinkering with one thing or another. The walls of his garage were adorned with Cypriot paraphernalia. His vintage radio was tuned to his favourite Greek station and his TV was also broadcasting his favourite cable channel from Cyprus. He looked very content.

ACKNOWLEDGEMENTS

I would like to thank Costas and Chrysoula Karatzas for their hospitality and for sharing their memories about the past with me. I would also like to thank their daughter Anastasia Karatzas Constanti for all her support. Special thanks to Costa Constanti for his help with double-checking the facts of his grandfather's life story.

32226

Kyriacos & Giorgios MICHAELIDES

ABOVE: *Kyriacos Michaelides. c.1930*

LEFT: *Giorgios and Philia Michaelides on their wedding day in 1919. Alexandria, Egypt.*

Kyriacos and Giorgios Michaelides were two of five sons born to Eleni and Michalis Tsangari in the village of Katokopia, near Morfou, at the turn of the twentieth century. Their mother Eleni Karayianni was from the village of Milia and was married to their father Michalis when she was only fourteen years old.

Not much is known about the Michaelides family from Katokopia other than Michalis Tsangari (originally from the village of Politiko), was a successful spice merchant who became very wealthy importing and exporting goods between Cyprus and Egypt during the Ottoman Era. By the time of his death, Michalis was affluent enough to give each of his sons a very comfortable inheritance. One story tells how he would loan money to many poor peasant fathers in Katokopia so they could afford to marry off their daughters. Remarkably, he would never go back to collect the money that was owed to him. Many young brides in Katokopia were better off because Michalis was able to pay for their dowry.

Giorgios Michaelides was born in 1899 and was the youngest of the five brothers; namely Kostas, Kyriacos, Vovos and Yiannis. He followed in his father's footsteps and was trained as a spice merchant. When he turned sixteen, he was sent to live in Alexandria, Egypt, to set up a permanent overseas base for the family business. In 1919, he met and married fifteen year old Philia Tsoukala, a refugee from Smyrni in Turkey. Philia had migrated to Alexandria with her parents.

Giorgios and Philia had two children: Mary, born in 1922, and Michael (Michaelakis) born in 1925.

The children were raised in relatively wealthy surroundings and lived a life of prestige thanks to the successful business fortune amassed by their father. Giorgios and Philia were part of the Greek-Egyptian aristocracy and high society. They owned a furniture shop and a number of restaurants in Alexandria.

Giorgios had a deep passion for photography. His accumulated wealth helped him to afford many cameras and take many photographs of his family. It is a rare and remarkable feat that he was able to record so many important moments in his life and be able to compile many albums full of photographs.

Giorgios' son Michael was apparently very athletic, musically gifted and highly intelligent. One story claims that after he graduated from college he left Egypt to join the British Secret Service during the Second World War and was never heard of again. It is not known how or why this happened. Another story suggests he was working for the British Government in the 1950s as a nuclear scientist. Although Giorgios took hundreds of photographs of his son in Alexandria, he never mentioned or spoke of him again after the war had ended. There is the ominous presence of a real family mystery here – or perhaps a great family secret.

Giorgios and Philia Michaelides with their baby daughter Mary and Philia's father k.Tsoukalas. Alexandria. c.1923

Giorgios Michaelides. Alexandria, c.1918

Giorgios' daughter Mary, on the other hand, stayed close to her parents throughout her life. In 1949, aged twenty-six, she married an English officer named Edward Charles Bradbury (Charlie) who was eleven years older than her. Mary met Charlie at her workplace in Alexandria. He was an accountant and living in Suez at the time. Mary and Charlie did not have any children of their own.

In 1953, the Egyptian President Nassar issued an edict to expel all Greeks and Jews from his country. The government seized all the property that belonged to the Michaelides family in Alexandria. Giorgios Michaelides was forced to flee Egypt with his wife, daughter and son-in law and return to Cyprus.

Despite losing almost all of his accumulated wealth, Giorgios opened a bar in Nicosia in 1954 and for a while it seemed that things were starting to look prosperous again. His daughter Mary found work as a typist at the Civil Labour Office of the Royal Air Force in Nicosia.

One fateful day in the early 1960s, some local youths who shared anti-British sentiments took offence that Giorgios had a British son-in-law and decided to detonate a homemade bomb in his bar. Giorgios escaped with a few cuts and bruises but a young female patron died in the blast. Fearing the worst, Giorgios uprooted his family for the second time, and left Cyprus onboard the migrant ship SS Aurelia bound for Australia. They docked in Melbourne in April, 1964.

Giorgios and Philia settled into a quiet life of retirement in Melbourne, sharing a house with their daughter Mary and son-in-law Charlie in Wantirna South. Mary and Charlie both secured administrative work for the Department of Defence. Philia died in Melbourne in 1982, aged seventy-eight. Giorgios died three years later in 1985, aged eighty five.

Giorgios' older brother Kyriacos was born in 1895, in Katokopia. When he was seventeen years old he married Milou

Mitzika. Together they had eight children: Michaelis, Giorkos, Maritsa, Electra, Christalla, Philia, Ioanna and Lampidona.

Kyriacos became the chief mechanic and salesman at the Singer sewing machine factory in Nicosia. He was often seen riding his Rayleigh bicycle from village to village repairing and servicing sewing machines upon request. Some say that he was the first person in the village of Katokopia to own a bicycle.

Kyriacos was also an accomplished machinist, mechanic, sculptor and inventor. Always creative and busy with his hands, he became well known in Cyprus for his plaster models of fruit and other ornamental objects including buildings. His plaster scale model of the Apostolos Varnavas and Ilarionas church from Peristerona won first prize at the Limassol Fair in 1963. In fact, President Makarios presented him with the award. But it was his hand-painted imitation fruit

Giorgios Michaelides at the wheel with friends in Alexandria. c.1935

sculptures made from gypsum that were widely sought after by various hotels across the island to display in their foyers.

After his retirement from Singer, Kyriacos worked mainly as a farmer. He was able to supplement his income by undertaking various small building and engineering works and by painting walls or manufacturing plaster statues.

In 1968, tragedy struck when Kyriacos broke his hip in a tractor accident. There was very little the local doctors could do to remedy such an injury and Kyriacos was crippled and unable to walk again. After three years confined to his bed he finally succumbed to his bedsores and infections and died in 1971 aged seventy-six.

ACKNOWLEDGEMENTS
I would like to thank Andreas and Mary Aristidou for sharing their stories about the Michaelides family with me and for kindly allowing me to scan their precious family photographs. I would also like to acknowledge Koullis Aristidou for his valued contribution before he passed away in 2014. Kyriacos Michaelides was the maternal grandfather of Andreas and Koullis Aristidou.

Kyriacos and Milou with one of their eight children. c.1920

Kyriacos and Milou with their neice Mary and nephew Michael. Alexandria, c.1930

Maria
CHRISTOFOROU

Maria Christoforou (nee Haralambou Moustaka) was born in the village of Moni in the district of Limassol on the 10th of September 1908. Her mother Styliani Sanithyiotis came from a very strict traditional Greek Cypriot family of four girls. She was engaged to Haralambos Moustaka when she was sixteen years old, however he was not allowed to go anywhere near her for four years until they were married.

Maria was the youngest of five children and was required to look after her sick mother from a very young age. No one really knew what was wrong with Styliani as she refused to see a doctor although it was suspected that she might be suffering with thalassemia. Apparently, she had been quite weak and anaemic for most of her adult life. Styliani would never have allowed a male doctor to examine her and there were no female doctors in her village. She was quite prudish, to say the least; as were most women from her generation. Apart from her husband Haralambos, no other man had ever seen more than her face, hands or ankles.

It is said that the day before Styliani passed away, she mustered the strength to ask her seven year old daughter Maria an unusual request. "Go and saddle our donkey and take me out to the fields to find the *nero patimata* (water steps)." Maria was unsure what the water steps were but nevertheless, did what her mother had requested. After searching

all day without success they returned back home. As she lay on her bed, Styliani spoke with laboured breath. "Maria my child; we did not find the *nero patimata*. It is time for me to die." The next morning she was gone. Maria was devasted. She would feel guilty for the rest of her life because she never found the water steps her dear mother was looking for.

After her mother's death, Maria's father Haralambos was unable to care for his children, so he sent them to be raised by relatives. Maria was separated from her siblings and raised by her father's brother and his wife in Limassol. Maria's brother Lucas and her eldest sister Sophia were sent to Egypt, where they remained until they returned to Cyprus in their later years. They both remained single. When Maria was older, she went to live with her sister Salomi and husband Loisos Christodoulidis in Limassol.

In 1939, when Maria was thirty-one, her uncle arranged for her to be married. After realising she had little in common with the would-be suitor, Maria decided to break off the engagement. This was not well received by many of the locals. In those days, it was a cultural taboo to break off an engagement - regardless of the reasons. As a result of her 'tarnished' reputation there was an absence of other available or suitable suitors.

At thirty-one years of age, Maria considered herself too old for marriage and threatened to join a monastery to become a nun. Her uncle would not hear

Panayiotis Christoforou. Cyprus. c.1940

of it, as all his children were married. What would people think of him if he did not marry off his niece? He immediately arranged another marriage with a man named Panayiotis Christoforou who was ten years younger than Maria.

Panayiotis was born on the 25th of March 1918 in the village of Lofou. He was a charismatic and renowned rascal in his village who was often in trouble with the law. Somehow, he was able to use his quick wit and natural charm to get out of trouble, time and time again.

Maria's sister Sofia (left). The other woman and girl are unknown. Sofia left Cyprus to live and work in Egypt with her older brother Lucas. Alexandria, Egypt. c.1946

Although Maria protested against marrying a younger man, her protests fell on deaf ears and in 1940, she was promptly married to Panayiotis.

After a simple village ceremony, Panayiotis rushed to join the war effort in Europe and enlisted with the Cypriot Volunteer Regiment (CVR). After seeing some action in Tobruk he was captured in 1943 by German soldiers and was sent to a Prisoner of War camp in Germany.

Incredibly, Panayiotis was able to use his natural charm to convince a German officer at the prison camp to recruit him as his personal handyman. The officer took a liking to the charismatic Cypriot and allowed him to stay at his home, thus sparing him the horrors of the prison camp.

In a dangerous feat of daring, Panayiotis began a secret affair with the German officer's young wife and she became pregnant. Apparently, sometime after the war, she sent Panayiotis a photo of the child and wrote that her husband never suspected anything and believed that the child was his. Panayiotis had once again fooled the authorities and managed to escape the severe consequences of his actions.

In 1945, Panayiotis returned to Cyprus and was reunited with his wife Maria. According to many reports, he was a changed man. He was once found standing in a field completely naked. No one knew why he was behaving this way or if he indeed sought medical help.

Numerous Cypriot volunteers who had served with the British army during the Second World War are reported to have received no counselling or special medical attention upon their return. Post-traumatic stress was as

yet an undiagnosed side-effect of war at that time.

Maria and Panayiotis moved to the village of Alassa where they owned and operated a *kafenion* (coffee house) for five years until 1950. Maria, at forty-two years of age, had now given up hope of having any children.

Panayiotis had heard many stories about Australia and started making plans to migrate there. Ignoring his wife's concerns, he decided to sell their business in Alassa to pay for a new suit and his ship fare to Australia. At this time, Maria had been feeling unwell and went to see a local doctor. She was shocked to discover that she was pregnant.

Maria was devastated that her husband was leaving to travel abroad in her time of need. With no income and now pregnant, what was she to do? Panayiotis went to the local village square and announced to all those gathered there that his wife was pregnant and that he was indeed the father. Apparently, he did not want any of the locals suspecting and gossiping that his wife fell pregnant after his departure.

Once her husband left Cyprus, Maria went to live with her sister Salome in Limassol. Her miracle baby, which she named Andrulla, was born in February 1950. Ten months later, Maria and baby Andrulla boarded a cargo ship called the SS Jenny for the long and arduous (two and a half month) journey to Australia.

Panayiotis managed to establish a business everywhere he went In every State of Australia. Whether he opened up a café, fish and chip shop, or barbershop, he was mostly successful. He was a barber by trade but he could turn his hand to just about anything. He even tried his luck at fortune telling and being a psychic. His daughter Andrulla believes that her father must have had gypsy blood in his veins, for he hated to stay in one place for too long. Her family moved all around Australia, having many adventures along the way.

The constant shifting from state to state and from house to house meant that Andrulla was unable to receive a proper education. She didn't start school until she was seven years old. In a bold move, her father pulled her out of school completely when she was thirteen. She was then engaged at fifteen, married at sixteen and had her first child at seventeen. It seemed her father was adopting the Cypriot village mentality. He expected his daughter to stay at home to help with the daily chores and to work in the family business.

Life with Panayiotis was never dull. He was very lucky when it came to business. He always managed to earn a living wherever he went. His weakness, however, was pretty women. He always employed and surrounded himself with many pretty waitresses while his poor wife was relegated to the kitchen, where she would slave away cooking, cleaning, filleting fish and chopping up chips all day. Amazingly, Maria never complained and never had a bad word to say about her husband.

In 1970, Andrulla and her husband Nick decided to return to Cyprus with their daughter Hayley. Their son Peter was born there in December 1971.

Many Cypriots living abroad had a yearning to return to the island of their birth.

In 1973, Maria and Panayiotis decided to join their daughter in Cyprus. When the Turks invaded the island in 1974, Andrulla and her family were evacuated to London before returning to Australia. Her parents on the other hand, stayed in Cyprus. After the troubles and tensions had eased somewhat, Panayiotis decided to become a professional psychic and spiritual medium. He was never short of customers. Despite being very religious, many Cypriots could not resist the lure of a good coffee cup reading.

Maria Christoforou holding her baby daughter Andrulla. The young girl standing is twelve-year-old Nina (Andrulla's godmother). Limassol, 1950

Maria and Panayiotis separated in 1976. Maria returned to Australia to live with her daughter Andrulla in Adelaide. Panayiotis stayed in Cyprus and married again, this time to a woman that he met at one of his spiritual readings. She was not much older than his own daughter.

Panayiotis died in 2012 at the ripe old age of ninety-two. He had lived an interesting and colourful life indeed. Even in old age it was said that Panayiotis had a roving eye for pretty young women.

Maria died in Adelaide in 1994 aged eighty-six. Like so many Cypriot women of her generation Maria had lived an extraordinarily selfless life. She demonstrated remarkable resilience and strength of character to bear witness to

Two monks from Agios Georgios monastery in Alamanos. The older monk is Papa Dimitris Baisios (Maria's uncle). He apparently helped to build the monastery doing a lot of the manual work himself. c. 1905

so much heartache from a young age; from the premature death of her mother to marrying a restless man who seemed to treat her more like a servant than a loving partner. She was forever grateful to always have her miracle child Andrulla close by her side and in her later years was surrounded by her loving grandchildren and extended family until the end.

ACKNOWLEDGEMENTS
I would like to thank Andrea (Andrulla) Johns for her kind assistance in helping me to write and document her mother's life story. I would also like to acknowledge her help in scanning her precious old family photographs.

Eleni Symeou and her family. From top-left is her sister Despina, her mother Orthodoxia and sister Maria. Bottom left is her grandmother Mariou, and her father Symeos Kyriakides holding baby brother Costas. Eleni is standing next to her brother Kyriacos. c.1926

BELOW:
Paraskevou with her mother (Eleni's neighbours in Ora). Year unknown.

Costas & Eleni
MICHAELIDES

ORA-LARNACA

Costas Michaelides was born in the village of Morfou in 1914. He was one of five brothers including a half-brother named Solon. When Solon was eight years old, his mother Eleni died from puerperal fever. After the required period of mourning, his father Michalis Hadjikyriakos remarried. Her name was Despina (Costas' mother).

Solon Michaelides was an extremely gifted musician who eventually went on to become an international success as a teacher, composer and one of the greatest musical talents to emerge from Cyprus. He first started playing music on a guitar when he was thirteen. The guitar was a gift from a school friend for helping

him with his school work. Solon was a natural and gifted musician. His talent was recognised by other teachers and musicians and before long he started earning distinctions and awards. Such awards included the gold medal from the 'Greek Brotherhood of Cypriots in Egypt' and a Diploma from the prestigious Trinity College of Music in London.

Like his famous half-brother Solon, Costas was also musically gifted and could play the violin exceptionally well. Once at a wedding in Ora, Costas was asked to replace the usual violinist who had suddenly become quite ill. A blind man at the wedding recognised that the sound of the music was different and remarked

ABOVE: Costas Michaelides aged about fifteen. Possibly in Orounda. c.1930

LEFT: Eleni's parents Orthodoxia and Symeos Kyriakides and her grandmother Mariou. The man standing at back is Orthodoxia's brother Andreas. Location unknown. c.1930s

Ora primary school. Costas (with cigarette) and Eleni Michaelides are standing in the middle at back. The children are about to embark on a school excursion. c.1945

to all the guests that the violinist was extremely talented.

Unlike his half-brother, Costas did not pursue a career in music. As a boy, he moved from Morfou to Orounta when his father (a policeman), was posted there. In Orounta, Costas began his apprenticeship as a shoemaker. His master was a Turkish Cypriot cobbler who also taught him to speak Turkish. Many of their customers were policemen and Costas was often required to make their boots.

On the 11th November 1945, Costas was married by *proxenia* (arranged marriage) to Eleni Symeou in the village of Ora. By coincidence, their fathers had met years earlier when they were serving together in the Cyprus Mule Corp.

Eleni Symeou was born in Ora in 1917 and was one of five children. When she became of age, she was taught to embroider lace of exceptional quality just like the women of nearby Kato Drys and Lefkara. Her older sister Despina taught her dressmaking. Eleni was known to ride her donkey around Ora and to all the neighbouring villages seeking out

Above and right: Eleni (in the middle) outside Ora village. c.1937

customers or teaching dressmaking to other young girls.

Costas and Eleni's first child Michael was born in September 1946. Three months later they boarded the passenger ship SS Arcadia and arrived in Liverpool, England in January 1947. They took a train from Liverpool to Victoria Station where they were met by Eleni's older sister Despina. London was experiencing a very cold winter in 1947 - quite a shock for the Mediterranean family accustomed to a warmer climate.

Their first residence was in Kilburn in North London. A year after they had arrived, Costas and Eleni welcomed the arrival of their daughter Orthodoxia (Thoxoulla), who was born in January 1948. Their second daughter Despina (Despo) was born in July, 1951.

Eleni's Uncle Andreas and Aunt Ayiro. Year unknown.

Slaughtering a pig at the house of Polyvios Mylonas in Ora. Costas Michaelides is second on the left. The two children are Christos and Constantinos Mylonas. c.1945

Eleni (far right) with her children Orthodoxia and Michael. From left is Anastasia with her son George, unknown woman and Eleni's sister Despina. Trafalgar Square, London. c.1949

For unknown reasons, Costas decided to leave his violin behind in Cyprus. In fact, he would never play a musical instrument again. Instead, he concentrated on caring and raising his family and establishing a new life for them in England. His children grew up in London never once hearing their father play the violin.

Once he was settled in London, Costas used his existing skills as a shoemaker to open up a makeshift workshop in the basement of his flat in Kennington. Not surprisingly, many of his customers were Greeks and Cypriots from the local area. He eventually established his first business in Brixton where he continued to reap the benefits of his shoemaking skills until he retired. Costas and Eleni lived a content and happy life in Thornton Heath surrounded with their family and many friends.

ACKNOWLEDGEMENTS

Special thanks to Thoxoulla Varellas and her sister Despina MIchaelides for their generous hospitality in London and for sharing their parent's story and precious family photographs with me.

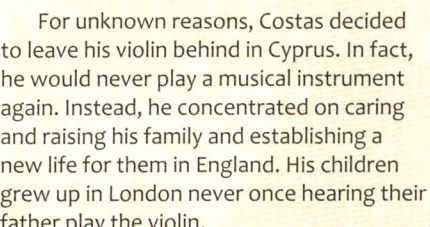

Eleni (far left) sitting next to her best friend Christalleni with two other friends dressed in traditional costume. c.1930s

Eleni's brother Costas Smoleskis (left) with his uncle and aunt. He was a Policeman in Cyprus. c.1940

Christoforos & Eleni
KIKKIDES

Christoforos Yiannis Kikkides was born in the village of Pano Arodhes in Paphos on the 15th of March 1915. His parents Yiannis Kyriakou Kikkides and Maria Savva (nee Panayiotou) were humble, self-sufficient farmers who harvested their own crops, spun wool and wove garments to sell and barter for goods with other villagers.

Christoforos and his siblings (Savvas, Despina, Anastasia, Panayiota and Xenia) did what they could to help their parents with the daily chores, on and off the land. By all accounts, they were a united and caring family.

Except for the eldest child, all the siblings completed primary school. When Christoforos finished primary school, it was said that he could read and write exceptionally well. He had a reputation of being mild-mannered and kind at all times.

Although life was difficult enough in the village, the early death of the children's father Yiannis made it even more challenging for the family. Some of the children now needed to leave the village to become child workers in order to help their widowed mother with the expenses of raising a family. When Christoforos was only five, he was recruited by his older brother Savvas to shine shoes at a *kafenion* (coffee house) in Ktima where he worked.

The 1920s was a particularly harsh decade for the rural population in regards to health. At a nearby village, numerous people died after eating contaminated broad beans. The villagers also had to deal with locust plagues and droughts.

Christoforos' older sister Anastasia married a widower named Xenios Economides sometime in the late 1920s or early 1930s. His first wife had passed away giving birth to their third child, (who, tragically, also died) and so his mother-in-law set out to find her son-in-law a new wife. Anastasia embraced her new role as mother to Xenios' two surviving children, Andreas and Theopisti. She eventually had seven children of her own: Haralambos, Christakis, Dimitrakis, Fostira, Anthoulla, Maroulla, and Niki.

Christoforos worked hard to make a living for himself and to help his family in whichever way he could. He was particularly kind to his sisters.

As the youngest male in his family, he was entitled to some property in Pano Arodhes. He decided however, to leave his inheritance to his favourite sister for her dowry as his other sisters were already married.

Christoforos worked with his brother Savvas for many years in Ktima; starting as a shoe shine boy and later becoming a waiter at a number of restaurants and *kafenia* in the town. When he was in his late teens, he moved to Limassol, where he continued to pursue work as a waiter. During the 1940s, he worked in the Troodos mountain region at a number of prestigious hotels and resorts including the Forest Park Hotel and the Helvetia Hotel in Platres. He became a first-class

Passport photo of Christoforos Yiannis Kikkides. 1950

waiter at both the Hotel Atlanta and the Astoria Hotel in Nicosia in the early 1950s.

When his brother Savvas opened his own café in Limassol together with his brother-in-law, Christoforos was probably disappointed that he was not included in the venture. True to his character, not a harsh word was ever spoken or heard.

On the 19th April 1951, thirty-six year old Christoforos boarded the ship Hellenic Prince in Limassol and arrived in Melbourne a month later on the 17th of May 1951. His migration to Australia was sponsored by George Tsindos, who

Anastasia Economides (Christoforos' older sister) holding her daughter Fostira. The little boy in the robe is her son Pambos. The other woman is Choratina, her husband's former mother-in-law. Akourdalia, Paphos. c.1928

Christoforos Kikkides, (back row, far right). Next to him is perhaps his sister Panayiota. His other sister Anastasia is seated up front wearing a light coloured dress. Location unknown. c.1938

had migrated to Australia in the 1920s as a young child. Tsindos had established himself as one of the Melbourne's most successful and distinguished restaurateurs.

A Cypriot migrant named Savvas Peter Krassaris provided accommodation for Christoforos and helped him find employment at one of Tsindos' restaurants. Krassaris became his lifelong friend. Christoforos also worked as a waiter at the popular Cypriot clubhouse called the Democritus Club which was located on Russell Street in Melbourne. He enjoyed listening to the political discussions and debates at the club which spurred his interest in reading all things socio-political. Like many Cypriot migrants, Christoforos sent funds on a regular basis to help his family in Cyprus.

When Christoforos moved into a shared house in Prahran, he was introduced to Eleni Agathokli Minas.

Eleni was born in the suburb of Agia Trias in Rizokarpaso on the 9th of December 1920. She was the daughter of Stavrinos Minas Agathokli, who was born in 1884; a few years after the British took

over the acquisition of Cyprus from the Ottoman Turks.

Eleni's great grandfather was Haji-Tassou, who owned a large area of land next to the monastery of Apostolos Andreas. Eleni's mother Maria Yianni Vasiliou Treti was nicknamed *Pallikarou,* in reference to her husband's stature. In his later years Stavrinos was called *levendoyeros* (handsome old man). It was common in Cyprus to address people by their nicknames, especially if there were others in the village or town with the same name. Nicknames were usually made up in reference to somebody's occupation, physical features, behaviour, or even a particular character trait.

Eleni's mother Maria was also born in Rizokarpaso. She had six siblings (Emilia, Stella, Lucia, Yiannis, Andriana and Nikolaos). Her younger brother Nikolaos died very young.

Eleni's parents were farmers of sheep, tobacco, olives and wheat. They were also mulberry and textile weavers of silk, cotton, wool and linen.

When Eleni was a young girl, her father made her work alongside her

siblings in the fields and on the family farm. For this reason, the children did not have a lot of time to attend school.

At school, Eleni was taller than the other children in her class. Self-conscious about her height, she often skipped class and would go and sit in a tree by the sea

Christoforos Kikkides, (aged about twenty-three). Location unknown. c.1938

watching the waves break on the beach. She would stay hidden in the tree until it was time to go home. At times, she would sell chicken eggs to buy lollies as a special treat. Apparently, her parents were unaware of her absence from school. As well as the wrath of her parents if they ever found out, Eleni had to be careful of other dangers too. There was a dangerous wild boar that killed a villager in the 1930s and plenty of snakes lurking in the cane fields. Despite skipping school so frequently, Eleni did manage to attend enough classes to learn both Greek and English and her handwriting attracted much praise from those who knew her.

At thirteen, Eleni's parents sent her to Varosi (Famagusta) to become a 'nanny' for the merchant Prastitis family, where she was required to care of their young son, Nikos. The family grew very fond of Eleni and bought her a bicycle. In Varosi, she studied to become a seamstress and gained a certificate specialising in shirts and machine embroidery.

Eleni continued to work in Famagusta and then decided to migrate to Australia. She was a lot older than most women who chose to migrate. Her delay was the result of an interested suitor who decided to put off his marriage to her until his own sister was married; as was the tradition back then. Apparently, the sister remained single on purpose, and Eleni tired of waiting, left

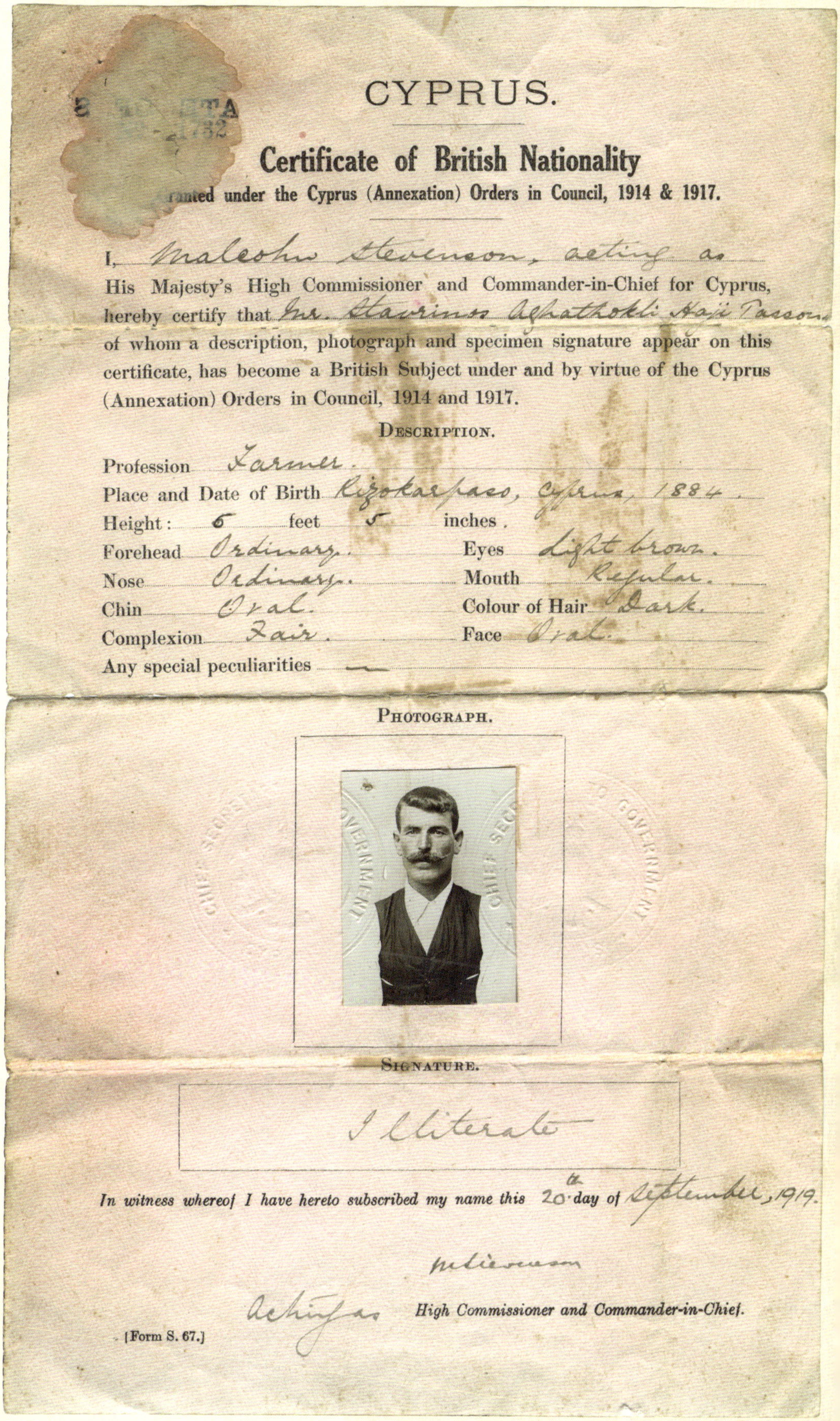

RIGHT:
Certificate of British Nationality for Eleni's father Stavrinos Agathokli Haji Tassou, (Minas). Dated 20th September 1919

CYPRUS.

Certificate of British Nationality

granted under the Cyprus (Annexation) Orders in Council, 1914 & 1917.

I, *Malcolm Stevenson, acting as* His Majesty's High Commissioner and Commander-in-Chief for Cyprus, hereby certify that *Mr. Stavrinos Aghathokli Haji Tassou,* of whom a description, photograph and specimen signature appear on this certificate, has become a British Subject under and by virtue of the Cyprus (Annexation) Orders in Council, 1914 and 1917.

DESCRIPTION.

Profession *Farmer.*
Place and Date of Birth *Rizokarpaso, Cyprus, 1884.*
Height : *5* feet *5* inches .
Forehead *Ordinary.* Eyes *Light brown.*
Nose *Ordinary.* Mouth *Regular.*
Chin *Oval.* Colour of Hair *Dark.*
Complexion *Fair.* Face *Oval.*
Any special peculiarities ———

PHOTOGRAPH.

SIGNATURE.

Illiterate

In witness whereof I have hereto subscribed my name this *20th* day of *September*, 1919.

M. Stevenson

Acting as High Commissioner and Commander-in-Chief.

[Form S. 67.]

for the furthest place possible; Australia.

On the 19th August 1951 Eleni boarded the Italian-owned ship SS Ionia Florentia in Limassol. It is said that the would-be suitor, upon realising that he might lose Eleni for good, drove all the way from Famagusta to the port of Limassol with a small delegation of family members to try and talk her out of her trip. Eleni stood firmly on the deck, resolute in her decision to leave Cyprus. She was thirty years old and had had enough. She turned her back and refused to acknowledge the suitor. Her ship sailed away. Apparently, the suitor and his sister never married.

Eleni arrived in Melbourne on the 29th September 1951. At Station Pier, she was met by three female cousins who convinced her to stay in Melbourne instead of sailing on to Sydney (as she had planned) to meet her sponsor Stelios Agathokli. After suffering weeks of nausea and sickness at sea, Eleni was relieved to get off the ship in Melbourne and onto dry land. One of her cousins needed babysitting so she asked Eleni to stay with her family in Albert Park. This was short lived, as Eleni was eager to work in her chosen field.

Eleni eventually moved to Abbotsford where there was work in the many textile factories nearby. She sent money home to her father to purchase land and to educate her younger sisters, who later moved to England. Eleni enjoyed being independent and being in a large city. Her mother Maria passed away eleven months after she had arrived in Australia.

Christoforos Kikkides and Eleni Agathokli Minas were married on the 26th August 1956 and settled down in a large house in Windsor. He was thirty-nine years old and she was thirty-five. Their first daughter Maria was born in April 1960 and their second daughter Joanna was born in May 1961. They worked hard to get ahead in Melbourne and to provide a good start for their family.

As toddlers, their daughters would wait at Mangos' Café in Windsor for them to finish their shifts, before they would all walk home together.

On the weekends during the Australian summer, they would all catch the train to Brighton and Sandringham beach and spend the day picnicking on the sand and swimming in the ocean. Christoforos was a keen swimmer. He also swam at the St Kilda indoor baths during

Eleni's mother Maria Treti who died in September 1952, just after Eleni arrived in Australia.

Eleni Kikkides standing in the back of her boarding house in Nicholson Street, Abbotsford. Melbourne, 1953

Eleni Agathokli Minas. Varosi. c.1942

the colder winter months.

Sometime in 1967, Christoforos' older brother Savvas wrote to him stating that the civil war in Cyprus was over and insisted that he should return. "Come back to your homeland," he wrote. "You will have a good life here and be able to buy a house and business." Christoforos did not budge. He had read enough in the Greek newspapers to know that the political tensions on the island were in fact, getting worse. He had no intention to return to Cyprus. Besides, he was now married and had two young daughters to raise and educate.

The Kikkides family home in Windsor was large enough to convert into a boarding house during the 1960s. Christoforos decided to rent a number of rooms to Greek migrants to earn a bit of extra money and in turn, help the new arrivals settle into Melbourne. A relative helped him to build a wood-fired oven in his already verdant backyard. At times, Christoforos practiced being a backyard beekeeper and had a few beehive boxes.

For Christoforos and Eleni, their traditional way of life was never too far away as they had successfully converted their backyard into a little slice of rural Cyprus. They shared all their home grown produce with the neighbours in the street. They concerned themselves with keeping a good home, looking after their children and leading a simple but contented life.

In the 1960s, Christoforos began work as a labourer at the Commonwealth Aircraft Corporation located at Fishermen's Bend. He subsequently moved to the General Motors Holden plant in Port Melbourne, working as a spray painter. It was at this time that he decided to start smoking – but just to get the same 'smoko' breaks that the other smokers at the factory enjoyed.

Unfortunately, in early 1985, Christoforos was forced to sell his house to the Victorian Government to make way for a new State School. He was sent a compulsory 'Notice to Treat' that

Eleni aged twenty. This was intended to be a Christmas greeting card. Famagusta, 1940.

grossly undervalued his home. Stressed and depressed, Christoforos passed away on the 25 April 1985. His beautiful Victorian family home was demolished. His castle was gone and so was he. The State School was never built.

Eleni was never truly content living in Australia. She did not return to Cyprus however, because she felt a lost connection with her past, especially her home town of Rizokarpaso after the Turkish invasion. Although, never naturalised (most likely due to the language barrier) Eleni still regarded Australia as her home. Even in her eighties she would refer to herself as a 'new Australian'.

Christoforos often stated that his greatest achievements were getting married, raising and educating

his children, having a fridge full of food, owning his own home and being on good terms with the people in his life.

Many elderly Cypriots had made

Eleni's brother Yiannis Stavrinos Minas during his time in the Cypriot Volunteer Regiment. Rizokarpaso c. 1940

similar sentiments to those expressed by Christoforos. Getting married and raising children was viewed as their ultimate achievement and perhaps the only validation of a life worth living. Achieving a debt-free existence came a close second. For those Cypriots who left Cyprus and migrated to other countries, there was an even greater sense of achievement. Most of them started new lives with nothing more than a fierce ambition in their hearts and a burning determination to succeed against all odds.

ACKNOWLEDGEMENTS

I would like to thank Maria Axiomakarou and Joanna Kikkides for helping me to write their family history and for allowing me to scan their family photographs. Without their efforts, their parents' story would not have been told.

Christoforos Kikkides, at rear wearing apron. Limassol. c.1946

The Wonder of
VINTAGE
PHOTOGRAPHY

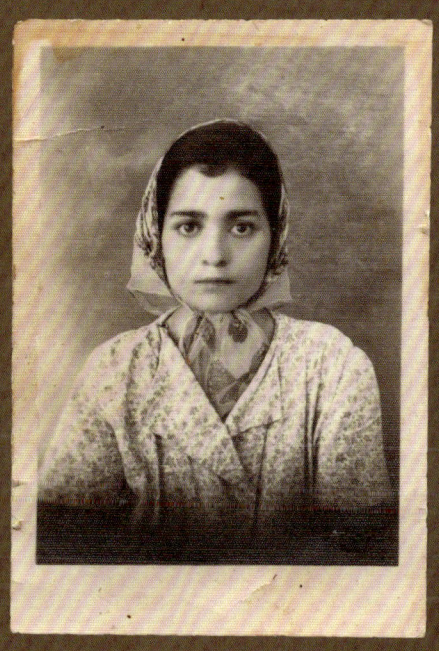

I have always been fascinated by old monochrome photography. When I visit an elderly family friend or relative, my attention is always drawn to the old photographs hanging on their walls or sitting on their mantelpiece.

My love for photography began when I was a boy and my father brought home a camera from the Kodak factory where he worked. After high school, I studied art and design at Phillip Institute where I was taught how to use medium-format and 35mm cameras and how to develop prints in a darkroom. After college, I began my creative career working as a studio and wedding photographer. In those analogue years, one had to know everything about aperture settings, shutter speeds, focal points and depth of field. I had to know how to frame a shot by understanding viewpoint and composition and I had to know how to master and control light.

This authentic and pure form of photography seems like a lifetime ago. It is certainly a far cry from today's automated 'point and shoot' methods that are synonymous with digital cameras.

My parents' generation had very little experience or exposure to photography. Cyprus during the British Era (1878-1960) saw only a few dedicated people adopt photography as a serious profession. The camera was a technical and expensive piece of equipment best left to the experts to operate. Developing a printed photograph was an even greater and more complicated mystery. The local population regarded photography as a luxury reserved for only the most special and important occasions. Furthermore, they did not have the financial means to afford the privilege, which explains the scarcity of family photographs from that period in Cypriot households.

In my quest with *Tales of Cyprus*, I have barely met a Cypriot who owns more than three or four original photographs taken prior to 1950. My father, who was born in 1921, had his first photo taken in 1947 when he was twenty-six years old. I therefore have no photographs of my father as a young man. In stark contrast, I have taken thousands of photos of my children. Most of those photographs are stored and hidden away on hard drives and memory cards. I fear that the traditional photographic album with its valuable assortment of printed photographs has become a relic of the past. Gone too, are the printed photographs that adorn the walls or are sent through the mail to loved ones.

When I look at old photographs, like the ones in this book, I am in awe of this antique art form. I marvel at the quality of the exposures as well as the tone and the texture of the paper. I am fascinated by the expressions of the people in the photographs. Time, mortality and memory are captured in such decisive moments. To my eyes, nothing has more character than an old sepia photograph.

One of the challenges faced by vintage photographers using early model cameras was the need for long exposures. Their subject had to stay perfectly still (up to eight seconds) to avoid any motion blur. So, photographers set up some simple rules: No talking; no moving and - just to be safe - no smiling.

The absence of electricity also meant indoor photography was avoided or altogether impossible for many photographers. Despite these constraints, the early photographers in Cyprus did an incredible job, taking some truly remarkable photos. The technical skill and mastery of their craft, together with their creative innovations, have helped record some of the most magical portraits of Cypriot people that I have ever seen.

The photographs shown in this section of the book are from my private collection. Many were taken in the districts of Paphos and Larnaca between 1910 and 1950. Amongst this extraordinary collection are some studio photos where the sitter would have paid around half a shilling or more to have their portrait taken. There are also photographs that appear to be unplanned or taken on impulse by a travelling photographer, perhaps at a village fair.

Professional studio photographers knew a thing or two about how to create a classic portrait. As well as having a high degree of technical expertise many were self-taught in terms of technique and composition. Tricks of the trade included setting up mood lighting using side or backlit lamps, having the subject look away from the camera and gaze into the distance and having the subject hold a prop like a book, a cane or a bouquet of flowers.

In 2016, I was fortunate to meet Monica Voulgaris, granddaughter of Leopold Glaszner. Mr Glaszner is regarded by many as one of the great names in early Cypriot photography along with the likes of John P. Foscolo and Theodoulos N. Toufexis.

Monica was able to share with me some of the methods employed by her grandfather in his popular Glaszner Studio in Larnaca. "My grandfather understood light and how to use a camera with technical efficiency," she said. "He was also gifted in knowing how to pose a person. He knew almost instantly and instinctively what was their best side or position. He knew how to read a face and direct the sitter to look or face a certain way in order to capture the ideal pose. This is why everybody who came back to collect their photos was always pleased with the results."

From the age of fourteen, Monica was required to work at her grandfather's studio in Larnaca. Some of her tasks included serving customers, helping to prepare the camera and setting up the props. She was also trusted in handling the large glass plates and even retouching the photographic prints using special pencils and paints. "With one plate, you get six photos," explains Monica. "That might cost someone ten shillings."

The Glaszner studio was unique in that it had a large glass ceiling allowing plenty of natural light to fill the room. Only if the weather was foul or large group photos were required did Glaszner use his photographic lamps.

The studio also boasted a large dressing room where patrons could go and get fitted and made up.

The other well-known studios in Cyprus during the British era included Edwards of Limassol, Mangoian Bros., Foto Fevzi, Foto Deanna and Foto Ümit

- to name a few. Each portrait taken in these studios was treated with the same delicate flair and sensitivity as a theatrical performance. Each photograph was meticulously planned and crafted with the same artistic reverence that a theatre manager might employ when positioning actors on stage within a particular scene.

These studio photographers had every conceivable prop and set design to create beautiful and detailed compositions based on an endless array of themes. The classic composition was that of the patriarchal family; father seated in a chair, mother standing with a hand gently placed on the shoulder of her husband and the

children sitting doe-like and demure at the feet of their parents. The extraordinary and complex sets constructed for each photographic shoot is testament to their technical genius. Combined with their innate ability to use natural light, was their command over shadows and an intimate understanding of glass-plate photography. These photographers created images that defined the style and genre for their generation.

Wedding photography was especially popular and sought after in Cyprus. The studio photographers were masters in this genre, servicing both Christian and Muslim couples. Those who could afford the five or ten shilling fee in 1935 would get the full treatment; sets, props, costumes, hair and makeup as well as

six beautifully crafted photographs. Poor people from rural areas were often photographed without fancy props and sets. The simple and plain surrounds that were used were carefully chosen to match (but not undermine) the equally plain traditional clothing worn by the sitters.

Many old photographs that I have scanned for this book do not have writing or inscriptions on the back. Perhaps this is testament to the fact that a lot of people in Cyprus were illiterate and could not read or write at the time.

Sometimes, although rarely, there is a hand-written message or perhaps a note that simply reads; "To my loving daughter (or son). To remember me, with love."

One of the tragic outcomes of digital photography, as well as eliminating the need for technical skill and knowledge, is that quite a few modern-day photographers seem to put little thought into the composition or artfulness of the image. In fact, they ignore the basic rules of good photography. They simply set their camera to AUTO and point and

shoot. To make matters worse, hardly any digital photographs make it to print. Most are viewed on screen.

Another menacing trend that has emerged - largely, I think, in response to social media, is the somewhat addictive desire by some to use the camera as a narcissistic tool. These people use their phone cameras to take hundreds of digital self-portraits (or selfies). Some people even take photographs of their food to post and share online. The obsession for recording images this way has to me lessened the value of photography.

It would appear that my parent's generation – not just in Cyprus, but around the world - did not have such a personal need or a vanity-driven obsession for photography.

Photographs were either required for Government-issued documents such as identity cards and passports or taken as commemorative tokens to be given to family members, friends and relatives.

Many people sent photographs of themselves and their families to loved ones living abroad. For this reason, photographs served as a reminder of home and were treated as precious mementos or keepsakes.

It never ceases to amaze me that so many beautiful old photographs in Cyprus are now lost. Were they stolen? Were they thrown out with the rubbish? Many Cypriots have admitted to me that their precious old family photographs had been destroyed or thrown away by other family members. Whether deliberate or accidental, countless prints have been lost to us – just like the ancestors they portrayed.

In addition to fading caused by light, many vintage photographs bear the ravages of age, time, and sometimes, neglect. There are tears, scratches, spots, burn marks and stains caused by mould. Some photos are corrupted by the acidic adhesive found in cheap albums.

If you are the custodian of an old family album or any old photographs for that matter, then I firmly believe that you

have an obligation to cherish and preserve these special, delicate images of the past. If possible, try and discover and document the origins of each photograph and the stories they hold. These photographs are the only physical reminders of people who have long since passed away. They are the only way that future generations will ever get to know those early relatives.

If you are interested in learning more about the importance and process of preserving old photographs please feel free to contact me or visit my website.

conemmanuelle@talesofcyprus.com
www.talesofcyprus.com

ACKNOWLEDGEMENTS
Thank you to Kadir Kaba for his input.

Glossary

A LIST OF THE COMMON CYPRIOT WORDS FOUND IN THIS BOOK

agora – a market place

agrophylakas – a rural guard

anari – a type of dried cheese

babutsa – prickly pear

bakaliko – grocery store

baklava – a Middle-Eastern pastry sweet with syrup and nuts.

balaska – a shoulder bag

basturma – cured spicy meat

bigginou – a children's game involving stones

chaoush – a Turkish Cypriot police sergeant

chobani – a goat herder

chouraki – junior apprentice

dekares – Cyprus currency equalling one quarter of a piastre

deratcha – carobs

flaounes – special Easter cheese pies

galaktoboureko – A Greek sweet made with custard and filo pastry

gatsarolla – a large cooking pot

grosi – currency used in Cyprus (9 groshia = 1 shilling)

gylko – spoon sweets made from fruit

haloumi – a traditional Cypriot cheese made with goat's milk

hodja – a devout Muslim who may perform some religious duties

hronia polla – live a long life

jami – mosque

kafejis – coffee maker or coffee shop owner

kafenion – coffee house or coffee shop

kapnistiri – incense burner

kataifi – a Greek pastry sweet

katzara – wood kindling

keftedes – Greek meatballs

kolokasi – taro

koulourakia – Easter biscuits

koulouria – sesame bread rings

koumbaros – wedding sponsor / best man

koupepia – vine leaves stuffed with rice and mince meat

kourabiethes – Greek shortbread biscuits

kouzma – a pick axe

kyrie eleison – Lord have mercy

kyrios – master

lefkaritika – special lace embroideries that originate from the village of Lefkara

levendoyeros – handsome old man

lingri – an outdoor game similar to baseball played with sticks and stones

loukoumades – Greek doughnuts

loukoumi – Turkish Delight sweets

mahalla – neighbourhood

mandra – a special pen for goats and sheep

mappa – football (soccer)

mou – my

mukhtari – the village headman

oka – a unit of measurement for weight

pablomatas – a quilt maker

pakira – Turkish word for currency like grosi

panayiri – festival

pantopoleio – grocery store

pappou – grandfather

papoutsosiko – prickly pear

passatembo – lightly roasted pumpkin seeds

perivoli – field

piastres – same as grosi

pilafi / pilaf – crushed burghul wheat

pirilia – marbles

plateia – town square

prika – the dowry

prikosynfonon – dowry agreement

prosklisi – invitation

proxenia – an arranged marriage

pryoni – a saw

psaltis – cantor in church

rashi / rasha – a special firewood ideal for wood fire ovens

resi - wheat and lamb pilaf typically served at weddings

samari – wooden cradle used on a donkey

scadouya – a game similar to marbles played with sheep droppings

shemé – a popular card game

soujouko – a special Cypriot sweet made from boiled grape juice, then dried

souvla – meat on skewers cooked over coals

stifado – a Greek stew dish

stroumulla – a children's game similar to blindman's bluff

trahana – a soup made with sundried wheat and yoghurt

tavli – backgammon

tsendi – wallet / purse

voufa – loom

vraka – traditional baggy pants mostly worn by elderly men

yiasou – a greeting meaning hello or goodbye

yiayia – grandmother

zivania – a strong alcoholic home brew

A time to remember

This school photo was taken in the village of Arsos (Limassol) in April 1974. That's me with the striped jumper trying to look mysterious and worldly.

I am grateful to have witnessed and experienced Cyprus before the war and before the authentic cultural and rural way of life changed forever. The changes are mostly due to displacement, tourism, commercialism, immigration, globalisation and the desire to modernise.

During my time in Arsos, I discovered some home truths about life in a Cypriot village that would ultimately change my opinion about my ancestral home. For example, I discovered that family unity and community engagement were strong,

children played outdoors, a hard day's work was expected and valued, people ate what they produced and nearly everybody I met was somehow content and grateful with the little that they had.

I only attended the school in Arsos for a few weeks. I remember playing *mappa* after school with the local lads on a dusty, flat and sad looking pitch.

My time in Cyprus had sparked a love affair with my culture and my heritage that would influence and shape my creative practice in ways I could never have imagined.

I can still smell the fresh goat's milk and the fresh oven-baked bread that I consumed on a daily basis.

I can still recall the late night debates between the old men at the village *kafenion*. I remember waking up to the crows of a dozen roosters and the braying of the donkeys. I remember the village festivals, banquets and feast days. I remember my old *yiayia* smothering me with kisses while my *pappou* in his *vraka* would smile and calmly sip his *zivania*.

Most of all, I remember witnessing the love and joy in my father's eyes as he sat with his father on a hill overlooking the family vineyard while a few stray goats nibbled grass at their feet.

I remember it all.

ABOUT THE AUTHOR

Constantinos (Costas) Emmanuelle is an Australian-born Cypriot artist living in Melbourne.

Before *Tales of Cyprus*, Costas was busy creating culturally-inspired art and exhibiting his work in a number of successful group and solo exhibitions.

Over the past twenty-five years he has been teaching art and design at various tertiary institutions both in Australia and overseas. He has also enjoyed an illustrious career working as an illustrator, graphic designer, visual artist and photographer.

He is married to Dr. Christina Pavlides, an archaeologist and London-born Cypriot.
He has four children and a cat called Stampy.

conemmanuelle@talesofcyprus.com
www.talesofcyprus.com
www.facebook.com/talesofcyprus